Praise for *Zest for 1*

The framework for zest for learning created by L
is the integration of a wealth of ideas on creativity, curiosity and resilience into a
meaningful, holistic approach to curriculum design that will galvanise our work on
museum learning and enrich the lives of the children and young people in our trust.

Rhodri Bryant, Executive Principal, The Arbib Education Trust

The Royal Yachting Association works hard to instil a healthy zest for learning in
its young sailors and associated support staff – and the impact of this approach
has been profound, helping Britain to win fifty-eight medals at Olympic level,
many of them gold. This book is an essential read for anyone who wants to succeed
in any walk of life.

Alistair Dickson, Director of Sport Development, Royal Yachting Association

Zest for Learning is a powerful call to action for a kinder, more joyful school
experience: one in which the emphasis is rightly on helping all young people
flourish and thrive. I strongly commend it.

Revd Nigel Genders, Chief Education Officer, the Church of England

This book is an excellent invitation to revisit the whole purpose of learning in our
schools and to discover what the key to zest is in all our students.

Trinidad Aguilar Izquierdo, Director, Colegio Kopernikus

Zest for Learning reminds us of the true purpose of education – to nurture curious,
passionate young people, putting the co-curriculum at the centre of their lives.
Holyport is delighted to be at the forefront of the kind of expansive education
advocated by Lucas and Spencer.

Ben McCarey, Head Master, Holyport College

Bill Lucas and Ellen Spencer brilliantly synthesise the latest thinking on how to
produce balanced, curious, purposeful young people to help us imagine a richer,
kinder, more sane pedagogy.

Al McConville, Director of Learning and Innovation, Bedales School, and co-author of
Learning How to Learn: A Guide for Kids and Teens

Lucas and Spencer effortlessly bring to life the literature insights and exemplary practices for the idea of zest for learning so that we know how to practically support students in building this capability for a purposeful and fulfilling life.

Matt Pfahlert, co-founder and CEO, Australian Centre for Rural Entrepreneurship

Zest for Learning is a practical resource for policy-makers, educators and parents wanting to co-create a space for children and young people to connect to the world in deep and profound ways; the research has been invaluable in inspiring FORM's Creative Learning programme in Western Australia.

Lamis Sabra, Creative Learning Manager, FORM

Focusing on zest is the single most powerful thing we've done as a leadership team; this book shows how all schools can make similar changes to their ethos.

Andrew Wood, Deputy Head Teacher, Steyning Grammar School

Zest for Learning

Developing curious learners who
relish real-world challenges

Bill Lucas and Ellen Spencer

Crown House Publishing Limited
www.crownhouse.co.uk

First published by

Crown House Publishing Limited
Crown Buildings, Bancyfelin, Carmarthen, Wales, SA33 5ND, UK
www.crownhouse.co.uk

and

Crown House Publishing Company LLC
PO Box 2223, Williston, VT 05495, USA
www.crownhousepublishing.com

British Library Cataloguing-in-Publication Data

A catalogue entry for this book is available from the British Library.

Print ISBN 978-178583401-1
Mobi ISBN 978-178583483-7
ePub ISBN 978-178583484-4
ePDF ISBN 978-178583485-1

LCCN 2019955152

Printed and bound in the UK by
TJ International, Padstow, Cornwall

Acknowledgements

Our huge thanks to:

All the pioneering school and organisation leaders who have contributed case studies, including:

The Arbib Education Trust – Jenny Blay, head of museum learning; Grace Shaw, deputy head teacher, the Langley Academy Primary; Lawrence Hyatt, deputy head teacher, the Langley Heritage Primary.

Australian Centre for Rural Entrepreneurship – Matt Pfahlert, co-founder and CEO; Michelle Anderson, director, Interface2Learn.

Bedales School – Alistair McConville, director of learning and innovation.

Colegio Kopernikus – Trinidad Aguilar Izquierdo, director.

Explorer Scouts – Matt Hyde, chief executive; Chris James, brand and ambassador manager of the Scouts.

FORM – Lynda Dorrington, chief executive; Lamis Sabra, creative learning manager; Vanessa Bradley, creative learning coordinator; Viet Nguyen, creative technology; Mags Webster, writer and researcher; Paul Collard, chief executive, Creativity, Culture and Education; Paul Gorman, creative director, Hidden Giants; Mathilda Joubert, academic and creative learning consultant and Creative Schools programme evaluator.

Forest School Association – Sarah Lawfull, director.

Holyport College – Ben McCarey, headmaster.

Planet Poetry – Daniel Phelps, author of *Xientifica: SOS*.

Portsmouth Museums – Christine Taylor, curator of natural history.

Royal Yachting Association – Alistair Dickson, director of sport development; David Mellor, coaching and development manager.

Shireland Collegiate Academy – Mark Grundy, CEO, Shireland Collegiate Academy Trust; George Faux, principal, West Bromwich Collegiate Academy (previously senior vice principal, Shireland Collegiate Academy).

Steyning Grammar School – Andrew Wood, assistant head teacher.

West Rise Junior School – Mike Fairclough, head teacher.

All the thought leaders on whose shoulders we stand, including:

Ron Berger, Guy Claxton, Paul Collard, Art Costa, Anna Craft, Angela Duckworth, Carol Dweck, Anders Ericsson, Chris Fadel, Michael Fullan, Howard Gardner, Leslie Gutman, Andy Hargreaves, John Hattie, James Heckman, Lois Hetland, Bena Kallick, Tim Kautz, Geoff Masters, David Perkins, Lauren Resnick, Ron Ritchhart, Ken Robinson, Pasi Sahlberg, Andreas Schleicher, Ingrid Schoon, Tom Schuller, Martin Seligman, Tom Sherrington, Robert Sternberg, Louise Stoll, Matthew Taylor, Paul Tough, Bernie Trilling, Chris Watkins, Dylan Wiliam and David Yeager.

The Comino Foundation for generously supporting our work to develop young people's personal capabilities at the Centre for Real-World Learning, University of Winchester.

Contents

Series Introduction

Developing capable young people

Ensuring that all people have a solid foundation of knowledge and skills must therefore be the central aim of the post-2015 education agenda. This is not primarily about providing more people with more years of schooling; in fact, that's only the first step. It is most critically about making sure that individuals acquire a solid foundation of knowledge in key disciplines, that they develop creative, critical thinking and collaborative skills, and that they build character attributes, such as mindfulness, curiosity, courage and resilience.

Andreas Schleicher and Qian Tang, Education Post-2015: Knowledge and Skills Transform Lives and Societies (2015, p. 9)

Changing roles for schools

Across the world there is a great shift taking place. Where once it was enough to know and do things, our uncertain world calls for some additional learning. We call them capabilities. Others call them 'dispositions', 'habits of mind', 'attributes' or 'competencies', words we find very helpful. Some refer to them as 'non-cognitive skills', 'soft skills' or 'traits', none of which we like given, respectively, their negative connotations, tendency to belittle what is involved and association with genetic inheritance.

Our choice of capabilities is pragmatic. A country in the northern hemisphere like Scotland is actively using the term, as is Australia at the opposite end of the earth. If we had to choose a phrase to sum up our philosophy it would be 'dispositional teaching' – that is to say, the attempt specifically to cultivate in learners certain dispositions which evidence suggests are going to be valuable to them both at school and in later life.

We know that the shift is underway for four reasons:

1. One of the 'guardians' of global comparative standards, PISA, is moving this way. In 2012, as well as tests for 15-year-olds in English, maths and science, they introduced an 'innovative domain' called 'creative problem-solving'. This became 'collaborative problem-solving' in 2015, 'global competence' in 2018 and will become 'creative thinking' in 2021.

2. Researchers the world over are beginning to agree on the kinds of capabilities which do, and will, serve children well at school and in the real world. We'll explore this increasingly consensual list later on, but for now we want to share just some of the key thinkers to reassure you that you are in good company: Ron Berger, Guy Claxton, Art Costa, Anna Craft, Angela Duckworth, Carol Dweck, K. Anders Ericsson, Charles Fadel, Michael Fullan, Howard Gardner, Leslie Gutman, Andy Hargreaves, John Hattie, James Heckman, Lois Hetland, Bena Kallick, Tim Kautz, Geoff Masters, David Perkins, Lauren Resnick, Ron Ritchhart, Sir Ken Robinson, Andreas Schleicher, Ingrid Schoon, Martin Seligman, Robert Sternberg, Louise Stoll, Matthew Taylor, Paul Tough, Bernie Trilling, Chris Watkins, Dylan Wiliam and David Yeager. We would include our own work in this field too.

3. Organisations and well-evidenced frameworks are beginning to find common cause with the idea of capabilities. The Assessment and Teaching of 21st Century Skills Project, Building Learning Power, Expeditionary Learning Network, the Global Cities Education Network, Habits of Mind, New Pedagogies for Deeper Learning, Partnership for 21st Century Learning and the Skills4Success Framework are just a few examples. We would include our own Expansive Education Network here too.

4. Inspirational leaders across the world are very gradually showing us that you can powerfully embed capabilities into the formal, informal and hidden curriculum of schools, if you have a mind to do so. Here are seven examples: Col·legi Montserrat in Spain, Hellerup School in Denmark, High Tech High in the United States, School 21 and Thomas Tallis School in England, and Rooty Hill High School and Carey Grammar in Australia. You'll doubtless have your own favourites to add in. We love these schools and their courageous teachers. Throughout the series we hope that their

stories and our grounded practical advice will serve to ensure that hundreds of thousands of schools across the world see the value of systematically cultivating capabilities *as well as* deep disciplinary knowledge and useful academic and practical skills.

Increasingly 'character' is the word used to describe the cluster of capabilities which are useful in life, with a further clarification of the term, 'performance character', suggesting those attributes which are associated with excellence in situations where performance is called upon – an academic test, examination, sports match or any extra-curricular activity in which concentrated demonstration of skill is required.

Indeed, character education has seen a popular resurgence among politicians in the UK in recent years, with former Secretary of State for Education Damian Hinds (2019) arguing that character education is as important as examination success, and promising the development of 'a new framework to help teachers and school leaders identify the types of opportunities that will help support their pupils to build character. The framework will also provide a self-assessment tool for schools to check how well they are doing.'

The UK's Jubilee Centre for Character and Virtues argues that teacher education must encompass preparation to teach character education (Arthur, 2014). England's Department for Education's *Strategy 2015–2020: World-Class Education and Care* (2016a) holds as one of its twelve strategic priorities 'build character and resilience'. Character education is seen as a means to:

> support the development of character traits associated with: improved attainment at school; improved employability skills; making a valuable contribution to British society as a good citizen. Embedding character education within the school system will create opportunities for all pupils to develop the skills they need to succeed in education and in adult life. (Department for Education, 2016b, p. 10)

In the second of Art Costa and Bena Kallick's book series on the habits of mind, Curtis Schnorr (2000, p. 76) argues that character education should have thinking at its centre because 'Successful character education is grounded in thoughtful processes.' Thinking processes and the capabilities of good thinkers – like persisting or managing impulsivity – are foundational to character education.

All this means that as well as ensuring that, as Andreas Schleicher and Qian Tang put it, all young people develop a solid foundation of knowledge and skills while at school, they also need to acquire a set of important capabilities.

The purposes of education

Parents, educators and policy-makers alike have many hopes for the education of children and young people. But with so many ideas about what schooling might achieve, it is hard to reach any kind of consensus. Nevertheless, in late 2015/early 2016, the UK parliament initiated an inquiry into the 'purpose of education'. On the one hand, it's a telling admission if a government has to ask such a fundamental question. On the other, it could be construed as a sign of strength, as a recognition that times are changing.

At the Centre for Real-World Learning, we worked with a number of national bodies to see if common agreement could be reached. The following list is what we came up with and is indicative of the sorts of things we might all wish for our children's education to achieve (Lucas and Spencer, 2016). The first half a dozen are particularly relevant to this series of books, but the remainder also give a sense of our values. We want educational goals which:

1. Work for all young people.

2. Prepare students for a lifetime of learning at the same time as seeing childhood and school as valuable in their own right.

3. See capabilities and character as equally important as success in individual subjects.

4. Make vocational and academic routes equally valued.

5. Cultivate happier children.

6. Engage effectively with parents.

7. Engage well with business.

8. Use the best possible teaching and learning methods.

9. Understand how testing is best used to improve outcomes.

10. Empower and value teachers' creativity and professionalism.

11. Proactively encourage both rigorous school self-improvement and appropriate external accountability.

Which capabilities matter most?

Let's look in more detail at the third item on our wish list: seeing capabilities and character as equally important as success in individual subjects. In the last decade, we have begun to understand with greater clarity those capabilities which are particularly useful. Here are two lists, the first from an economic perspective (Heckman and Kautz, 2013) and the second through the eyes of educational researchers (Gutman and Schoon, 2013). Both sets of researchers are trying to describe those capabilities – or, in some cases, transferable skills – which will improve outcomes for individual learners and so for wider society.

Heckman and Kautz:	Gutman and Schoon:
Perseverance	Self-perception
Self-control	Motivation
Trust	Perseverance
Attentiveness	Self-control
Self-esteem and self-efficacy	Metacognitive strategies
Resilience to adversity	Social competencies
Openness to experience	Resilience and coping
Empathy	Creativity
Humility	
Tolerance of diverse opinions	
Engaging productively in society	

The striking thing about these lists, to us, is how similar they are. With regard to this book's focus on zest, we will see how important some of these transferable skills or dispositions are, including perseverance, openness to experience, empathy, tolerance of diverse opinions, self-control, engaging productively in society, motivation, social competencies and creativity, and how they contribute to our thinking.

While we may want to interrogate these terms more closely, the general direction is clear. The demand side, from employers, is similar in its emphasis. In 2012, the Confederation of British Industry (CBI) launched a campaign suggesting the kinds of capabilities it wanted young people to acquire at school. Their list included grit, resilience, curiosity, enthusiasm and zest, gratitude, confidence and ambition, creativity, humility, respect and good manners, and sensitivity to global concerns. This book takes the CBI's idea of zest and provides a theoretical and practical underpinning to the concept.

Lifelong learning

As well as preparing pupils for their next immediate steps on leaving, we argue that schools also have a role in preparing young people to be learners throughout their lives. That this is an important aspect of school life has become clearer over the last two decades (Lucas and Greany, 2000; Schuller and Watson, 2009). Specifically, it is appreciated that much of the preparation for lifelong learning is informal, experienced based and often coordinated by organisations outside school. In *Zest for Learning*, we focus on the role of these often charitable organisations in enriching the lives of young people and instilling a love of learning beyond school. In particular, we are keen to understand how schools can best interact with outside bodies.

The progression from classroom to life outside school via interest-led activities is shown in the figure below.

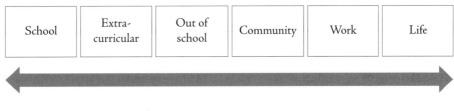

Learning beyond the school

The idea of signature learning experiences

If we are reaching consensus as to the kinds of capabilities increasingly being seen as valuable, what about the kinds of teaching and learning methods that might cultivate them? In the first two books of the series we asked you to consider these two questions:

+ If I wanted to teach a student how to become more creative and better able to solve problems, what methods would I choose?

+ If I wanted my students to become more resilient, what methods would I choose?

To help you think about them we introduced the idea of signature pedagogies, as suggested by Lee Shulman, in the context of preparing learners for different vocational routes. These are 'the types of teaching that organize the fundamental ways in which future practitioners are educated for their new professions' (Shulman, 2005, p. 52). He talks of the three dimensions of a signature pedagogy:

1. Its surface structure: 'concrete, operational acts of teaching and learning, of showing and demonstrating, of questioning and answering, of interacting and withholding, of approaching and withdrawing' (pp. 54–55).

2. Its deep structure: 'a set of assumptions about how best to impart a certain body of knowledge and know-how' (p. 55).

3. Its implicit structure: 'a moral dimension that comprises a set of beliefs about professional attitudes, values, and dispositions' (p. 55).

It's not much of a leap to think not about the fundamentals of a particular profession but instead of a particular capability. Suppose it were perseverance: how would you model and demonstrate it? What know-how does someone who is a good 'perseverer' show, and how can you impart the clues of persevering to students? What are the underpinning self-belief and can-do dispositions that reinforce perseverance?

Signature pedagogies are the teaching and learning methods which are most likely to lead to the desired capability, and in books 1 and 2 we explored these in some depth. But with zest, as we have begun to indicate, it is slightly different. Pedagogy is not quite the right way of describing the more informal ways of learning encountered in the more informal learning associated with extra-curricular and out-of-school activities. So instead we suggest the phrase 'signature learning experiences' to characterise them. The question we invite you to consider is:

+   If I wanted my students to be full of zest for learning, what learning experiences would I want them to have?

In this book you will encounter a variety of answers to this question with some common themes. The experiences are often outward-looking and involve making things, giving time voluntarily, being outdoors, meeting new people and going on journeys. Or they might be more inward-focused, such as reading, practising, reflecting or even meditating.

Within and beyond school there are core techniques that need to be mastered, just as students will need to become comfortable with their times tables, irregular verbs or acids and bases. These include:

+   Giving and receiving feedback.

+   Practising deliberately.

+   Drafting and prototyping.

+   Using design processes.

- Goal-setting.

- Mentally rehearsing.

- Verbalising the processes of learning.

- Reflecting on processes and progress.

- Self-testing.

- Working in groups.

- Teaching others.

In each of the books in this series, we explore the many ways in which such techniques can be cultivated in many different contexts.

About the series

The Pedagogy for a Changing World series is action oriented and research led. The books are guides for teachers, school leaders and all those working with schools who want to develop capable young people. Each book offers practical suggestions as to how key capabilities can best be developed in learners, building both theoretical and practical confidence in the kinds of pedagogies and methods which work well. The books are aimed at both primary and secondary levels.

The first two in the series are:

1. *Teaching Creative Thinking: Developing learners who generate ideas and can think critically*

2. *Developing Tenacity: Teaching learners how to persevere in the face of difficulty*

This is the third book and will explore the idea of zest for learning and how this can be developed in young people in and beyond school.

It is structured in the following way:

+ A clear definition of zest and why it matters.

+ A framework for zest for learning, with some practical examples for getting started.

+ An overview of the signature learning experiences which cultivate zestful learners.

+ Promising practices – case studies of schools which are adopting these approaches.

+ A focus on the brave leadership needed by schools consciously looking outside their gates.

+ An A–Z of ideas for developing zest.

Chapter 1
Zest for Learning

What it is and why it matters

zest, *n. figurative*. Enthusiasm for and enjoyment of something, esp. as displayed in speech or action; gusto, relish. Frequently with *for*.

Oxford English Dictionary

We wrote this book for teachers because it seems to us that there is an absence of zest and an abundance of both blandness and examined predictability in too many schools at the moment. For many young people, their learning stops just when it is getting really challenging and engaging. The bell goes and out they file. Where their learning interests might ideally take them is beyond the scope of a particular subject or syllabus. And in these form-filling, litigious times it is ever more tricky to organise educational forays out into the real world.

We like the word 'zest' because it suggests the kind of engaged curiosity we see as being at the heart of all good learning. We have looked hard at the evidence to understand more about zest. Research suggests that it is a valuable capability, central to human flourishing and eminently learnable.

This book draws together a far-reaching literature exploring zest and zest-like attributes, offering schools and organisations working with schools a model of how it could be at the heart of children's educational experiences. We hope it will give encouragement to head teachers, teachers, proactive parents and all those in the many voluntary, charitable and business organisations who work with young people to be expansive in their thinking. *Zest for Learning* is a call to action for us to broaden our horizons of what school can be and to take heart from the ideas which others are already using.

We believe there are two essential outcomes of education: flourishing and real-world challenge-readiness. By flourishing we mean thriving and growing with an underlying sense of direction and purpose. By being ready for the world's tests we mean prepared both morally and practically for the challenges of living in complex times. We need to understand where we've come from, how we've arrived at this place in time, and where we want to be as a society. It is not just about being able to come up with a creative solution to an engineering or biomedical problem. Beyond problem-solving is problem-setting: asking which problems are worth looking at, and seeking knowledge, understanding and wisdom that allows ethical decisions to be made based on more than just blind progress. Both flourishing and meeting real-world challenges are about embracing learning with both hands.

So what do we mean when we say a person has 'zest for learning'? Using the definition of zest on page 11, such a person might take a certain enthusiastic enjoyment in their learning; they are hungry to learn and find it a stimulating end in its own right. They enjoy the way learning opens up a richer understanding of other aspects of their life, seeing the interconnectedness of things. They are deeply satisfied when something that was formerly fuzzy and grey becomes clear to them, like the pieces of a jigsaw fitting together. They are keen to develop themselves, to experience new things, to try some and to master others. They try not to be discouraged by setbacks. To some degree, they are discontented with the status quo, with their own understanding of things, if not with the world at large. Zestful learners use hand, head and heart in much of their lives.

We know that human beings are born with an instinct to learn, boosted by the feedback they receive from every encounter with the objects and people around them. It's more than a proclivity; small babies *are* learners. In this book we will be wondering how best we can help young people to maintain a child-like fascination with the world as they grow older, wiser and more experienced in the ways of the world. The amount of zest for learning we each possess will, of course, be down to both nature and nurture. Positive learning experiences will impact people in different ways. There is much in the psychology literature to unpick here.

You could be forgiven for wondering whether this book's focus represents more fanciful territory than either creative thinking or tenacity, which we dealt with in our two earlier books. Are we really going to argue that all children, whatever their background, can benefit from zest? Or that schools can cultivate it? The answer is yes! In *Zest for Learning* we argue that zest is a public good, that learners with zest are more likely to be keen learners in and beyond the classroom, and that teachers deep down want to help foster zest in any way they can.

Bodies of knowledge

Perhaps because zest is used as shorthand for something everyone is assumed to understand, definitions of zest are conspicuous by their absence in the bodies of literature that use the word. In this book we offer a framework for zest: a practical guide for teachers, underpinned by theory. We draw on a number of areas of knowledge and practice that each have something to contribute to the concept of zest for learning, clarifying the concept of zest and bringing together ideas in concrete and actionable ways. As we do this we will constantly be asking: *what might this tell us about developing zest for learning in and from schools?*

More than fifty years ago, John Holt (1967, p. 175) came close to putting into words the essence of zest for learning:

> Since we cannot know what knowledge will be most needed in the future, it is senseless trying to teach it in advance. Instead we should try to turn out people who love learning so much and learn so well that they will be able to learn whatever needs to be learned.

The concept of zest for learning sits broadly within two large fields of knowledge: psychology and education. We are interested in the specific contribution each makes to our understanding of zest for learning, represented by the area where the two intersect:

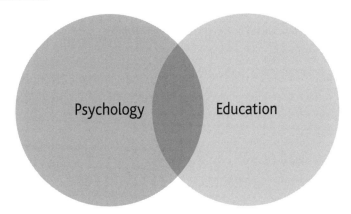

Our understanding of zest for learning comes from two broad areas of knowledge and research

These two fields are, of course, broad, encompassing many different and unrelated areas of research and knowledge. Because there is very little that speaks explicitly to a concept like zest for learning, this book carves out new territory, uncovering what the two fields have to say about human flourishing. The figure below shows some of the relevant topics within each body of knowledge. There will, of course, be cross-fertilisation of ideas as some topics have links to more than one knowledge area.

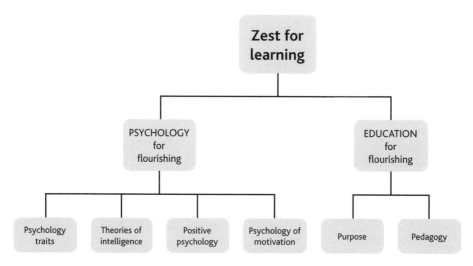

Two bodies of knowledge and their most relevant topics

In this chapter we unpack each of the areas of literature in terms of their relation to zest for learning. We look first to the field of psychology and its multidisciplinary and loosely collected studies called the 'learning sciences'. This is where we find ideas like habits of mind, grit, optimism and their cultivation.

- We explore the psychological study of traits. If, as we have suggested, it is possible to cultivate zest, we need to understand what aspect of it – if any – is related to the relatively fixed notion of personality traits.

- Theories of intelligence is a broad area in which we look at embodied cognition and the study of learning to learn.

- Positive psychology offers us the concept of 'flow', which is also relevant to learning to learn. Character strengths are also explored in this field.

- We explore the psychology of motivation where the concept of flow is, again, important. Mastery goals and a sense of purpose are also important ideas from this area.

The field of education also has a number of contributions to make, particularly in terms of ideas regarding the ultimate purpose of education as they concern meaning, situating oneself within the world and the development of virtues and values.

- We explore ideas relating to finding purpose, including lifelong learning and character.

- In terms of pedagogy, the learning sciences have important concepts for zest, including metacognition, real-world learning and habits for learning.

Developing a model of zest for learning

In this book we have created a model that describes the habits for learning, or dispositions, that together make up a person with – specifically – zest for learning. This moves beyond what it is to be a good or powerful learner into understanding what makes a skilful, effective, motivated, ethical, life-wide and lifelong learner. We try to look beyond the confines of whatever curriculum is currently in play, and ask a bigger question about what might be important to learn. In trying to narrow down what these dispositions or habits might be, we have scanned much of the literature, especially focusing on psychology and education.

You will notice that within the discussion of each area are a number of concepts which bring something significant to bear on the idea of zest for learning. These can be distilled down into six themes that relate to habits for learning:

1. Valuing relationships.

2. Maintaining perspective.

3.   Exploring the world.

4.   Embracing novel experiences.

5.   Finding meaning.

6.   Deepening understanding.

We signpost these themes along the way. Chapter 2 explores the framework and Chapter 3 asks how we might cultivate these valued habits in school. Having a framework through which to consider these habits is important for teachers because what they do in the classroom *really* matters. Talking of curiosity, a close cousin of zest for learning, Susan Engel (2015, p. 127) makes it clear how what teachers do makes all the difference:

> from an early age, some children are more curious than others. But there is also great fluctuation from one setting to another. A child who is usually timid about opening things or asking questions can be beckoned into inquiry. Children who are ordinarily inquisitive can be hushed into a kind of intellectual listlessness. The characteristics that fuel curiosity are not mysterious. Adults who use words and facial expressions to encourage children to explore; access to unexpected, opaque, and complex materials and topics; a chance to inquire with others; and plenty of suspense ... these turn out to be the potent ingredients.

Psychology for flourishing

In linking together areas of literature that speak to the broad concept of zest for learning, there is much that falls under the label of psychology. Within this broad field we might look at psychological traits, theories of intelligence, positive psychology and the psychology of motivation. Each of these has something to contribute. There are relationships between these fields which mean that sometimes we talk about a particular concept where it sits best.

Psychological traits

Psychological approaches to zest (in a broad sense, not constrained to zest for learning) examine it from a personality trait perspective. Traits are relatively enduring characteristics. The 'most widely used taxonomy of personality traits in psychology' (DeYoung et al., 2014, p. 46) is the Five-Factor Model, or Big Five, which can be remembered by the mnemonic OCEAN: openness, conscientiousness, extraversion, agreeableness and neuroticism.

Embracing novel experiences: openness to experience

In terms of the Big Five psychological traits, the openness to experience trait has provoked extensive debate in terms of its labelling and naming. DeYoung et al. (2014, p. 46) tell us that it 'has been described variously as Culture, Intellect, Openness to Experience, and Imagination' but that 'the compound label Openness/Intellect is increasingly in use'.

When psychologists talk about intellect here, they are describing a tendency to think in a certain kind of way:

> The psychological function that appears to be common to all of the traits encompassed by the Openness/Intellect factor is cognitive exploration ... Individuals high in Openness/Intellect display the ability and tendency to seek, detect, comprehend, and utilize more information than those low in Openness/Intellect. (DeYoung et al., p. 46)

This notion of cognitive exploration processes that drive learning about the world is closely related to the idea of zest for learning.

Outside of the field of psychology, the personality trait of extraversion is frequently used as a proxy for 'sociable'. There is a known link between extraversion and positive emotions, and so people might expect an extravert to have more zest in general. Psychologist Carl Jung first coined the phrase extravert – and its opposite, introvert – in the 1920s, and the trait has been the subject of a great many studies since. In fact, extraversion is more than just being confidently sociable. It suggests that an individual draws their energy from what happens outside them as opposed from looking within.

It is important to recognise that individuals sit on an introversion–extraversion spectrum, and nobody is 100% one or the other. It is also important to stress that the two types are different and neither is superior – for example, a mixture of both approaches to thinking and speaking is often most effective in a work situation (Cain, 2012).

In explaining zest, Peterson et al. (2009, p. 161) mention various other terms that have been used to describe the psychological 'dispositional influence on work satisfaction' that they call zest. It has also been referred to as energy, liveliness, vitality, exuberance, *joie de vivre*, vigour and engagement (in work). Zest in adults and young people, as defined by Peterson, can be measured using a self-report scale that uses ten statements such as 'I have lots of energy'.

Peterson's study found that measuring highly for zest predicted that an individual would also view their work as a calling, and claim satisfaction in their work and in their life more generally. The reason for this is because work satisfaction is more than a function of the job itself. While there are all sorts of factors inherent to the job that may influence work satisfaction, the literature is clear that:

> what a person brings to his or her work is also important. Those who are generally happy – due to their biological, psychological, or social makeup – are more likely to be satisfied at work … Those who are extraverted and socially engaged are also more likely to be satisfied … especially if they find close friends in the workplace … Zest as a construct captures many of these characteristics. (Peterson et al., 2009, p. 162)

The authors called for scholars to pay more attention to the study of zest in order to develop its presence in the workplace, something we are pleased to be doing in the wider context of education.

Peterson and Seligman (2004) struggled to conceptualise the character strength they finally labelled 'open-mindedness'. Collected under this theme from an array of categorisations of character, both ancient and modern, were labels like judgement, critical thinking and rationality. Whatever label is used, the authors were clear that open-mindedness should not be taken to a foolish extreme and should represent a careful mix of appropriate judgement: 'He or she is not indecisive, wishy-washy, nihilistic, or permissive. Neither does the open-minded thinker bring this style to bear on all matters. Red traffic lights mean stop, and viewing this signal from all possible angles is simply stupid' (p. 101).

It seems reasonable to suggest that zest for learning in particular can be developed in both introverts and extraverts, albeit with a recognition that extraverts tend to be more open to new experiences than introverts. It is important, therefore, that individuals recognise their own strengths and propensities, and not be limited by the responses to situations that their psychological make-up would tend to lead them to favour.

Zestful learners embrace novel experiences. They keep their minds open to the cognitive exploration of ideas using judgement, critical thinking and rationality. They recognise their own tendencies and push themselves to take on new challenges wherever possible.

Embracing novel experiences: restlessness, sensation-seeking and risk-taking

A term we came across that resonates with the concept of zest is 'restlessness'. Along with curiosity, openness and excellence, restlessness is identified as being a core value – for example, at Warwick Business School (WBS).

The idea of restlessness brings to mind imagery of dogged curiosity and a keenness to understand how things can be made better. The language WBS uses demonstrates this idea: 'We want to develop world-class business leaders that are constantly curious, open-minded and restless to make a positive impact on society'[1] and 'Restlessness: always challenging convention to find a better way.'[2]

More broadly as a concept restlessness has pathological connotations. Academic papers on the subject are predominantly published in journals like *Addiction*, *Psychopharmacology*, *Depression and Anxiety* and *Journal of Learning Disabilities* and cover such topics as physiological and neurological disorders. In the classroom

---

1   See https://www.wbs.ac.uk/news/executive-mba-ranked-in-world-s-top-25-by-ft.
2   See https://www.wbs.ac.uk/research.

it is generally a negative term too, indicating behaviour disorders, agitation, hyperactivity or poor lesson regulation (Westling et al., 2017).

Sârbescu and Boncu's (2018) paper looking at an alternative classification of personality types to the widely used Five-Factor Model uses the label 'restless' to describe someone with the trait of sensation-seeking. This is 'a personality trait defined as the tendency to seek varied, novel, complex, and intense sensations and experiences and the willingness to take risks for the sake of such experience' (Zuckerman 1979, p. 10). A 'normal' trait, it is nonetheless overrepresented in some kinds of personality disorder.

Given these potentially negative associations and its absence from more education-related journals, we suggest caution in using the term restlessness.

An obviously school-relevant aspect of sensation-seeking is risk-taking. Canadian academic, author and psychiatrist Jordan Peterson tells us that humans tend towards a preference for living life 'on the edge'. In this space we are able to benefit from confidence in our experience as well as 'confronting the chaos' from which we grow. An inbuilt enjoyment of risk, to varying degrees, means that we feel 'invigorated ... when we work to optimize our future performance, while playing in the present' (Peterson, 2018, p. 329).

Risk-taking is related to the psychological trait of openness to experience and the virtue of courage, both of which are aspects of zest for learning. Of course, when talking about teenagers it always going to be important to remember that the lack of development of the prefrontal cortex means that, despite adult teaching and coaching, young people are more likely to take risks at this period of their lives whatever their personality type (Kann et al., 2014).

In summary, by understanding the ideas behind psychological traits we can immediately see connections with the concept of openness to experience, which we build into our framework for the habits of zest for learning.

> Zestful learners embrace novel experiences. They demonstrate a willingness to take risks in order to seek varied, novel, complex and intense learning experiences. They are doggedly curious, with a keenness to understand how things can be made better.

Theories of intelligence

The nature of intelligence is one of the most studied areas of psychology. It has a controversial past, with many theories emerging that propose how to define it and what it comprises; debate continues around the degree to which it is possible (or desirable) to measure it. Changing conceptions of intelligence have moved beyond intelligence as a static test score to 'a dynamic concept of modifiable capacities, which can be continuously developed throughout a person's lifetime and cultivated deliberately in homes, classrooms, and learning organizations' (Costa and Kallick, 2000, p. xviii).

In *New Kinds of Smart* (2010), Bill Lucas and Guy Claxton explore current conceptions of intelligence, arguing that it is composite, expandable, practical, intuitive, distributed, social, strategic and ethical.

We consider four key topics to be of relevance to our understanding of zest for learning within the field of intelligence. These include embodied cognition, experiential learning, deliberate practice (expertise) and experiencing flow.

Finding meaning: embodied cognition

The title of the Centre for Real-World Learning's report *Bodies of Knowledge* (Claxton et al., 2010) made a play on the first word in the phrase embodied cognition. It recognised the resurgence of interest in practical learning and physical, bodily work, reflected in books by thinkers like Matthew Crawford, Richard Sennett, Mike Rose and Guy Claxton. This isn't merely a rebellion against a desk-bound knowledge economy, but an acknowledgement that the hand 'is the cutting edge of the mind' (Bronowski, 2011 [1973], p. 93) and a vital part of how human beings make sense of the world.

For us, embodied cognition – the idea that our minds and bodies are intimately connected – brings two ideas to the table. First, this school of thought recognises the rich connections between learning and doing. Our body is not just a useful vehicle for carrying around our brains. What we do with our bodies actually affects 'the quality of our thinking' (Claxton et al., 2010, p. 4). We recognise this when we take a break from a difficult problem to walk around the block and come back having figured it out. Second, the idea of embodied cognition values the human body and its place in the world. Again, we cannot leave aside our bodies when we think about how we plan to conduct ourselves in this world, the activities through which we learn and with which daily life is filled.

Zest for learning is going to involve the body in a number of respects. It might be helpful to explore the origins of our current cultural understanding of mind and body to understand why authors like Crawford and others have come to think of work that involves the human body as requiring genuine intelligence and of deep value.

Although there has long been an understanding in Christendom that human beings comprise both body and soul, the academic world has been dominated by the philosophy of materialism: the idea that nothing exists beyond the material world. Indeed, Descartes' error was to locate 'authentic human identity in the mind alone', while the body was regarded as a mechanism operating purely by natural laws (Pearcey, 2018, p. 50) – which Claxton et al. (2010, p. 4) describe as the 'mind's container and perambulator'. In this materialist paradigm, the mind tends to be reduced to grey matter that simply reacts to its environment.

Christianity, which has long dominated our culture and underpins much of our taken-for-granted ways of thinking, holds that 'body and soul together form an integrated unity – that the human being is an embodied soul' (Pearcey, 2018, p. 20). This is to say, there is a mind–body dualism in that neither aspect can be reduced to the other, and the body is as important as the soul it holds. This alternative paradigm bestows enormous value on the body.

The common portrayal of the Puritans typically shows them as being 'averse to beauty because they rejected iconography, ornamentation, and personal display' (Robinson, 2018d, loc. 2790). In fact, the Puritans actually valued the body extremely highly as seen through their affirmation of the physical union of marriage. They 'idealized marriage and educated their daughters' (Robinson, 2018e, loc. 3899). King Edward VI of England – himself greatly interested in theology and a follower of Protestant reformer John Calvin – 'ended the requirement of clerical celibacy' (Robinson, 2018c, loc. 2184). He saw, like Calvin, that 'marriage as covenant was … the bond most favored by God' (loc. 2526). Thus, the importance of bodily intimacy in marriage is recognised as 'holy' and not 'base' as some had seen it. The valuing of the body was a natural consequence of the biblical teaching that we are all made in the image of God. Value and dignity of human life is therefore seen as inherent to all human beings.

This is in stark contrast to the materialistic philosophy that has given rise to personhood theory – another type of 'two-level dualism that sets the body *against* the person, as though they were two separate things merely stuck together' (Pearcey, 2018, p. 21). Under this paradigm, the human body (a part of nature not seen as God's handiwork but as the result of a blind, unconscious and automatic process) is 'reduced to a mere mechanism with no intrinsic purpose or dignity' (p. 25). As a consequence, 'it can no longer be assumed that the words *psyche* or *soul* or *mind* can be taken to correspond to anything real' (Robinson, 2018d, loc. 2733).

To summarise, the biblical understanding of the body is never that it is 'bad'. The central character, for Christians, Jesus, came to earth *in the flesh*, which he would not have done if flesh were inherently bad.

The idea of embodied cognition pushes us into the terrain of purpose. It recognises that we are not a mind detached from a body, but that thinking happens in a physical brain that is very much a part of the body; it is integrated into and wholly interconnected with the body. Thinking happens within brain–body connections. Embodied cognition reminds us that we are head, heart and hand, all of which combine to give us a sense of purpose. We might, for example, have a *feeling* or an *understanding* that we need to take an action, but only by action does it manifest in the world.

In *Love Thy Body*, Nancy Pearcey (2018, p. 202) argues that a teleological view of nature (one that explains phenomena – like bodies, for example – in terms of the purpose they serve) 'gives a basis for accepting the goodness of nature and affirming the value and dignity of the created order'.

The value and importance of the physical realm is where we get the 'Protestant work ethic' from, which stems from the reformers' recognition that the physical world and work with our hands is a vocation and a calling.

> Zestful learners find meaning. They recognise the inherent value of the body and the intelligence involved in – and dignity that comes from – working with it.

Exploring the world: experiential learning

Despite the name, experiential learning is not just about practical action. It is characterised by experience and reflection upon it; not just *doing*, but *thinking about doing*. While the idea of action and reflection is important in terms of exploring zest for learning, we need to recognise a bit about the way that the concept of experiential learning originated, and how an oversimplification of the ideas has led to some misguided thinking about how we learn.

Experiential learning has its origins in an eclectic mix of philosophical perspectives, including those of pragmatist John Dewey as well as Kurt Lewin and Jean Piaget (Miettinen, 2000). Like Dewey, Lewin and Piaget before him, David Kolb represented learning as a cycle, which can be depicted as a four-stage model (as in the figure on page 25). It was a synthesis of the work of 'nine foundational scholars from education, psychology, and philosophy to generate an ideal process of learning and developing from experience (the learning cycle)' (Peterson and Kolb, 2018, p. 230). The experiential learning cycle is one practical exemplification of embodied cognition in action: body and mind, action and thought working together as part of a learning process.

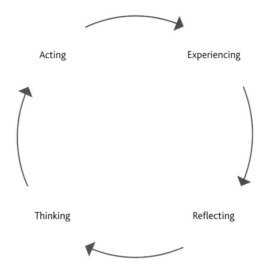

The experiential learning cycle

Source: Kolb and Kolb (2018, p. 8)

In fact, Kolb saw similarities between the human processes of experiential learning, the scientific enquiry process, problem-solving, decision-making and the creative thinking process. This similarity led him to suggest that 'there may be a great payoff in the integration of findings from these specialized areas into a single general adaptive model such as that proposed by experiential learning theory' (Kolb, 1984, p. 33).

In thinking about our concept of zest for learning, the explicit inclusion of experience alongside conceptualisation and reflection is helpful in showing how these modes of being complement each other, allowing us to process what we are learning and to abstract meaning from it.

Of course, it is not possible and probably not desirable for all lessons to be experiential – for example, there will be moments of expert demonstration and formal introduction of concepts that are essentially theoretical. Neither is it always possible for pupils to be spending school time off-site on a regular basis.

We need to recognise that the learning that takes place in school classrooms is of great value. Education is a privileged time in children's lives, when experts in various disciplines can immerse them in the intellectual exploration of complex ideas. The fact that it takes place in a classroom and not the workplace or 'real world' need not diminish its value. Knowledge is not reified into something more meaningful simply because it takes place 'on the job'.

John Kijinski, an English teacher at a US university, argues that offering 'real-life' experiences as credits for college can do students a disservice, and that they will be better served in the long term by taking the academic option:

> Almost all of us will eventually have to work for a living, and that will always require sustained 'real-life, engaged learning.' It will also call for immersion in interactions with average minds (like most of our own) working toward mundane ends. As educators, we should be proud that we give our students, while they are students, the opportunity to interact – through their reading and writing, their laboratory work, and our instruction – with what the best minds have discovered and developed within our various disciplines. This is something the 'real world' is unlikely to offer them regularly once they leave college. (Kijinski, 2018)

As with the two earlier books in this series, we find ourselves arguing against simplistic alternatives – *either* real-world engagement *or* deep disciplinary study – when we clearly need both. In *Zest for Learning*, we will see that deep study is one way in which learners can build a sense of purpose, while their curiosity will inevitably want to explore the world out there as well as discoveries from the past.

Zestful learners explore the world. They recognise that fulfilling practical and theoretical work both make cognitive demands, and value each equally. They reflect on their practical experiences in order to learn from them.

Performing well: deliberate practice (expertise)

By *deliberate practice*, as we explored in *Developing Tenacity*, we mean a series of highly structured activities, such as drafting, redrafting, prototyping and rehearsing, undertaken with the specific goal of improving performance. Deliberate practice involves breaking complex activities into their constituent parts (Ericsson and Pool, 2016). It requires a level of task motivation. It involves the provision of real-time feedback for learning and the repeated repetition of the same or similar tasks.

Sometimes such practice is a solo activity, but frequently it is social. It is worth remembering that for some 50% of the population who would describe themselves as introverted, practice can be more effective if done alone. Susan Cain makes a powerful case for introverts in *Quiet* (2012, p. 75), arguing that collaboration can suppress creativity: this 'New Groupthink elevates teamwork above all else'. But it is easy to see that if corporations demand it, it will be seen in the classroom. Without wishing to suggest that creativity happens in a vacuum, Cain makes the case that deliberate practice, in her view, 'is best conducted alone' (p. 81) – an idea corroborated by Anders Ericsson, who coined the term. She notes that even 'elite athletes in team sports often spend unusual amounts of time in solitary practice' (p. 81).

When we think of mastering something, we recognise that deliberate practice is needed. A person with zest for learning may aim, ultimately, at developing expertise in a particular area of learning. In this sense, deliberate practice which develops that expertise is relevant to our framework of zest for learning. The experience of expertise, or even a belief in its attainability, may even reinforce the thrill of learning that an individual seeks out. We will return to this idea when we consider motivation.

> Zestful learners perform well. They engage in deliberate practice with a view to improving their knowledge, expertise or performance.

Performing well: experiencing flow

At this point, we draw attention to the related concept of flow. Flow is a state in which the skill and challenge levels of a task are at their highest, producing such intense focus and immersion in a task that it is easy to lose track of time (Csikszentmihalyi, 1996). Angela Duckworth looks at an interesting distinction between deliberate practice and flow in terms of their relation to expertise in *Grit* (2016, p. 132). She suggests that the two rarely go together, and explains that while deliberate practice is important for preparation, it is in the performance that flow happens.

Flow is a wonderful state to experience. There is something hedonic about the feeling of flow, perhaps addictive. But it is not the same as deliberate practice. Computer science professor and author of *So Good They Can't Ignore You* Cal Newport (2012) says: 'the feeling of flow is different than the feeling of getting better. If all you seek is flow, then you're not going to get better. There is no avoiding the deliberate strain of real improvement.' Deliberate practice is planned; it involves intense concentration and self-generated deep motivation. It also involves selecting the parts *you* find difficult, not those that challenge someone else.

Flow can happen at any stage of expertise. Newport (2011) rather harshly describes flow as 'the opiate of the mediocre', and it is easy to see why. Think of a pianist who plays his Grade 5 piece beautifully over and over. He may get a buzz from being able to do it well, but unless he tries something harder, he remains perpetually at Grade 5. As Jordan Peterson writes in *12 Rules for Life* (2018, p. 88), success in every area of life might just mean you're not challenging yourself. Growth, rather than winning, 'might be the most important form of winning'.

The passion – the joy of performing – actually requires a lot of effort in the background. So the grittier you are, the more likely you are to experience flow. This isn't to say grit and flow always co-exist, but they are closely linked.

If we want to experience zest in our learning we need passion, which comes from positive performance and an experience of flow. It's a feedback loop where performance is the reward, fills up our bank of zest and enables us to keep going. We need to be gritty! This is why Duckworth (2016, p. 267) ultimately advises four things if we want to grow grit from the inside out (which we mentioned in our earlier introduction to the concept of grit):

1.   Cultivate your interests.

2.   Develop a habit of daily challenge-exceeding-skill practice.

3.   Connect your work to a purpose beyond yourself.

4.   Learn to hope when all seems lost!

In *Developing Tenacity*, we included the habit 'controlled' with its elements 'sticking to a routine', 'deferring gratification' and 'controlling impulses'. Much of this speaks to the importance of deliberate practice.

Zestful learners perform well. They are able, having practised deliberately, to experience an opportunity to enjoy the fruits of their work in a moment of things 'going well', whether alone or performing to others.

The idea of deliberate practice highlights a couple of points in terms of zest for learning. First, the need for deepened understanding that brings about satisfaction in a number of ways: 'Perhaps happiness is always to be found in the journey uphill, and not in the fleeting sense of satisfaction awaiting at the next peak' (Peterson, 2018, p. 94). Second, the need for balance in the way we use our time: some time will be spent with others, other time may best be spent alone in practice or in quiet contemplation and reflection.

Positive psychology

Finding meaning: self-actualisation and flow

Positive psychology is a branch of psychology devoted, essentially, to studying well-being. It poses the question: what makes life worth living? It looks broader than the cognitive, focusing also on the physical side of human activity and its relation to well-being.

Flow speaks to self-actualisation and to finding meaning. We discuss it here, while recognising that so many of these concepts cannot be cleanly shelved within a single body of literature. Indeed, they may inform several.

Connected to self-actualisation and flow is Ken Robinson's message in *The Element* (2009, pp. 86, 89) – that doing what we love puts us in a place called 'the zone', when activities are 'completely absorbing'. He recognises that these 'optimal experiences' are what Csikszentmihalyi described as 'flow'. Robinson adds:

Activities we love fill us with energy even when we are physically exhausted. Activities we don't like can drain us in minutes, even if we approach them at our physical peak of fitness. This is one of the ... primary reasons why finding the Element is vital for every person ... Mental energy is not a fixed substance. It rises and falls with our passion and commitment to what we are doing at the time. (p. 93)

In addition to those links we've made when looking at theories of intelligence, the field of positive psychology allows us to make links between flow and zest as we think about character strengths.

There are a number of concepts related to positive psychology that also link to flow: the 'good life', life satisfaction and subjective well-being (happiness). These three ideas are to some degree a proxy for zest for living.

There is a vast literature on the good life, asking questions about what makes for a good life, how it might be defined in different cultures, the significance of different factors (e.g. spirituality) and whether life satisfaction measures accurately capture it. It is associated with the development of character formation, and occurs mainly in the positive psychology literature in places like the *Journal of Happiness Studies*.

In *On Reading Well: Finding the Good Life Through Great Books* (2018), Karen Prior begins with the assumption that literature shapes and forms our approach to the world. Literature can offer 'images of virtues in action' as well as 'offering the reader vicarious practice in exercising virtue' (p. 15). The book centres on character formation, where the 'virtuous life' sits been two extremes – for example, bravery sits between cowardice on the one hand and brash behaviour on the other.

A notable finding in the good life literature comes from a study (Wirtz et al., 2016) which aims to ascertain whether people recognise the documented link between self-control and important life outcomes, or whether they attribute something else to those outcomes instead. Greater self-control has all sorts of research-validated benefits, from physical and mental health to the regulation of thoughts, feelings and behaviours, and to relationships.

There are obvious conceptual links from self-control to grit, tenacity and deliberate practice. In our discussion of the psychology of motivation we propose how these might contribute to zest for learning.

What Wirtz and colleagues found, however, was that people give more credence to self-esteem than to self-control in bringing about positive behaviours. This means that people's beliefs 'contradict the vast scientific literature that has repeatedly shown high self-control to be a critical trait for developing and maintaining social relationships, good physical and emotional health, longevity, healthy behaviours, and other positive outcomes' (p. 580). This has the unfortunate consequence that people are motivated to pursue the good life without recognising the importance of self-control, and risk pursuing self-esteem over self-regulation.

Teachers cautious about the self-esteem movement will be familiar with the predictable result that a focus on increasing self-esteem as the pathway to the good life may even, in some cases, fuel narcissism. Our own work on dispositions and character strengths recognises that subjective feelings wax and wane. We suggest that self-esteem is rooted in the innate value and dignity of human beings, as well as in genuine formation of good character, virtues and learning dispositions that lead to the pursuit of excellence at whatever level a child is capable.

Three ways of obtaining happiness are described in the literature going from ancient to contemporary times. These are pleasure, engagement and meaning. It could be argued that a state of flow provides all three of these means of obtaining happiness. Peterson et al. (2007) cite the 'Orientations to Happiness' scale that assesses all three. The scale has been well-researched (Buschor et al., 2013), such that it is possible to say that each orientation predicts life satisfaction. High scores on all three orientations give the highest life satisfaction score.

> Zestful learners find meaning. They spend time doing what they love.

Maintaining perspective: character strengths – hope, zest, curiosity, gratitude and love

Happiness is given the descriptive label 'subjective well-being' in psychological studies of adolescence. Subjective well-being is the 'global self-appraisal of the quality of an individual's life at any given point in time' (Telef and Furlong, 2017, p. 492), and subjective health and well-being and life satisfaction are closely related (World Health Organization, 2016, p. 75). In a comparative study of teenagers in the collectivist culture of Turkey and the individualist culture of California, the researchers found a number of factors (self-efficacy, self-awareness, family coherence) and the character strength of zest to be predictive of subjective well-being in both sets of teenagers. For the California sample, peer support, optimism and the character strength of gratitude were also predictors. Telef and Furlong found optimism and zest to be predictive of subjective well-being for students in both countries.

The authors note that the link between zest and subjective well-being is well-established. For example, a study of 5,299 adults (Park et al., 2004) found a consistent and robust association between life satisfaction and zest, as well as hope, gratitude, love and curiosity. A later study by an expanded team, surveying 12,439 US and 445 Swiss adults (Peterson et al., 2007), found the character strengths 'most highly linked to life included love, hope, curiosity, and zest' (p. 149). In the US, gratitude was among the most 'robust predictors' and perseverance operated similarly in the Swiss sample.

Research points to the idea that character strengths have an important role to play in terms of well-being, and there is strong empirical evidence that they are positively related to life satisfaction (Buschor et al., 2013). More specifically, of the twenty-four character strengths identified by leaders in the field, Peterson and Seligman (2004, p. 116) found that a number of the strengths (hope, zest, curiosity, gratitude and love) 'play key roles in the interplay of strengths and satisfaction with life'. Of the factors impacting 'orientations to happiness', the idea of flow was of key importance in predicting satisfaction with life. Bear in mind that this is zest for living in general, not the more specific zest for learning, but nevertheless the conceptual link to flow may be a useful one. A learner experiencing flow is more likely to put in the necessary investment of mental energy to reconnect with that optimal learning experience.

Solano and Cosentino have similarly explored conceptions of positive psychology with a focus on life fulfilment. Their 2016 empirical study found the character strengths of love, honesty and zest to be of major importance for personal well-being – that is to say, they are contributors to it.

In the field of positive psychology, vitality is a character strength of the individual 'whose aliveness and spirit are expressed not only in personal productivity and activity [but seen when] such individuals often infectiously energize those with whom they come into contact' (Peterson and Seligman, 2004, p. 273). This is clearly a hugely beneficial strength, and perhaps not a realistic aspiration for many. But beneath this complex construct, Peterson and Seligman choose four descriptive 'behavioural criteria' (p. 31): zest, enthusiasm, vigour and energy. They don't go on to define what they mean by zest, perhaps assuming that it is descriptive enough in its own right.

There are many aspects of character that we might conceivably link to zest. Peterson and Seligman help us to limit our focus. Their twenty-four strengths sit within six virtues based on extensive work to identify 'six core moral virtues that emerge consensually across cultures and throughout time' (p. 28). Their project, which spanned several years, looked at identifying components of good character and devising tools to assess individual differences within those components.

The authors leave the classification of the twenty-four strengths under the six virtues open to debate (p. 31), noting that their work is primarily aimed at deepening understanding of the twenty-four strengths themselves rather than demonstrating psychometric validity to the classification. They also note that the character strength and virtue relationship is not a causal one. This means that we should perhaps pay more attention to those character strengths that seem reasonably to have some relationship to zest for learning than we should to the broader virtue concept of courage.

Zest for learning then is not a straightforward trait or virtue, but is apparently forged through a combination of other character strengths that dispose an individual towards it. What is helpful about the classification is the way in which Peterson and Seligman have done much legwork in isolating a set of distinct strengths. Anecdotally, we might expect the likelihood of its emergence to be enhanced through a combination of a number of the strengths in the following list. The six virtues, with their twenty-four character strengths, are:

1. Wisdom and knowledge (creativity, curiosity, open-mindedness, love of learning, perspective).

2. Courage (bravery, persistence, integrity, vitality).

3. Humanity (love, kindness, social intelligence).

4. Justice (citizenship, fairness, leadership).

5. Temperance (forgiveness and mercy, humility and modesty, prudence, self-regulation).

6. Transcendence (appreciation of beauty and excellence, gratitude, hope, humour, spirituality).

Those aspects of character with an obvious link to zest for learning are shown below:

Character strengths that combine to dispose individuals towards a zest for learning

Zestful learners maintain perspective. They are disposed to act well in terms of character strengths in general, and in areas like creativity, curiosity, open-mindedness, love of learning, bravery, persistence, vitality, appreciation of beauty and excellence, hope, humour and spirituality.

Maintaining perspective: optimism and the importance of perception/mindset

Positive psychology isn't about thinking positively as much as it is about mindset. Thoughts and feelings are transient, so simply trying to think positively is not effective. Many psychological studies have found that individuals' negative mindsets are more powerful than their positive ones. There are some approaches that can be helpful in counteracting negative thought patterns, including cognitive behavioural therapy and using our own character strengths. Character strengths are more stable than fleeting thoughts and can be used to develop a mindset more conducive to zest for learning.

The VIA Institute on Character has free and paid-for surveys that can be used to create a profile of your character strengths.[3] If you are more aware of your own blend of character strengths you can use them to challenge negative mindsets. For example:

+ If you are naturally curious, be intrigued by your thought pattern and accompanying feelings. Can you identify negative thoughts and probe into where they are coming from? Can you question the truth of the dampening thoughts? Are they valid? Instead of being passive in your curiosity (which can lead to anxiety), can you be actively curious about the positive situation, replacing the negative thoughts with one thing that is positive?

+ If you are a naturally critical thinker, be questioning about the rationality of your thought pattern and accompanying feelings. Can you critique your assumptions about what other people might think? Could you be wrong? Using your logical thought process, what would you think if the situation were reversed, and why? Does some part of you actually want them to be envious? Is that an admirable quality in yourself? Does this say more about you than them? What might a reasonable person think? Does what an unreasonable person think really matter? How can you position yourself in such a way that you are innocent of wrong motives while still celebrating the good thing?

---

3   See https://www.viacharacter.org/character-strengths.

In a similar vein, adopting a zestful mindset to the extent that you exhibit some of the characteristics of living and learning with zest may actually help you to develop zest.

Carol Dweck's (2006) studies on mindset have shown that mindset – a way of perceiving your own efficacy in the world, in this case with regard to being able to get better at learning – actually leads to marked improvements in learning. The same can be true with zest. Our behaviours can prompt change. If you act in a way that points to a certain reality, then this behaviour can manifest in actual success.

We are embodied minds. For example, it is well-recognised that physical actions can actually change emotions. We know that emotion is, in part, bodily expression. Peterson's (2018) discussion of poor posture and its impact on a spiralling 'positive feedback' loop is a case in point. As Kleinke and colleagues (1998) found, emotion can be amplified or dampened by bodily expression, such that a person who is asked to present a sad expression actually reports feeling less happy.

The folk wisdom of this is recognised in the aphorism 'fake it till you make it', which is concretised in the principles of cognitive behavioural therapy. It's the idea of acting as if something is true as a means to highlighting a positive path forward to change, rather than self-delusion. It is about changing patterns of thought in a given situation in order to modify consequent emotions, their consequent behaviour and ultimately physical reactions, thus reinforcing 'good' thoughts next time the antecedent situation occurs.

Desirable outcomes (such as acting zestfully and the associated benefits of this) can therefore arise from zestful behaviour. If beliefs (and not mere decisions, instruction from a researcher or attempts to self-talk into actually being zestful) are the precursor for physical actions, then self-perception ultimately leads to those actions, which in turn lead to manifestation of the desired state. If you believe something about yourself and it causes you to act differently, then this can lead to actual success.

Unlike learnable intelligence in the example from Dweck, zest is not a phenomenon. But it *is* a positive thing. We don't need individuals to believe they are zestful, merely to believe that zest is a good thing and to behave accordingly.

In summary, the character strengths literature can contribute to our understanding of zest for learning through its concept of optimism. We suggest that the idea of maintaining perspective can be useful in developing a framework for the habits of zest for learning.

> Zestful learners maintain perspective. They recognise the degree of agency they have in order to improve in any learning situation. They use their own unique mix of character strengths to challenge thought patterns.

Maintaining perspective: optimism and the importance of action

In *12 Rules for Life* (2018, p. 1), psychologist Jordan Peterson's first rule is 'stand up straight with your shoulders back'. Why? Because brain chemistry is reflected in and affected by our posture. This positive feedback loop is also amplified by the social context. Peterson argues that poor posture not only makes a person look but also feel 'defeated and ineffectual'. Consequently, other people's reactions 'will amplify that … If you start to straighten up, then people will look at and treat you differently' (p. 37).

The connection between thought and action has long been recognised, and is fairly self-evident. In his famous *A Treatise Concerning Religious Affections*, first published in 1746, Jonathan Edwards wrote:

> Yea, it is questionable whether an imbodied soul ever so much as thinks one thought, or has any exercise at all, but that there is some corresponding motion or alternation of motion, in some degree, of the fluids, in some part of the body. But universal experience shows, that the exercise of the affections have in a special manner a tendency to some sensible effect upon the body. (Edwards, 2018, loc. 771)

When people are filled with joy, fear or some otherwise overwhelming affect, their bodily disposition is usually a giveaway. When individuals are defeated, their posture droops, their brain produces less serotonin and they become less happy and more anxious. According to Peterson (2018, p. 26), this produces a positive feedback loop 'adding effect to effect' so that they 'spiral counterproductively in a negative direction'. However, he also tells us that this works the same way in reverse:

> Change might be opportunity, instead of disaster. The serotonin flows plentifully. This renders you confident and calm, standing tall and straight, and much less on constant alert. Because your position is secure, the future is likely to be good for you.

In this posture, an individual no longer feels the need 'to grasp impulsively at whatever crumbs' might be offered (p. 17). They feel in control enough to make thoughtful plans, with the expectation that good things will come. Thus, learners maintaining perspective need to recognise the importance of their own posture.

Zestful learners maintain perspective. They take decisive actions and assume postures that reflect their desired situation.

Maintaining perspective: physical activity

Positive psychology also looks at the relationship between physical activity and psychological well-being/flourishing. Within this topic are the concepts of sleep, exercise and diet.

Sleep, especially deep sleep, is a crucial part of the mind–body's self-repair: 'During sleep we can process information, consolidate memories, and undergo a number of maintenance processes that help us to function during the daytime. Sleep is crucial to the health of individuals' (Robotham et al., 2011, p. 4).

Many teenagers are permanently underslept, running on several fewer hours of sleep than the recommended eight to ten hours needed per night. Exercise is similarly beneficial, enhancing well-being and, with regard to zest, having a clearly positive impact on energy levels. Exercise increases our heart rate and leads to an increase in endorphin levels, which in turn increases energy levels. Expending energy generates energy, as anyone knows who has set out on a jog or brisk walk feeling lethargic and returned feeling rejuvenated.

Eating well not only improves our health, but also has some relationship with mental well-being. For example, one systematic review (O'Neil et al., 2014) found that a diet with high levels of saturated fat, refined carbohydrates and processed food products was linked to poorer mental health in young people.

For many schools these three 'truths' about what makes for healthy learners are hardly new. While they rely on influencing parents to put them into practice at home, there are many practical things that schools can do to provide the necessary underpinning for their students, as we see later in the book.

In summary, the positive psychology literature in the area of physical activity contributes to our understanding of zest for learning through its understanding of the need for sleep, good diet and exercise for flourishing.

Zestful learners maintain perspective. They are developing good habits in terms of diet, exercise, rest and sleep.

Valuing relationships: social well-being (a strength of character)

Social intelligence is a character strength, but it is also what we might call a 'prosocial' outcome of education. It involves two concepts: social awareness (what we sense about other people) and social facility (what we do with that awareness).

Effective ongoing social contact requires both awareness (reading the emotions and wishes of those around you) and facility (knowing how best to interact with people). Jean Lave and Etienne Wenger (1991) have helped us to understand how the social elements of learning work and how context is important. How we learn on a sports field, in a science lab or in a drama studio is heavily influenced by the social situation and by the nature of the activity in which we are engaged. The way learning is organised in a school maths class, a competitive sports team, a rock band or an amateur dramatic society is very different, and these cultural differences strongly influence how people grow and think.

Lave and Wenger coined the phrase 'communities of practice' to describe the kinds of social learning that such cultures require. Members of a community pursue a common interest and help each other as they do so; as they work and solve problems together, so their learning habits and attitudes rub off on each other. New members watch carefully how the more established members talk, respond and deal with challenges, like children do when they want to join someone's 'gang'. Lave and Wenger have called this stage of joining a community 'legitimate peripheral participation'. As we become part of a group or community we necessarily go through a kind of apprenticeship in which we gradually learn how to do something. In order to do this we practise with others, learning from those more skilled (closer to the 'centre' of the community) than ourselves in their repertoires and insights. Practice also suggests that learning is a process, not an event – it takes time.

In summary, the character strengths literature can contribute to our understanding of zest for learning through the concept of prosocial outcomes and the character strength of social well-being. We suggest that the idea of valuing relationships is useful in developing a framework for the habits of zest for learning.

> Zestful learners value relationships. They develop their social awareness and social facility (what they sense about others and what they do with that awareness) to foster positive relationships for learning.

Psychology of motivation

Anyone with zest for learning is, by definition, motivated to learn. Motivation and performance are not the same thing, of course, because there are other factors of which performance is a function. Campbell and Pritchard (1976; cited in DuBrin, 1978, p. 38) proposed that performance is 'some function of' (i.e. f) at least four factors, including skill level and effort. Their equation can be shown like this:

performance = f (aptitude level × skill level × understanding of the task × choice to expend effort × choice to persist × choice of degree of effort to expend × facilitating and inhibiting conditions not under the control of the individual)

While each of the areas under the individual's control might speak to zest for learning in some way, the choice to expend effort and persist are the two areas that relate to motivation.

In one sense, motivation is an overarching concept. Whichever way we break down zest for learning into a set of habits that build it, motivation will have a part to play.

In this section we consider four factors that might be key motivators, and which help us to connect motivation to our framework. These relate to our two habits:

1. Performing well:

    +   The feedback from good performance in terms of experiencing flow.

    +   Expectation of good performance.

    +   Goals worth pursuing.

2. Finding meaning:

    +   A sense of purpose.

We will discuss each in turn.

As we think about motivation and its relationship with flow, it may be helpful to consider the relationships which exist between how challenging a situation is and the level of skill a learner is able to bring to bear. Csikszentmihalyi (1996, p. 30) reminds us that optimal experiences 'usually involve a fine balance between one's ability to act, and the available opportunities for action'. An optimal state of flow sits between the anxiety of too great a challenge and the relaxation of one that is too low (as shown in the figure on page 42).

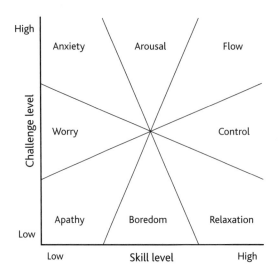

High challenge versus high skill = flow

Source: Csikszentmihalyi (1997, p. 31)

Performing well: the feedback from good performance in terms of experiencing flow

In the introduction we recognised that human beings are born learners and are motivated to learn in part by the feedback they receive from performance. It could be argued that one of motivation's most pertinent contributions to zest is in terms of the motivation that comes from performing well when effort has been expended in learning.

For our purposes, when we talk about performance we don't mean public exhibition, but successfully doing what it is you are trying to learn. This is partly what examinations measure, and also what public exhibition would hope to demonstrate. However, knowing you are performing is not just indicated by verbal feedback or recognition from others. Performance is also personal and speaks to the individual who is doing the learning. It is a culmination of their efforts to date and can represent a significant source of motivation.

It might be a sense of flow (that sense of hedonic being-in-the-moment during performance), achievement, satisfaction or pride. As you experience learning something new in the moment, it is about watching the dots connect, seeing a piece come together, and realising what you still don't know but being able to see the gaps more precisely as the fog of unconscious incompetence clears.

When we explored the literature on positive psychology and theories of intelligence, the concept of flow was seen to lead to a potential feedback loop of perpetuating deliberate practice, which in turn leads to performance, flow and so on:

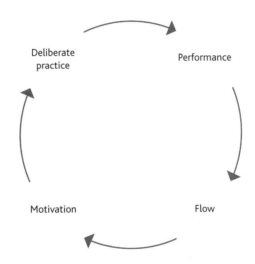

One possible relationship between motivation, deliberate practice and flow

The experience of flow that represents a positive performance could, for some, and under some circumstances, serve as a motivator of deliberate practice. But we recognised in our illustration of the pianist stuck at Grade 5 that this feedback loop is not automatic.

Another reason this feedback loop is not automatic is that engagement is not the same as motivation. Motivation is the 'psychological processes that cause arousal, direction, and persistence of voluntary actions that are goal directed' (Mitchell, 1982, p. 81). But engagement, like flow, does not necessarily lead to exertion of effort. Teachers often fall victim to the 'engagement trap'. We can all think of lesson plans that result in a fully engaged group of young people who are learning nothing!

While performance can be likened to flow, flow doesn't necessarily lead to deliberate practice. In motivation terms, flow does not necessarily motivate. Something else is needed. As such, we leave the contribution to our framework of flow to the theories of intelligence literature, and don't link flow and motivation. Motivation is important to teachers, not just in terms of getting students engaged with discrete tasks, but in terms of understanding what (other than the legal requirement for education) motivates learners to learn, and the degree to which that motivation drives performance on a broader scale.

> Zestful learners perform well. They allow an experience of flow to feed their motivation for more practice, better learning and a more complex performance.

Performing well: being motivated by expectation of good performance

How do we make it more likely that flow or performance will lead to deliberate practice? What literature might bring to bear helpful answers to this question? Within the psychologies of motivation literature are the concepts of hygiene factors and, more importantly, motivators.

Frederick Herzberg (1968) identified that certain factors motivated job performance, while others didn't actually motivate but their absence led to dissatisfaction. He called these 'hygiene factors'. Without extrapolating unreasonably from an employment context to a learning one, nor relying overly on an idea with limitations (e.g. Hinrichs and Mischkind, 1967), the idea that what prevents demotivation may not actually motivate is a useful one.

Herzberg found that factors preventing dissatisfaction were actually external to the job itself. They were concerned with pay and conditions relating to man's 'built-in drive to avoid pain from the environment, plus all the learned drives which become conditioned to the basic biological needs' – things like company policy, supervision, salary, status, security and interpersonal relationships. The factors that actually served to motivate related to job content – things like 'achievement, the work itself, responsibility, and growth or advancement' (Herzberg, 1968, p. 57).

What might these be in the context of zest for learning? Let's consider that there may be a whole range of hygiene factors whose absence inhibits zest for learning but whose presence does not actually motivate. For example, these might be certain combinations of personality traits, optimism, certain character strengths like tenacity, relationships with others and enjoyment.

An individual lacking the character strength tenacity won't necessarily persist to more deliberate practice. Nor will the individual lacking in optimism because he sees external factors as being of more import than his own efforts in leading to positive or negative performance outcomes. This external locus of control, or attribution bias, is a real motivation killer.

Rather than focusing on flow as a motivator, a more useful motivator to consider might be the expectation that good performance will arise from deliberate practice. We could add in a fifth point to the feedback loop:

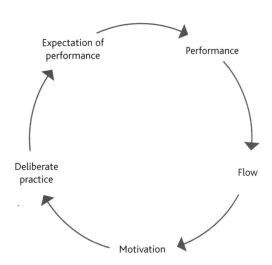

The relation of expectation of performance to motivation

If you have a process in your practice you know you will succeed eventually. An example is the sort of analysis and discussion of literature that goes into developing a conceptual framework like the one this chapter aims to culminate in. It doesn't materialise from the air, but is the result of careful and systematic checking to ensure that every concept discussed takes an appropriate place in the framework. Nothing can bypass the hard work, but you know you will get there eventually because rigour will take you to its logical end.

> Zestful learners perform well. They have good processes in their practice that they can be confident will lead to successful learning outcomes.

Performing well: goals worth pursuing (mastery goals)

A third key motivator could be the possession of goals worth pursuing. Moving away from fixed IQ theories, Carol Dweck's (1999) theory of motivation has been highly influential in understanding learner motivation and how to change it for the better.

Learners tend to split down the middle in terms of how they attribute ability. Those with a fixed mindset believe their ability is fixed at birth, relates to talent and/or genetics, and effort cannot really change their ability to grasp difficult concepts. Those with a growth mindset believe that so-called ability and success are due to learning, which can itself be learned. Differences in performance show up when challenges are particularly difficult, which may not be until learners move onwards to institutions of further or higher education. At this point (in the 'real world') it is clearly of great advantage to hold a growth mindset.

The purpose of teaching students about this theory is that they can change their attribution of ability, which will increase their motivation to learn in a way that is sufficiently robust to withstand setbacks and challenges. They will be more likely to practise and persist, knowing that this is materially efficacious to success. A review by Hattie and colleagues (1996) into the effectiveness of study skills programmes found that those with the greatest impact were those that focused on teaching students about this attribution relationship.

While having performance goals can, of course, motivate performance – and does so to a large degree – this type of goal doesn't lead to zest for learning. It is more likely to lead to success addiction, perfectionism or serious disappointment when learning does not go as planned.

> Zestful learners perform well. They set mastery goals for themselves, valuing the learning of something tricky over performing something they can already do.

Finding meaning: a sense of purpose and/or self-actualisation

A fourth key motivator could be a higher sense of purpose that orients you towards a goal larger than yourself. We talked about finding purpose in our discussion of the real-world learning and embodied cognition literatures.

Maslow's (1943) famous hierarchy of needs is a way of thinking about human needs that has remained influential over the 70 years following its proposal. Organising fundamental needs into a pyramid that goes from basic needs for food to the highest category of human need is intuitively appealing because it corresponds to our common sense (Peterson and Park, p. 320).

The degree to which self-actualisation is a human need, and should remain at the top of the hierarchy, was the subject of debate between psychologists in a special issue of the journal *Perspectives on Psychological Science* in 2010. Kenrick et al. proposed amendments to Maslow's framework that removed self-actualisation as a 'functionally distinct human need' (p. 293) and subsumed it within needs for status/esteem. Although the attempt to update the framework was broadly praised, with Ackerman and Bargh (p. 324) suggesting self-actualisation may now be 'in its proper place as a consequence of goal pursuit in other domains', Peterson and Park (p. 320) saw this move as 'premature'.

The need for self-actualisation or some higher purpose is, however, an important part of what it means to be human. Kesebir et al. drew attention to the way Maslow's description of self-actualisation 'is reminiscent of Aristotle's … concept of *eudaimonia*, which often translates as happiness, a well-lived life, and flourishing' (p. 316). This idea was the ancient philosopher's own attempt at understanding what it is about human beings that sets them apart from other species. Consequently, Kesebir et al. were critical of any theorising on human nature that results in 'stripping off the very things that make humans uniquely human' (p. 316). They argue that 'the need for meaning is another candidate for an ultimate human need' (p. 316). Meaning, they say, is 'derived from a sense of embeddedness, belonging, and relatedness'. It can come from social groups to which people belong and from personal relationships, but also from culturally embedded systems of meaning 'such as art, religion, or scholarly pursuits' (p. 316).

We would argue that the human need for meaning and purpose is a driver of human activity, and can hardly be separated from any quest for finding zest for learning. Maslow (1943, p. 382) described self-actualisation as the individual 'doing what he is fitted for. A musician must make music, an artist must paint, a poet must write, if he is to be ultimately happy. What a man can be, he must be.'

In 1970 Maslow identified fifteen characteristics of people who are able to self-actualise. Of these, eight are of special interest in understanding zest:

1. Unusual sense of humour.

2. Able to look at life objectively.

3. Highly creative.

4. Concerned for the welfare of humanity.

5. Establish deep satisfying interpersonal relationships with a few people.

6. Peak experiences.

7. Need for privacy.

8. Strong moral/ethical standards.

Some of these ideas stretch us beyond the self and into the realm of higher purpose. Operating at the very highest level of your being does not guarantee that you have a sense of purpose, but it is a strong indicator that you are likely to do so.

Zestful learners find meaning. They align their performance goals with a purpose outside of themselves.

Education for flourishing

The field of education is broad, encompassing thinking about such things as teaching, learning, curriculum, pedagogy, teacher education, technology, educational psychology, policy, history and the purpose of education.

In thinking about education for flourishing, for developing a zest for learning, there are two aspects of the field that we want to explore: the purpose of education and the connected area of pedagogy.

First and foremost is thinking within the field that relates to education's purpose. Purpose concerns the values and knowledge that education aims to instil in children and young people. It affects decisions about what are the desirable outcomes for a particular course of study or learning and what learners should be competent to do, or to know, as a result. It will also impact on the way learning is assessed and the value attributed to different subject areas.

Second, we will address the practical aspect of teaching – pedagogy: the science, art and craft of teaching and learning and the many decisions teachers make, both in their planning and in the moment, about how they are going to help learners learn particular material. We will first look at the literature that speaks to the purpose of education, in order to understand how zest for learning fits with this thinking.

We then progress to exploring what the field of learning sciences has to offer our understanding of zest for learning. Three areas of the learning sciences are relevant, and each contribute to thinking about pedagogy: metacognition (thinking about your own thought processes), real-world learning and habits for learning.

Purpose: how zest for learning explains education's purpose

Just prior to the turn of the millennium, the UK's then Labour government famously stated as its top three priorities: education, education, education. The green paper, *The Learning Age: A Renaissance for a New Britain* (DfEE, 1998), in which Secretary of State David Blunkett set out for consultation an agenda for lifelong learning, was very clearly couched in terms of zest, passion and love of learning: 'how learning throughout life will build human capital by encouraging the acquisition of knowledge and skills and emphasising creativity and imagination. The fostering of an enquiring mind and the love of learning are essential to our future success' (p. 7). The rationale for this relates to the idea of longer and more flexible working lives on moving trajectories: 'To cope with rapid change and the challenge of the information and communication age, we must ensure that people can return to learning throughout their lives. We cannot rely on a small elite … Instead, we need the creativity, enterprise and scholarship of all our people' (ibid.).

Our argument for encouraging zest for learning is not about ensuring young people will happily submit to becoming lifelong learners for some instrumental benefit. So, how can we relate lifelong learning to zest, particularly in the knowledge that lifelong learning can so often be driven by need rather than passion?

Finding meaning: lifelong learning

School education aims to prepare young people not just for employment or immediate further study, but for a lifetime of learning. At one time, progression through school and into a trade, vocation or career was relatively linear. It had a clear start and end point, with movement of individuals between organisations, but on the whole within the same sphere of work. Jobs were clearly defined and the age of retirement was fixed (give or take). But careers are no longer so predictable. Various changes in the world's work landscape, both figuratively and literally – as industries relocate, for example – have contributed to a great change in this traditional picture. Consequently, there is a need for flexibility in individuals as they seek to make themselves useful to society.

The idea of lifelong learning can be associated in people's minds with things such as opportunity and pursuit of interest, and with less positive ones such as the necessity of change and accompanying disruption to family life. In order to think about what lifelong learning means for zest in a world where lifelong learning may not always be seen in a positive light, we need to understand its many drivers in order to better comprehend what else those might be, other than a desire for learning. What are the reasons why (young) people may want to continue to learn? There are many, which might include:

+ Economic: to be employable; to gain promotion or to be more 'marketable'; to change personal/family circumstances.

+ Self-improvement: to develop an awareness of some area of human knowledge that helps them to become more understanding, wise, able to reason, think and make decisions.

+ Get better at learning: to develop character through new challenges; to develop learning skills to do better at exams or further qualifications.

+ Interest: to do something that requires a level of skill (surfing, performing a song, driving a car); to move into a new area of work – paid or otherwise – that better fits with their interests or skills as they develop through life experience and/or reading.

+ Active brain: to keep body and/or mind active; to relieve boredom or break up routine; to develop a new pastime or skill.

+ Social: to keep up with or help their own children; to come into contact with different types of people or a 'community of practice'; to make informed opinions in order to become better able to converse with others; to serve others.

This very last point is often missed out. One of our core arguments is that serving others, or some kind of higher meaning than the self, is the key to finding purpose and, ultimately, zest for learning.

This speaks to the concept of vocation. Since church reformer Martin Luther first challenged the secular–sacred divide, Christians have come to understand how their daily lives reflect a vocation just as critical as that of ordained clergy. A major theme in theologian Tim Keller's book on the purpose of work, *Every Good Endeavour* (2012), is that of vocation and purpose in work. Theologically speaking, vocation depends on there being something more important than you. He describes vocation as follows:

> The Latin word *vocare* – to call – is at the root of our common word 'vocation'. Today the word often means simply a job, but that was not the original sense. A job is a vocation only if someone else calls you to do it and you do it for them rather than for yourself. And so our work can be a calling only if it is reimagined as a mission of service to something beyond merely our own interests ... thinking of work mainly as a means of self-fulfillment and self-realization slowly crushes a person and ... undermines society itself. (p. 19)

Keller goes on to explain how sixteenth-century Protestant reformers stressed the way that 'God cared for, fed, clothed, sheltered, and supported the human race through our human labor' (p. 21). Therefore, fulfilling others' needs does not have to mean working for a charitable organisation, the public sector or within traditional 'caring' work domains. Nor does it exclude the aesthetic, educational or recreational aspects of life.

As we argued in our formal response to the Education Select Committee's inquiry into the quality of education in England, the purpose of education needs to be about helping children find their own sense of purpose – to 'know their "best self", and shape their own futures ... A good education uncovers and stimulates children's own innate, unique interests and talents, nurturing their passions and supporting them as they develop understanding' (Lucas and Spencer, 2016).

This idea of vocation, of purpose, resonates with an argument made by Richard Sennett (1998): that in an economic context characterised by the uncertainties of work, individuals are no longer afforded the opportunity to grow into a sense of sustained purpose. The integrity of the self is at stake without this purpose.

Zestful learners find meaning. They navigate through life learning what they need in order to serve a higher purpose.

As well as *who* might be the focus of your learning, the list on page 51 brings to mind the issue of *what* is being learned. These reasons for learning hint at the different sorts of things we might learn. For example, there is a difference between learning to do and learning to know, although we need not rehash debates about types of knowledge here.

What is important is that a person who is a prolific reader can demonstrate just as much zest for learning as a person whose goal is mastery of a particular skill or craft. In *Zest for Learning*, we do not esteem *knowing that* over *knowing how*, or vice versa. This means that the kinds of learning that might interest young people for all of the reasons listed, and which we wish to include in our discussion, might not fit neatly into a lesson timetable divided by subject. There is certainly a large amount of curious finding out about the world that lends itself to studying or trying things (i.e. learning) that might be better represented in out-of-school, extra-curricular or (if we may say it) less highly valued subjects.

> Zestful learners find meaning. They recognise that meaning might come from book knowledge or practical knowledge, and don't limit themselves to one or the other to achieve their goals.

Finding meaning: teaching for character, moral virtues and values

The Jubilee Centre for Character and Virtues (2017) has developed a Framework for Character Education in Schools – see figure on page 54.

The model sees four kinds of virtues producing practical wisdom which enables individuals and society to flourish:

> A society determined to enable its members to live well will treat character education as something to which every child has a right. Schools should consider questions about the kinds of persons their students will become, how the development of good character contributes to a flourishing life, and how to balance various virtues and values in this process. (p. 1)

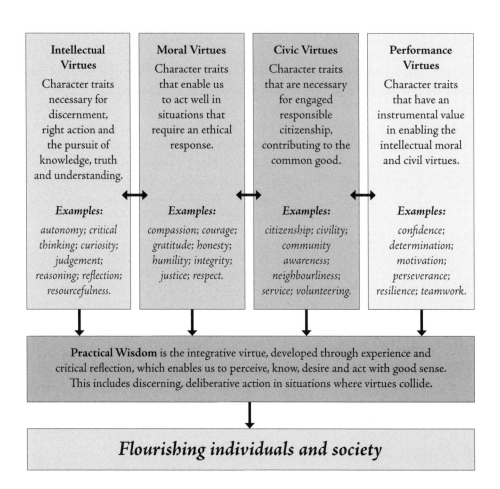

The Framework for Character Education in Schools

Source: Jubilee Centre for Character and Virtues (2017, p. 5)

While we are not convinced that the concept of virtue adequately captures all we are exploring, and nor are we enamoured of the word 'trait', with its associations of fixity, the list of examples encompass much of what we have been exploring.

In our formal written response to the Education Select Committee, we argued for the importance of developing 'performance character', and recognised that some form of formative assessment would be necessary in order for teachers and children to recognise whether they were developing the desired character:

> The capabilities most useful to young people are increasingly called 'performance character', rather than inaccurate descriptors such as 'soft' or 'non-cognitive' skills. They include resilience, positive attitude, self-control, 'grit' and craftsmanship. Valuable in their own rights, they also lead to better educational attainment. Carol Dweck offers strong evidence for the power of 'growth mindset' as a 'super-capability'.
>
> If capabilities and character are to be valued as much as examination results, then some formative and summative measures of their development are desirable ... Research to develop reliable and useful measures is needed. (Lucas and Spencer, 2016)

The literature on positive psychology has much to say about character formation, which we addressed earlier. It led us to suggest that in terms of the habits of mind:

Zestful learners find meaning. They are disposed to act well in terms of character strengths in general, in areas like creativity, curiosity, open-mindedness, love of learning, bravery, persistence, vitality, appreciation of beauty and excellence, hope, humour and spirituality.

The purpose of education literature leads us to consider that character is also important in terms of the habit of mind of finding meaning. Purpose in life has been defined as 'a stable and generalized intention to accomplish something that is at once meaningful to the self and leads to productive engagement with some aspect of the world beyond the self' (Damon, 2008, p. 33).

Bronk and colleagues (2010) helpfully identify two aspects of purpose: the degree to which engagement is focused on a personal goal and the degree to which such energy is focused outwards, beyond the self (see figure on page 56).

High	Beyond-the-self dream	Purpose
Prosocial reasoning		
Low	Drifting	Self-oriented life goal

| Low | Active engagement | High |

Purpose in life: active engagement and prosocial reasoning

Source: Bronk et al. (2010, p. 134)

> Zestful learners find meaning. They recognise that development of character is a valuable aspect of their learning journey and are disposed to develop their character strengths in general.

You will notice here the importance we attribute to character formation; its appearance in both the positive psychology literature and research that speaks to educational purpose demonstrates that in terms of zest for learning, character development can help learners to maintain perspective *and* find meaning.

Finding meaning: situating yourself in the world

In a 2015 Presidential Lecture at Stanford University, Marilynne Robinson argued against an instrumental vision of education and society:

> If it is no longer clear what [universities] should be doing, it is pretty clear what they should not be doing, which is disseminating knowledge and culture, opening minds. The dominant view now is that their legitimate function is not to prepare people for

citizenship in a democracy but to prepare them to be members of a docile though skilled working class. (Robinson, 2018b, loc. 1374)

Elsewhere, Robinson argues for a deeply humanising vision: the value of education for its own sake, the achievement of learning that broadens understanding, the joy of new experiences. The best educational experience will prepare children to be good thinkers.

Education is not about recognising the extraordinary in all children. They are unique, in the way that every human in history has been, but the vast majority of them will live ordinary lives. While those in the developed world may leave more trace of themselves than their ancestors ever did, let us not forget that most of us could not name our great-grandparents, and have far less idea of the occupation or political affinities of our ancestors prior to the last century. The best educational experience will open children's hearts and minds to things they find deeply interesting; those things that, through the accumulation of knowledge, they have learned to be interested in.

Let us consider that the best educational experience will encourage zest for learning as a lifelong mode of being. Teachers are not solely responsible either; parents and children themselves have a major part to play. In *Creating Learning without Limits* (2012), Mandy Swann and colleagues write of their experience reorienting their school away from fixed-ability thinking to focus on building a learning environment that enables everybody. They argue that the most important part of the process is actually the sense of moral purpose that arises when teachers recognise that all the hard work of learning is worthwhile when it serves the goal of 'mov[ing] towards something that people believe is worth striving for. This sense of moral purpose – the contribution that people believe they can make to creating a better world – comes from deep-rooted values; it gives rise to a passion that drives people on and makes the struggle not just worthwhile but even exhilarating' (p. 94). This sounds rather close to a zest for learning. They call this combination of vision and self-efficacy 'passion'.

In summary, a focus on the history and purpose of education with a view to developing zest for learning would lead us to consider ideas that are collectively about finding meaning – concepts like making a connection with the material world, lifelong learning and developing character.

Zestful learners find meaning. They read widely and take a broad interest in the past and present as well as the future. Their learning goals are not purely instrumental and 'career focused', but based on the desire to be educated in a way that is appropriate to develop people who hold humanity in high esteem.

Pedagogy: what the learning sciences tell us about teaching for zest – metacognition

In thinking through the areas of literature that contribute to an understanding of zest for learning, we have placed learning sciences within education rather than psychology. The reason for this is that the learning sciences cover areas like metacognition (understanding your own thought processes, or 'thinking about thinking'), real-world learning and habits for learning. These ideas become important as researchers and teachers think about pedagogy – how best to put these ideas into practice with real learners.

Learning sciences is an interdisciplinary field. In this sense it is neither a pure subset of psychology, nor of education, but uses knowledge and methods from various fields, including 'cognitive science, educational psychology, computer science, anthropology, sociology, information sciences, neurosciences, education, design studies, instructional design' (Sawyer, 2006, p. xi). It seeks to shed light on teaching and learning.

There are a number of academic journals in which work in this field is published, including *Cognition and Instruction, Journal of the Learning Sciences* and *Instructional Science.*

To educate people for flourishing, teachers recognise the importance of referring back to the overarching purpose of that education. In thinking about pedagogy, something we wrote a while ago may be helpful here:

> There is no such thing as 'good pedagogy' or 'best practice' in the abstract. The concept of good teaching and what it might look like makes sense only if we have already specified 'teaching for what?' We need to know what the goal is before we

can begin to think about what the resulting 'desired outcomes' ... might be, and how to achieve them. (Lucas et al., 2012, p. 32)

Exploring the world: thinking about thinking

To be able to explore the world in all its aspects effectively, to maintain a healthy sense of perspective on your learning and to practise well so that you can improve purposefully demands a range of learning strategies. These things require students not just to throw themselves into learning new things but also to be able to stand back and reflect on their thinking and learning processes. This process is what has become known as metacognition.

The term was first used by Flavell (1976, p. 232) to refer to an individual's awareness of thinking and learning:

> Metacognition refers to one's knowledge concerning one's own cognitive processes and products or anything related to them, e.g. the learning-relevant properties of information or data ... Metacognition refers, among other things, to active monitoring and consequent regulation and orchestration of these processes in relation to the cognitive objects or data on which they bear, usually in the service of some concrete goal or objective.

As we have begun to outline the many strands of thought underpinning zest for learning, it will have become clear that many of the opportunities learners have that feed their love of learning are informal and often occur outside school. In these situations, being aware of, and being able to control, their own thought and learning processes is especially important. Zestful learners need, as it were, to have an imaginary coach on their shoulders able to consider which learning method might be most suited to the context in which they find themselves and to deploy the method accordingly. Within school, much more recent meta-analysis by John Hattie (2009) echoes this finding that metacognition improves achievement levels.

In terms of zest for learning, and certainly flourishing in education, it would seem that metacognition is vital.

Zestful learners explore the world. They monitor their own comprehension, self-regulate and display self-control strategies in order to embed their own learning.

Exploring the world: 'playing the whole game'

In terms of zest for learning, two ideas connect well to the concept of metacognition we have just been exploring. The first is David Perkins' concept of 'playing the whole game', and the second is asking the right questions.

In *Making Learning Whole* (2009), Perkins makes an eloquent argument that the teaching of any subject should never be just about content; learners are trying to get better at doing something. Neither is it just about solving a problem; it is about finding it. In short, subject content and metacognition should go hand in hand.

Perkins proposes that any academic subject should be approached as though it were a game of sport. When learning a sport, the player is typically introduced to the whole game rather than isolated parts. This is not to say that the pitcher doesn't practise pitching at a net for hours without ever a game in sight. He suggests there are seven ways that this analogy can work in a school context, and number 7 speaks to metacognition:

1. Play the whole game – engage in an authentic, full version of the thing you are trying to learn.

2. Make the game worth playing – think about what will motivate you.

3. Work on the hard parts – engage in deliberate practice (see the earlier section on theories of intelligence).

4. Play out of town – think about how you can transfer the learning to other contexts.

5. Uncover the hidden game – learn the underlying rules, processes and strategies.

6. Learn from the team – think about how the social context of the learning environment can assist you.

7. Learn the game of learning – use metacognitive strategies as you learn.

> Zestful learners explore the world. They play the whole game as they engage in learning something.

Valuing relationships: asking the right questions

What does good teaching look like? In *The Hidden Lives of Learners*, Ian Wilkinson and Richard Anderson (2007) summarise what is known about teaching *for* learning. In short, the teacher's task is to provide opportunities for students to process and reprocess information in ways that allow them to be better learners:

+   Design learning activities with students' memories in mind: students need to interact with information so that it is embedded in their memories. Learning *how to learn* is important here. By prompting recall of a prior lesson, students become used to this process and start self-questioning 'when they need to cue their own recall' (p. 161).

+   Engage students in activities that enable them to revisit concepts and make connections between them.

+   Monitor individual students' evolving understanding of concepts so that we can decide what to do next.

+   Focus on 'big questions'. Covering fewer of these, but in depth, is better than skimming the surface of the entire curriculum.

+   Capitalise on the peer culture (i.e. by creating a learning culture) to foster learning.

+   Over time, encourage students to manage their own learning activities. Again, this speaks to the importance of learning how to learn, or metacognition. As the authors say: 'A dual goal for teaching, then, is to teach the curriculum content as well as effective procedures for learning the content. Over time, students internalise the procedures into productive "habits of mind" that they can apply on their own to learn new concepts' (p. 163).

Asking the right questions in the appropriate moment is important. In *The Book of Beautiful Questions* (2018), Warren Berger discusses the sorts of questions we might ask if we want to become better decision-makers, to spark creativity, to connect with others or to be a stronger leader. Whatever your purpose for asking questions, the act of enquiring can lead to interesting answers and reveal more questions. For Berger, if a question causes a shift in a person's thinking, it counts as beautiful. This sort of question prompts you to think at a slower pace and widen your aspect beyond what might be a typical reaction, limitation or judgement stemming from emotion. Beautiful questions can give you a nudge in a more productive direction at a crucial juncture in your thinking.

Some of Berger's (2019) questions might be used in the classroom to help learners connect better with others. For example, the 'WAIT question' reminds learners to ask themselves, 'Why am I talking?' and so to think about listening rather than wondering what their own next words might be.

Another metacognitive approach that values the asking of questions is Philosophy for Children, which aims to develop children's thinking and language skills through philosophical enquiry.[4] The approach values letting others speak, careful listening, formulation of clearly articulated questions and precise speech in a social context.

Zestful learners value relationships. They ask interesting questions that value the other person, and are genuinely interested in the answers.

---

4   See https://p4c.com.

Pedagogy: what the learning sciences tell us about teaching for zest – real-world learning

For more than ten years the Centre for Real-World Learning has been at the forefront of developing the idea of real-world learning. By this we mean learning that prepares you for anything you might want to do throughout your life at school, at home, in the community or at work. Real-world learning is authentic and relevant. It is what you do when you are faced with a problem or challenge. It might be as functional as tying a shoelace or sending an email, or as complex as thinking about climate change or global migration. To be a successful real-world learner you need the kinds of capabilities we have been exploring throughout this three-book series.

Maintaining perspective: practical learning

We have already discussed the idea of embodied cognition, that our minds and bodies are intimately connected. But in schools this connection often seems to be a broken one, with much teaching defaulting to more cerebral activity. Where practical learning is found it is often in colleges or, if within schools, aimed at a vocational pathway.

Across the world, schools – especially secondary or high schools – are becoming ever more conscious of the importance of academic achievement: the results. Health and safety concerns coupled with the cost of workshop and lab facilities have also contributed to a general reduction in the number of subjects which have an obviously practical component. Hand and heart work is increasingly being squeezed out in favour of head work. One of our case study schools, Bedales, shows how this need not be the case (see Chapter 4).

We know that an emphasis on practical learning is beneficial in a number of ways: for our health, in understanding and communicating emotions, in expressing our creativity, in the development of expertise, in balancing intellect and intuition (Claxton, 2015). Yet too often in schools it is seen as somehow of second-order importance and not the kind of chosen course for those students who are described as more 'academic'.

> Zestful learners maintain perspective. They actively seek balance in their learning by using hands as well as head.

Maintaining perspective: outdoor learning

In 1987, Bill Lucas founded an organisation called Learning through Landscapes (LTL) in the UK (so at least one of us needs to declare a possible bias here!). LTL's focus was, and is, on getting outdoors at school in the easiest way possible – by using school grounds. Being outdoors in school grounds offers opportunities for experiential learning, for developing an understanding of the natural world and its ecology, for survey work, for first-hand landscape development and for a whole range of applied learning – science, geography, archaeology and so on.

As well as school grounds, outdoor learning includes going to the coast, environmental centres, farms, mountains, rivers, wildlife reserves and many more. Many of the case studies in Chapter 4 explore the wide range of opportunities, from residential activities to learning to sail, going on expeditions and volunteering within the community.

The benefits are widely established. According to Learning and Teaching Scotland (2010, p. 5), outdoor learning 'provides relevance and depth to the curriculum in ways that are difficult to achieve indoors'. The rationale for offering outdoor learning – particularly well-constructed and well-planned activities – is multifaceted. To name just a few, outdoor learning experiences:

+ Are enjoyable to children.

+ Motivate children to become successful learners.

+ Motivate children to develop as healthy, confident, enterprising and responsible citizens.

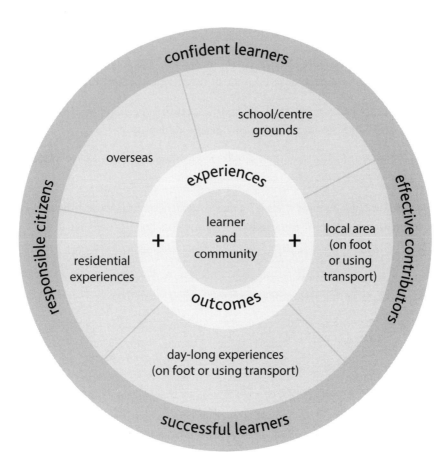

Planning for outdoor learning

Source: Learning and Teaching Scotland (2010, p. 12)

- Connect young people with the natural world, with our built heritage, culture and society, and encourage lifelong involvement and activity in the outdoors.

- Utilise pedagogy that has challenge, enjoyment, relevance, depth, development of the whole person and an adventurous approach to learning at its core.

- Develop professional relationships and networks that contribute to the continuing professional development of teachers and educators.

- Provide clear pathways for delivering the sorts of experience and outcomes that a good and rounded curriculum should demand.

- Contribute to the well-being of children, enabling them to become resilient, responsible citizens and successful lifelong learners.

The figure on page 65 shows how learner experiences and desired outcomes are core to planning, whatever the outdoor learning context.

> Zestful learners maintain perspective. They relish the challenge of learning in unfamiliar outdoor environments, often in all-age groups.

Maintaining perspective: co-curricular and extra-curricular activities

The terms co-curriculum and extra-curriculum have come to be used almost interchangeably in schools. But although they have much in common in terms of their focus on activities and hobbies which are not taught as part of the school timetable, they are different. Co-curricular activities take place during the school day – for example, choir, orchestra, drama and sports practice. There may be choice as to whether students are involved, but they fall within the school day. Extra-curricular activities are discretionary and take place after school, at the weekend or during school holidays. They often involve travel. Many arts activities and sports fixtures fall into this category because more time than can be found within the busy school day is needed. Steyning Grammar School, one of the case study examples in Chapter 4, believes that the co-curriculum is so important that it includes five hours every fortnight of specific character learning to ensure that all students benefit from these experiences.

Co- and extra-curricular activities tend to be less formal than lessons and are often driven by the passions of either teacher or students, or both. They offer wider horizons to young people than can be found within the timetable and a chance to form new relationships. Often they are organised by activity rather than according to age group, providing useful opportunities to develop social skills.

There is clear evidence that out-of-school activities of the kind accessed through the co- and extra-curriculum increases learner engagement and motivation (Washor and Mojkowski, 2013).

> Zestful learners maintain perspective. They engage in co- and extra-curricular activities that keep the goals of education expansive.

Exploring the world: learning through play

There is an enormous body of literature on the study of learning through play. Most associated with the early years of education, playful approaches can serve us well throughout our lives.

Child-centred educational philosophies include those of well-known names like Friedrich Froebel (programme created in 1837), Maria Montessori (method developed in Italy in 1897), Reggio Emilia (introduced in Italy just after the Second World War) and Rudolf Steiner (first school opened in Germany in 1919).

The work of German pedagogue Friedrich Froebel – developer of the 'kindergarten' concept – is a good example. In a piece on his legacy, Eugene Provenzo (2009, p. 85) writes that Froebel's work is not widely recognised in modern education or play theory, beyond acknowledging him 'as a pioneer in early childhood education'. However, he argues that 'those interested in educational reform, in the improvement of our schools, and in the play of our children would do well to reconsider the insights of Froebel' (p. 97).

Zestful learners explore the world. They discover rules, connections, patterns and ideas through playful interactions with objects, ideas and people.

Finding meaning: connecting to the world through your hands

Matthew Crawford's exploration of modern education, *The World Beyond Your Head* (2015, p. 256), makes a compelling argument for learning with your hands and 'reclaim[ing] the real' that educators should take seriously. He writes:

> To reclaim the real in education would be to understand that one is educating a person who is situated in the world and orients to it through a set of human concerns. This is more effective than addressing oneself to a generic 'rational being' and expecting him or her to get excited. (p. 257)

He uses the example of a young boy at school who 'admires the skill and courage of race car drivers', because our 'rational capacities are intimately tied into our emotional equipment of admiration and contempt' (p. 257). The boy knows that this kind of 'human greatness may not be available to him realistically', but he also knows:

> If he learns trigonometry, he can put himself in the service of it, for example by becoming a fabricator in the world of motor sports. He can at least imagine such a future for himself, and this is what keeps him going at school. At some point, the pleasures of pure mathematics may begin to make themselves felt and give his life a different shape. (p. 257)

Crawford's earlier book, *The Case for Working with Your Hands* (2009), is a critique of post-industrial capitalism. His central argument is that we live in a society that is increasingly alienated from the means of production. While he avoids 'the kind of mysticism that gets attached to "craftsmanship"' (p. 5), Crawford believes that the way of life available to the tradesman 'provides many of the same satisfactions' that craftsmanship, an 'ideal', is able to offer. Disillusioned with intellectual work in the city, Crawford opened a motorcycle repair shop. His book is 'an attempt to understand the greater sense of agency and competence I have always felt doing manual work, compared to other jobs that were officially recognized as "knowledge work" ' (p. 5). He adds: 'Perhaps most surprisingly, I often find manual work more engaging *intellectually*' (p. 6; original emphasis).

In *Intelligence in the Flesh* (2015, p. 288), Guy Claxton suggests that real-world learning is often embodied and practical:

> Intelligence is getting things done that matter to you. It is finding good resolutions of those three sets of factors: your concerns, your capabilities and your circumstances. And to do that well you need your body, and you need the kind of broad, detailed integration of its messages that gives rise to conscious awareness. In routine situations we rely, quite rightly, on habit and precedent. It is intelligent of me to operate on automatic pilot most mornings as I prepare to go to work. Intelligence is what allows effective, economical, elegant and appropriate interaction with the world. It is intelligent to accumulate a wide repertoire of such routines.

In one sense, then, manual work connects us to real, tangible, satisfying work. In another, the promise of meaningful manual work can motivate young people to learn the necessary intellectual skills to be able to progress into a field they value.

> Zestful learners find meaning. They value practical problem-solving and find working with their hands satisfying, developing a repertoire of practical routines.

Valuing relationships: craftsmanship for the future

Crawford's (2015, p. 210) argument for rejecting the twenty-first century understanding – that because an appropriate education 'must form workers into material that is … indeterminate and disruptable. The less situated the better' – is persuasive. He writes: 'But consider that when you go deep into a particular skill or art, it trains your powers of concentration or perception. You become more discerning about the objects you are dealing with and, if it all goes well, begin to care viscerally about quality' (ibid.).

Thinking about a person whose work situates them in a long tradition – Crawford uses the example of pipe organ manufacture – he finds that the 'historical inheritance … seems not to burden these craftspeople, but rather energize their efforts in innovation'. It's an orientation towards the future (noting the longevity of what they make) that 'requires a critical engagement with the designs and building methods of the past' (ibid.).

One point in Crawford's narrative that strikes us is the way in which those situated in the real world – the material world of organ repair – are less concerned about getting the job done and more concerned about making the repair in such a way that in years to come, long after they are gone, others will be able to make the necessary repairs that wear and tear make necessary. They have sought out the traditional methods of adhesion of leather to wood because with 'modern glue, you'd be bleeding trying to get it off' (p. 228). To care for the people they have never even met, and may not yet be born, shows a real relish for doing a job properly: 'the recovery of traditional techniques [in much of their work] seems to be motivated not by a hankering after the past, but rather a concern for those who will come later' (ibid.).

What does all this tell us about zest for learning? Some thoughts:

+ It's not just about others who are present; it's about those who are past and those yet to come that motivate zest for learning and doing a job well.

+ Seeing how something – that at first glance seems dull and of no relevance to you – might fit with a hoped-for future, can lead to a zest to master it.

> Zestful learners value relationships. They care about people who will come after them to work on something they are learning how to do.

Valuing relationships: communities of practice

Implicit in Crawford's chapter on pipe organ manufacture is the notion of communities of practice, an idea we met earlier (see page 40). This is a group of people who share a concern or passion for something they do. They learn to do it better as they interact. There is a shared degree of competence and, for those not yet initiated into competence, the concept of 'legitimate peripheral participation' sees them observing from the edge of the community, with a gradual increase in the number of, and importance of, interactions with the work of the group.

These are not just people who share an interest. The clue is in the name: a community of *practice* includes practitioners – people who have real problems to solve. From a communities of practice perspective, school education is not just about what happens in the school, but the community itself forms an unspoken curriculum. The school 'is not a self-contained, closed world in which students acquire knowledge to be applied outside, but a part of a broader learning system. The class is not the primary learning event. It is life itself that is the main learning event' (Wenger-Trayner and Wenger-Trayner, 2015).

This quotation is key to the sort of learning we are writing about in *Zest for Learning*. Learning at school is not limited to the classroom, but must stretch beyond it and always hold the real world close to hand. Combining all these things together we can say that in terms of zest for learning:

+ Children in schools are part of a learning community, but for each child that community will differ slightly. Each child will move along their own trajectory, bringing in different experts at different times, but all in service to the goal of finding their niche.

+ In this respect we can say that there is, in fact, a web of learning communities of which school is a part.

> Zestful learners value relationships. They recognise their ever-shifting place within a community of learners, learning from some and guiding others.

Valuing relationships: imitation

The psychological idea of 'social contagion' (Lucas and Claxton, 2010) helps to explain the transfer of both mood and behaviour among people. Could zest for learning be 'caught' by social contagion?

Much of our learning takes place by observation and imitation. Bandura's (1977) social learning theory describes how children learn by observing models, encoding behaviour (both positive and negative) into their memories and later imitating, depending on mediational processes like attention, retention and ability, to reproduce a behaviour and motivation.

If a zest for learning can be demonstrated through behaviours that show enthusiasm, engagement and focus, it can be observed, encoded and imitated by learners.

> Zestful learners value relationships. They choose to spend time with others who relish learning.

Valuing relationships: grit and passion

Angela Duckworth brought the concept of grit into popular parlance in the education world. Its link to zest is through the passion element of grit.

There are two ways of growing grit: outside in and inside out (Duckworth, 2016, p. 269). The outside in way is where relationships with others are key. For example, Duckworth notes the importance of creating a culture (a group's shared attitudes, values, goals, and practices). This happens through leadership, but also through the presence of others. If a team is gritty, joining it is a good idea, because there is much to be said for conformity. The human motivation to conform increases your chances of acting gritty if you're in a gritty team.

In terms of finding a passion, a close cousin of zest, Duckworth found an interesting thing. There was no light-bulb moment for most of the people she interviewed. Instead, most spent a number of years seeing where other interests took them. They eventually came to find that a single interest occupied their thoughts, and this one 'wasn't recognizably their life's destiny on first acquaintance' (p. 100).

But it's not as simple as trying new things. Duckworth's colleague Barry Schwartz told her:

> There are a lot of things where the subtleties and exhilarations come with sticking with it for a while, getting elbow-deep into something. A lot of things seem uninteresting and superficial until you start doing them and, after a while, you realize that there are so many facets you didn't know at the start, and you never can fully solve the problem, or fully understand it, or what have you. Well, that requires that you stick with it. (p. 102)

What do these quotes tell us about zest for learning? Some ideas come to mind:

+ Having others alongside you on the journey supports the process of embedding yourself sufficiently deeply in an experience to develop a passion for it. It's hard to have zest, grit and passion on your own.

+ Experiences are necessary. Schools that aim to expose their students to a broad curriculum and offer a variety of extra-curricular options are attempting to give them an opportunity to try new things and see what piques their interest. But ...

+ Time is also necessary. Finding your passion usually takes time and arises from a gradual acquaintance with a field of interest, topic of study, type of environment, object, sport, phenomenon, language, culture, concept, creature, whatever, that comes to dominate your thoughts.

As Duckworth summarises: 'here's what the science has to say: passion for your work is a little bit of *discovery*, followed by a lot of *development*, and then a lifetime of *deepening*' (p. 103; original emphasis).

> Zestful learners value relationships. They stick with people who keep going.

Finding meaning: grit and purpose (aligning your goals with a higher purpose)

There is another point worth mentioning about grit. Duckworth (2016, p. 269) suggests that grit can be fostered by connecting your work with some purpose outside of your own self. She defines purpose as 'the intention to contribute to the well-being of others' (p. 146). There tends to be a progression from self-oriented interest, to self-disciplined practice, to an integration of this work with an 'other-centred purpose' (p. 143). What keeps the spark alive in gritty people seems to be the sense that there is a larger purpose than themselves.

In terms of zest, we might conceive that the need for meaning is an important element. This might manifest itself in a number of different ways. From finding an other-centred purpose, to developing your understanding of the world so that you can situate yourself within it, to connecting physically with the material world through the use of your hands, to a development of your moral virtues as well as your performance virtues. All of these things suggest that finding meaning is important.

> Zestful learners find meaning. They connect their learning to the well-being of others in some way.

Pedagogy: what the learning sciences tell us about teaching for zest – habits for learning

Successful learners develop habits which help them to learn well. When they get stuck they do not go to pieces but instead have a repertoire of strategies to get themselves unstuck. When they are working with others on a task, they appreciate that they will need to play different roles, each calling on different routines or habits if the task is to be successfully completed.

In *Redesigning Schooling 2: What Kind of Teaching for What Kind of Learning?* (2013), Claxton and Lucas identify two types of commonly desired outcomes of education: prosocial and epistemic. Into the former category are things like being kind, generous, forgiving, trustworthy and brave. Each of these call upon certain patterns of behaviour: kindness suggests active checking of another's needs, generosity requires a giving disposition and so on.

The outcomes in the latter category relate to the qualities of mind of a learner. They are more than just behaviours, but influence the way in which learners tackle the challenges of life both during and beyond school. Therefore, they are important outcomes of schooling itself. These epistemic outcomes (e.g. inquisitive, resilient, imaginative, craftsmanlike, sceptical, collaborative, thoughtful, practical). They are part of the knowledge, abilities, attitudes, dispositions and values that young people need in order to thrive.

Explicitly seeking to cultivate both prosocial and epistemic dispositions, propensities to think and act in a certain way, is part of helping children to be properly socialised, develop enhanced coping skills and, ultimately, flourish.

Maintaining perspective: dispositions for learning/epistemic outcomes

In Japan, a recognition of the link between behavioural problems and a lack of daily life skills has contributed to a countrywide focus on zest for living, which 'seeks to promote the qualities and abilities necessary to steadily acquire the basics of education and to have self-learning abilities, as well as to develop problem-solving skills and to acquire skills for relating to others' (Kobayashi et al., 2013, p. 123).

It is concerned with supporting a set of life skills that enable children and young people to function well to such a degree that they can thrive. Skills include things like self-discipline, kindness, care for one's own health, the ability to problem-solve and to work with others.

Kobayashi and colleagues found that it was possible to measure zest for living in children using a scale with questions fitting into seven categories:

1. Problem-solving/synthesis (e.g. able to solve a problem by reasoning or to examine and compare various options).

2. Relationship with friends (e.g. able to have an honest discussion with a friend).

3. Personal manners (e.g. able to be polite to older people).

4. Decision-making and future planning (e.g. able to consider self-development needs).

5. Self-learning (e.g. able to plan for doing homework).

6. Collecting and using information (e.g. able to find and summarise sources of information).

7. Leadership (e.g. able to summarise everyone's opinion in a discussion).

Intuitively, we can see why each of these examples might indicate zest for living. In fact, the polar opposite of these sorts of behaviours – for example, inability to prioritise, closed off from relationships, inability to think about the future, lacking motivation, lethargy and inability to inspire others – could demonstrate a depressed individual.

Not all the factors that comprise zest for living are necessarily relevant to zest for learning. Relevant factors might be problem-solving, decision-making, self-learning and collecting and using information. The figure below summarises where the zest for living connection leaves us.

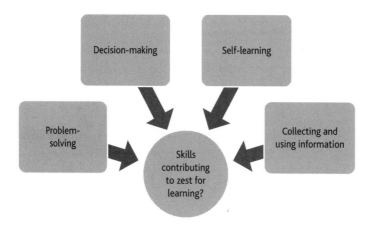

A subset of the skills that measure zest for living might also be indicative of zest for learning

In summary, the skill for effective living literature can contribute to our understanding of zest for learning through its own concept zest for living. The dispositions identified in the figure on page 76 show how the literature contributes to our understanding of what it might mean to have a zest for learning by identifying what zest for living means.

> Zestful learners maintain perspective. They develop dispositions for learning that enable them to learn well generally in areas like problem-solving, decision-making, self-learning and the ability to collect and use information with discernment.

Maintaining perspective: tenacity

In *Developing Tenacity*, we used the word 'tenacity' to draw together a number of related concepts. The grit concept has obvious links to tenacity, but remains conceptually distinct because it encompasses the element of passion. Our focus was on synthesising a framework of learnable elements.

Our framework included the habit of committed, with its sub-habits of keeping things in context, staying optimistic and seeing beyond the immediate.

The dispositions for learning literature can contribute to our understanding of zest for learning through its concept of tenacity. We suggest that the idea of being committed to the pursuit of knowledge and expertise can be useful in developing a framework for the habits of zest for learning.

> Zestful learners maintain perspective. They are committed to the pursuit of knowledge and expertise.

Exploring the world: creative thinking

In *Teaching Creative Thinking*, we looked closely at the learning disposition of creative thinking. There is a natural crossover between the idea of a zest for learning and the epistemic curiosity of an individual who thinks creatively.

Novelty, writes Susan Engel in *The Hungry Mind* (2015), is what helps human infants survive. Young children 'actively seek explanations in the phenomena around them' (p. 30). But the disposition to welcome novelty is a function of temperament. If it is not used, it risks being further quashed:

> Given that a core feature of curiosity is not only the ability to detect novelty, but an impulse to explore novel events and objects, children who are distressed or shrink back from new experiences will have far fewer opportunities to sate their curiosity, and may in fact feel it in a more muted way, or less often, because it competes with a sense of tension or fear. (p. 33)

We also know that curiosity is neither wholly a cognitive nor wholly an emotional experience. Furthermore, 'children with greater emotional and self-governing resources ... exhibit more curiosity as they get older' (p. 40).

Curiosity, Engel tells us, 'is an expression, in words of behaviors, of the urge to know more – an urge that is typically sparked when expectations are violated' (p. 17).

Zestful learners explore the world. They are curious about things and want to explore. They seek out explanations for things happening around them.

Summary

This chapter has brought together thinking from two large and key bodies of knowledge: psychology, and education, particularly the literature relating to education for flourishing.

As we read and mapped out the common themes within these areas of literature, we noticed a number of dispositions, or habits, of zest for learning coming to the fore.

These were: valuing relationships, maintaining perspective, exploring the world, embracing novel experiences, finding meaning and deepening understanding. Both literatures, psychology and education for flourishing, have contributions to make in terms of our understanding of these dispositions.

In the preceding sections, these six dispositions were signposted within each of the topics that our reading of the relevant research literature brought to light. In Chapter 2, we develop these themes into a framework. Chapter 3 then looks at how these can be developed in school by allowing learners to have relevant 'signature experiences'.

Chapter 2
A Framework for Zest for Learning

A noble purpose drives a person to make a positive difference in the world.

William Damon, *The Path to Purpose* (2008, p. 28)

We begin this chapter with our conceptual framework for zest. In our usual style, this is a practical framework drawn from research with six habits arising directly from a very broad range of literature. It has taken us a little longer to get here than in the earlier two books as the concept has needed more teasing out than either creative thinking or tenacity.

A particular challenge is that zest for learning, as we are defining it, requires a holistic engagement from schools encompassing all aspects of curriculum, from formal to co- to extra- and ultimately to the hidden curriculum.

Now that we have laid out carefully where the concepts have come from, we are in a position to put aside the labels that describe those bodies of literature (like 'learning sciences' or 'positive psychology'). We have distilled these into six key themes to describe the dispositions of an individual with zest for learning:

1. Valuing relationships.

2. Maintaining perspective.

3. Exploring the world.

4. Embracing novel experiences.

5. Finding meaning.

6. Performing well.

If you go back now to Chapter 1, you will see these themes identified in subheadings and grey summary boxes within each section.

We propose that these six themes pair up such that three habits of the individual with zest for learning become apparent. We call these three habits: *balanced, curious* and *purposeful*. The framework below is essentially our definition of what it means to have zest for learning.

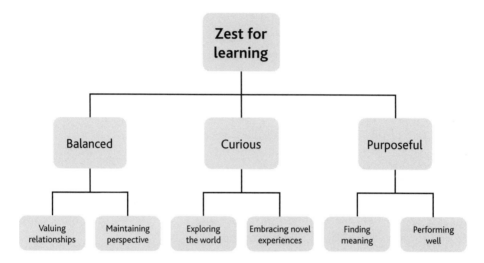

A three-dimensional model of zest for learning: balanced, curious and purposeful

In the following tables, we draw together the explanations of what each of the six dispositions mean from the grey boxes throughout Chapter 1. These explanations allow teachers to be sure of how we are defining each one, based on the literature that speaks to the concept.

Balanced

Zestful learners are balanced: they value relationships and maintain perspective.

Balanced learners value relationships

This means that learners ...	Based on literature that speaks about
... care about people who will come after them to work on something they are learning how to do.	Craftsmanship for the future.
... recognise their ever-shifting place within a community of learners, learning from some and guiding others.	Communities of practice.
... choose to spend time with others who relish learning.	Imitation.
... stick with people who keep going.	Grit and passion.
... develop their social awareness and social facility (what they sense about others, and what they do with that awareness) to foster positive relationships for learning.	Social well-being (a strength of character).
... ask interesting questions that value the other person, and are genuinely interested in the answers.	Asking good questions.

To illustrate using examples from organisations whose case studies appear in Chapter 4:

Learners at Explorer Scouts, part of the UK's Scouting movement for 14–18-year-olds, learn to value relationships through communities of practice when they take on the role of being a Young Leader. Young Leaders are mentored and trained as part of their learning journey.

Learners in Forest School programmes – which run in and beyond the UK – benefit from outdoor opportunities with others where grit is modelled and contagious. Watching adults struggle to get a fire lit on a damp day is a great leveller. Those same adults can be appreciated by young people who witness this struggle both for their empathy and their determination to get the fire lit.

Learners at the Langley Heritage Primary in Slough, England, benefit from the opportunity to do something practical that will be valued by the community that comes after them. Each cohort takes its turn to make annual repairs to the replica Iron Age roundhouse. Learners come to recognise the significance of their own work, and the care and attention to detail that will be needed if the roundhouse is to last another year for the benefit of future cohorts. Knowing that their work matters to others contributes to a sense of pride in a job well done.

The Australian Centre for Rural Entrepreneurship – operating in Victoria with the purpose of building a thriving rural Australia – aims to develop a sense of craftsmanship for the future, and also social well-being, by helping to turn young people's ideas into mini enterprises that benefit their own rural communities rather than being purely for-profit. Learners need to be thoughtful enough to recognise the needs of others and think about how they can meet them.

Learners experiencing the Creative Schools programme at FORM, in Australia, develop their social well-being as they are challenged to think from others' perspectives. Collaborative learning activities encourage them to look at the world from the standpoint of their peers, learners from a different age group, or refugees.

Balanced learners maintain perspective

This means that learners ...	Based on literature that speaks about
... develop dispositions for learning that enable them to learn well generally in areas like problem-solving, decision-making, self-learning and the ability to collect and use information with discernment.	Dispositions for learning/epistemic outcomes.
... are committed to the pursuit of knowledge and expertise.	Tenacity.
... are disposed to act well in terms of character strengths in general, in areas like creativity, curiosity, open-mindedness, love of learning, bravery, persistence, vitality, appreciation of beauty and excellence, hope, humour and spirituality.	Character strengths – hope, zest, curiosity, gratitude and love.
... recognise the degree of agency they have in order to improve in any learning situation. They use their own unique mix of character strengths to challenge thought patterns.	Optimism and the importance of perception/mindset.
... take decisive actions and assume postures that reflect their desired situation.	Optimism and the importance of action.
... are developing good habits in terms of diet, exercise, rest and sleep.	Physical activity.

This means that learners …	Based on literature that speaks about
… actively seek balance in their learning by using hands as well as head.	Practical learning.
… relish the challenge of learning in unfamiliar outdoor environments, often in all-age groups.	Outdoor learning.
… engage in extra- and co-curricular activities that meet the goals of a good education.	Co- and extra-curricular activities.

Learners at West Rise Junior School on the south coast of England develop their ability to maintain perspective through a combination of practical and outdoor learning opportunities. Outdoor learning reminds them of nature and the changing seasons, which offer unique and powerful learning opportunities for the children. Ewes will give birth to lambs on the school playing field in the spring; in the summer months the children will paddleboard and swim in the lake; and in the autumn and winter the children learn to appreciate the need for a fire and warm food as they gather wood and build shelters.

At Steyning Grammar School in West Sussex, England, students benefit from five hours of specific character learning each fortnight. This aims to develop their character, including their zest for learning, by offering the opportunity for balance through extra- and co-curricular activities that help them to develop their own interests. These lessons focus on the impact learners can have on the lives of others in their community, which gives them a developing sense of purpose.

Steyning's students are also familiar with the concept of optimism. They are taught it specifically, and mentoring interventions are in place to enhance the optimism of those measuring low in it.

Curious

Zestful learners are curious: they explore the world and embrace novel experiences.

Curious learners explore the world

This means that learners ...	Based on literature that speaks about
... are curious about things and want to explore. They seek out explanations for things happening around them.	Creative thinking.
... recognise that fulfilling practical and theoretical work both make cognitive demands, and value each equally. They reflect on their practical experiences in order to learn from them.	Experiential learning.
... monitor their own comprehension, self-regulate and display self-control strategies in order to embed their own learning.	Thinking about thinking.
... play the whole game as they engage in learning something.	'Playing the whole game'.
... discover rules, connections, patterns and ideas through playful interactions with objects, ideas and people.	Learning through play.

Young sailors involved with the Royal Yachting Association, Britain's national governing body for boating sports, are given the opportunity to develop their curiosity by learning through play. Coaches for the under-18s use a 'deliberate play' approach, providing experiences that allow sailors to explore and test different solutions.

Pupils at the Langley Academy Primary benefit from a 'museum learning' approach that uses hands-on experience to teach ideas. The concept of prehistory, and the way we can learn about it, is taught through the use of real archaeological artefacts and practical introduction to its various methods of study and the thinking and decisions involved.

Holyport College in Berkshire, England, seeks to inspire curiosity and a passion for the world in its young people. The vehicles it uses for this include exchanges, field trips and day trips, museum visits and conferences. Students are also able to try out some of the societies on offer at Eton College.

Learners at Shireland Collegiate Academy in the West Midlands, England, benefit from a remodelled curriculum called Literacy for Life. A reorganisation of subjects into themes engages learners' curiosity and encourages them to explore the world. A 'connected curriculum' helps them seek out and make connections between areas in the real world – for example, they might explore the practical skills of buying a house in real life, the economics of house design or aesthetics in art.

Curious learners embrace novel experiences

This means that learners ...	Based on literature that speaks about
... keep their minds open to the cognitive exploration of ideas using judgement, critical thinking and rationality. They recognise their own tendencies and push themselves to take on new challenges wherever possible.	Openness to experience.

This means that learners …	Based on literature that speaks about
… demonstrate a willingness to take risks in order to seek varied, novel, complex and intense learning experiences. They are doggedly curious, with a keenness to understand how things can be made better.	Restlessness, sensation-seeking and risk-taking.

Learners with the Royal Yachting Association develop their curiosity because they are open to experiences. The team's culture supports sailors to be 'curious and willing to try new things'. Leavers who move into the Olympic programme are expected to 'learn from mistakes and embrace learning opportunities'. Coaches are also expected to be 'fascinated with how people learn and make decisions.'

Children at Colegio Kopernikus in Chile come to appreciate that opportunities for learning come from all sorts of places, and not just school. Like many schools, Kopernikus recognises that today's students are tomorrow's global citizens and need to be educated to embrace novel experiences. The school takes every opportunity to engage learners with the community and cultural environment, and to bring in new ideas from external visitors.

Learners experiencing the Creative Schools programme, which brings together teachers and creative practitioners in Australian classrooms, are challenged every week to stretch outside of their comfort zone. They might be undertaking team-building challenges or filming adverts to grow their understanding of other cultures.

Purposeful

Zestful learners are purposeful: they find meaning and perform well.

Purposeful learners find meaning

This means that learners ...	Based on literature that speaks about
... value practical problem-solving and find working with their hands satisfying.	Connecting to the world through your hands.
... connect their learning to the well-being of others in some way.	Grit and purpose (aligning your goals with a higher purpose).
... recognise the inherent value of the body and the intelligence involved in – and dignity that comes from – working with it.	Embodied cognition.
... read widely and take a broad interest in the past and present as well as the future. Their learning goals are not purely instrumental and 'career focused', but based on the desire to be educated in a way that is appropriate to free people who hold humanity in high esteem.	Situating yourself in the world.

This means that learners …	Based on literature that speaks about
… are disposed to act well in terms of character strengths in general, in areas like creativity, curiosity, open-mindedness, love of learning, bravery, persistence, vitality, appreciation of beauty and excellence, hope, humour and spirituality. … recognise that development of character is a valuable aspect of their learning journey and are disposed to develop their character strengths in general.	Teaching for character, moral virtues and values.
… spend time doing what they love.	Self-actualisation and flow.
… align their performance goals with a purpose outside of themselves.	A sense of purpose and/or self-actualisation.
… navigate through life learning what they need in order to serve a higher purpose. … recognise that meaning might come from book knowledge or practical knowledge, and don't limit themselves to one or the other to achieve their goals.	Lifelong learning.

At Bedales School in Hampshire, England, students find meaning through practical work that connects them to the world. A philosophy, religion and ethics student might find themselves in the design department making a model to illustrate their theory of mind–body interaction for a presentation, or a global awareness student might find themselves working in a group on an awareness-raising campaign about a global health issue.

At West Rise Junior School, in Eastbourne, England, learners find meaning through the use of practical tools that connect them to real world of making and eating. All of the children learn to light a fire, cook on it, forage and use tools to make wooden objects.

Learners with Explorer Scouts engage in purposeful learning as they find a purpose beyond themselves with which to engage. They choose their own community impact projects, engaging in a range of social action themes that enable them to develop aspects of their character, such as empathy. A group in Cumbria carried out an accessibility audit of their local community.

A very immediate example of purposeful learning is demonstrated by teenagers with attention deficit hyperactivity disorder (ADHD) working with Forest School programme instructors. Unable to sustain attention in the classroom, the teenagers were able to focus intently on the learning skills involved in lighting a good fire. While perfecting the process may take weeks of concentration, the director of the Forest School Association, Sarah Lawfull, explains that the result is worth the effort: 'bread has never tasted as good as when cooked on a fire you have built and lit yourself'. Feeding yourself is one of the most fundamental of all practical problems that requires hands-on efforts.

Purposeful learners perform well

This means that learners ...	Based on literature that speaks about
... engage in deliberate practice with a view to improving their knowledge, expertise or performance.	Deliberate practice (expertise).
... are able, having practised deliberately, to experience an opportunity to enjoy the fruits of their work in a moment of things 'going well', whether alone or performing to others.	Experiencing flow.

This means that learners ...	Based on literature that speaks about
... allow an experience of flow to feed their motivation for more practice, better learning and a more complex performance.	Experiencing flow (the feedback from good performance).
... have good processes in their practice that they can be confident will lead to successful learning outcomes.	Motivation by expectation of good performance.
... set mastery goals for themselves, valuing the learning of something tricky over performing something they can already do.	Goals worth pursuing (mastery goals).

Learners with the Royal Yachting Association are purposeful about their learning through deliberate practice as coaches set challenging problems. Through deliberate training, coaches learn to expose sailors systematically to learning environments that vary the conditions of practice, trying out different approaches in different situations.

Learners at the Langley Academy have the opportunity to build the study of real-life histories into their development of drama performance pieces through exposure to artefacts and archives. This helps learners to engage in purposeful thinking. It gives them the goal of producing a more meaningful and mature performance, one that reaches empathetically into the experiences and emotions common to man.

Learners who benefit from the Australian Centre for Rural Entrepreneurship's social enterprise programme experience the sense of accomplishment that arises when real community members see, and engage in, an up-and-running social enterprise that impacts on their own lives. These meaningful connections are goals learners can see are worth pursuing and that give their enterprise genuine purpose.

Our framework for zest has been developed both from the literature and empirically through the exploration of existing practices in schools and in those working with schools. In the next chapter we consider those learning experiences which are most likely to cultivate zest in young people.

Chapter 3
Cultivating Zest

Focusing on signature experiences

Zest predicts not only general life satisfaction but also work satisfaction and the
stance that work is a calling.

Christopher Peterson, Nansook Park, Nicholas Hall and
Martin Seligman, 'Zest and Work' (2009, p. 167)

Let's go back to one of our questions in the introduction. If you wanted to teach
someone how to develop zest, what methods would you choose? What, in short,
are the kinds of experiences you would want to offer young people to develop their
zest for learning?

There are four key steps:

1. Develop a real understanding of the capability – zest.

2. Manage the learning: signature experiences and engaging methods chosen
   to expand horizons.

3. Harness learner engagement and commitment to the capability: create
   opportunities for student leadership.

4. Establish a supportive climate: leadership that is outward facing; expansive
   learning embedded in the formal curriculum; co- and extra-curricular
   opportunities; partnership working with outside organisations; a
   programme of outside trips; engaged adults modelling their own zest for
   learning; and a reward system which values zest.

In the previous chapter we outlined a framework for zest for learning, providing
lots of help with step 1. In this chapter we explore in more detail the kinds of
methods, or signature learning experiences, that are likely to cultivate zestful

learners and the opportunities these afford for deep learner engagement. In Chapter 4 we showcase an array of schools and supporting organisations who are really taking these ideas seriously, and in Chapter 5 we summarise the leadership implications of everything we have been describing.

We have arrived at this set of signature learning experiences by considering all of the key concepts that came to light when we explored the literature (the appendix lays this out in full). For example, the concept of connecting to the world through your hands came from the literature on real-world learning which told us something about what it means to have zest for learning. This concept led us to consider that a signature learning experience that might lead to a young person finding meaning – given what we know about the importance of real-world learning for zest – is the experience of making something tangible with your hands and with tools. Our shorthand for this is the learning method 'learning by making'.

Signature learning experiences

Here is the whole list of the experiences/methods we will now explore:

+ Learning by making (and by the promise of making).

+ Learning through the arts.

+ Learning by volunteering.

+ Learning in and through worship.

+ Learning through sports.

+ Learning by reading (widely).

+ Learning in and through museums.

+ Learning by following.

+ Learning by practising.

+ Learning by deliberate searching.

- Learning by performing.

- Learning through conversation and listening.

- Learning by explicitly developing life skills.

- Learning by travel/being away from home.

- Learning by joining clubs/trying something new.

- Learning by planning and following through.

- Learning by researching.

- Learning through reflection.

- Learning by teaching.

- Learning by being mentored.

- Learning from others' experiences.

- Learning by being coached.

- Learning through play and games.

- Learning by exercising.

- Learning by being outdoors with nature.

- Learning by imitation.

- Learning by socialising.

Some of these signature experiences are linked to one sub-habit (balanced, curious or purposeful), some to two and others to all three. We also illustrate each signature experience with one or more examples, which are listed in Chapter 6.

As we researched this book we found many organisations which share some or all of these ideas. They offer their own interpretation of what zest for learning means and the multiple ways they seek to engender this in the young people with whom they interact. By probing their descriptions we have been able to validate our list of signature experiences, expand our thinking and identify key messages for schools and those with whom they are working in partnership.

In this way, we have generated what we believe to be a comprehensive list of signature learning experiences, informed by both the literature that speaks to zest for learning, as well as by practices in the field. What is noticeable is that there is a great degree of overlap: nothing arises in practice that could not be deduced from the literature, and our exemplar organisations use a whole range of experiences. But there is always room for improvement, and we provide this full list with the aim that keen teachers, schools and the leaders of outside organisations involved with young people can be inspired by the practices to which the research gives rise.

While some teachers may wish to focus on signature learning experiences that develop a particular sub-habit (for example, purposeful learners), it is perhaps more useful to teachers to have the full list of signature learning experiences from which to choose, with the hope of developing zest for learning more generally. But breaking down zest for learning into three sub-habits means we have been able to consider the ways in which it can be developed more thoroughly. Now that has been done, there is no need to be prescriptive now about which experience leads to which sub-habit. Experience tells us that these ideas are springboards from which teachers can explore the development of zest more broadly.

The rest of this chapter is an ordered analysis showing how each of the key literatures and the concepts that emerge from them can be linked to real, practical teaching and learning methods. We lay out a number of methods or signature learning experiences to help develop purposeful, curious and balanced learners.

+ Purposeful learners find meaning and perform well. There are a number of key concepts for the learner who finds meaning, including embodied cognition and lifelong learning.

+ Curious learners embrace novel experiences and explore the world. Key concepts include risk-taking and learning through play.

+ Balanced learners value relationships and maintain perspective. Key concepts for the balanced learner include ideas of craftsmanship and imitation.

In some cases we have already talked about these approaches to learning in Chapter 1. In other cases, a signature learning experience is mentioned for the first time, and we draw on some related literature to illustrate.

Learning by making

Learning that develops purposeful learners involves helping them to find meaning. One of the key concepts from the literature that tells us about this is the idea of connecting to the world through your hands: *learners value practical problem-solving and find working with their hands satisfying.* This is about connecting to the physical material world as well as connecting to the social world across time. A signature learning experience we think might be useful here is learning by making. Examples might be:

Public art. This might involve making something tangible with your hands and with tools, or making something that the school or organisation needs and will use and keep for a long time. For example, learners might make a piece of public art as the outcome of a project in the community. The project might seek to understand the identity of places that visitors have come from.

Artefact project. This might be something like an artefact project. The WJEC exam board (WJEC CBAC, 2015, p. 78) gives examples of 'well framed artefact projects':

+ To produce a scale model of a trebuchet for under £100 that is capable of throwing a tennis ball over ten metres.

+ To manufacture a leather bomber jacket for under £100 using the school laser cutter.

+ To write and produce a short film on the Syrian refugee crisis aimed at learners of sixth form age.

Another aspect to learning by making is the idea that being able to make, construct and interact with the 'real world' depends on other foundational knowledge. Matthew Crawford's (2015) real-world learning example told us of a boy who learned to be keen on maths because of the promise it provided. He recognised that the practical application of more abstract learning about trigonometry could lead to a fulfilled goal of practical work with cars. Courses in design and realisation or design technology work in the same way. Learners are able to develop and use their knowledge of materials and tools in the construction of something tangible. The promise of making that background theoretical learning provides can also therefore help learners to find meaning.

> **Multifunctional practical project.** Learners might collaborate on a practical project to build raised beds in their school playground that serves multiple purposes: utilising recycled materials, providing a barrier between different play zones, 'greening' the playground environment and providing ingredients for the school kitchen or plant specimens for science lessons.

Learning through arts

Another signature learning experience for helping learners to find meaning through the connection of the world with their hands is that of learning through the arts. There is an obvious sense in which the arts have a contribution to make in developing zest for learning. Alexander (2017, p. 1) tells us: 'at their best the arts excite, amaze, inspire and move us ... they compel us to step out of the here and now into the realm of the possible and barely apprehended ... they are unique and powerful ways of making sense of ourselves and our world'.

Art serves different purposes in education: on the one hand, there is the subjective teaching of art as creative self-expression; on the other, a more objectivist approach sees art education as an induction into 'conventions, techniques, and discipline' or 'making, responding, performing, and appraising' the value of art (Fleming, 2010, pp. 52, 56).

The inclusion of learning through arts in our list of approaches for developing zest for learning is based on the assumption that art is an essential part of human expression. It is arguably an important tool for developing cognition and innovative thinking (UNESCO, 2005) and for teaching emotional intelligence (Ivcevic et al., 2014).

Artists need to have openness, which means they look 'at the world with interest and receptiveness' (Ivcevic et al., 2014, p. 9). A case could be made that art offers space for individuals to remain open to how a piece of work will unfold – that is, to get used to tolerating uncertainty. And perhaps if art can help develop openness, then it can also develop zest for learning.

Art may take many forms, but we are thinking of something that leads to a tangible product reflecting the use of the hands or body in its creation.

Sculpture and the body. Learners participating in the 14–18 NOW learning programme – commemorating the centenary of the end of the First World War – worked with artists and heritage specialists exploring themes of the Great War, connecting the global conflict with their experiences today.[1] Using themes from an exhibition called 'The Body Extended: Sculpture and Prosthetics' as a catalyst for enquiry, the students wrote their own poems and performed them, made films, created an art newspaper and made their own sculptures, which were displayed at Leeds City Museum.

Learning through arts may also be helpful in developing curious learners by helping them to embrace novel experiences. Curious learners *keep their minds open to the cognitive exploration of ideas using judgement, critical thinking and rationality. They recognise their own tendencies and push themselves to take on new challenges wherever possible.* An example might be something that helps them be inspired to look at the world with interest or from a different angle.

---

1   Learning resources and projects from 14–18 NOW are available at: https://www.1418now.org.uk/learning-engagement/learning-resources.

Creating art with the body. In the twentieth century, the links between the body and art went beyond the concept of beauty to explore how the body could be used to create art. Performance art is an extension of this. A skilful example of use of the body in art is Texan artist Natalie Fletcher, who uses the human body as a canvas for painting people into their surroundings. Young dancer/artist Josh Hoffman combines contemporary and street dance with art to create unique canvases.[2] Learners at school might work on an art piece that expresses some connection between their own body and the natural world.

Learning by volunteering

Learning that develops purposeful learners involves helping them to find meaning. One of the key concepts from the literature that tells us about this is the idea of grit and the alignment of your goals with a higher purpose. A signature learning experience we think might be useful here is learning by volunteering, which can help *connect their learning to the well-being of others in some way.*

This might involve helping learners to find something to volunteer for which holds importance or personal significance. It might be in school, through after-school clubs or extra-curricular activities and responsibilities, or it might be out of school.

Elected positions. An example in school might be standing for an elected role. At Claypole Church of England Primary School, volunteering is seen as an activity that everyone can be involved with and benefit from.[3] The school encourages pupils to contribute to the school and its community. In particular, it offers pupils roles that give them individual responsibility, where they can support the life and work of the school. Pupils can stand for election to be representatives on the pupil parliament or to be house captains. Older pupils

---

2   Watch Josh at: https://www.lastbusmagazine.com/post/sonder-presents-a-dance-with-paint.
3   See http://www.claypoleprimary.org/curriculum-overview.

can apply and be interviewed for positions of responsibility including phone duty, fruit monitor, librarian, sports ambassador and playground leader. Pupils in class can volunteer to take on duties at lunchtime or organising equipment for collective worship.

Unfortunately there is a remarkably low uptake of the sorts of volunteering activities secondary schools in England offer through extra-curricular programmes. The Sutton Trust, a UK foundation set up to improve social mobility through education, recommends means-tested vouchers for low-income families, either from the government or through schools' own pupil premium funding (Cullinane and Montacute, 2017).

The Duke of Edinburgh's Award, which requires participating young people to engage in volunteering, can take place during school hours. It can be used by schools as a way of creating an alternative curriculum, particularly with young people for whom exclusion is a risk.

Duke of Edinburgh's Award. Volunteering that develops purposeful learners might be something like the Duke of Edinburgh's Award.[4] This requires participating young people (aged 14–25) to take part in a volunteering activity which is about 'choosing to give your time to help people, the community or society, the environment or animals'. Some schools have even adopted a Duke of Edinburgh's Award programme as their curriculum for certain challenging cohorts to develop 'positive citizenship', among other outcomes. Activities included:

+ Planning, budgeting, marketing and carrying out a fundraising event to produce a sensory garden at an old people's home, and creating a coastline conservation garden at the local Royal National Lifeboat Institution (RNLI) station.

---

4   Further information on the Duke of Edinburgh's Award volunteering requirements are available at: https://www.dofe.org.

- ✦ Highlighting the dangers of using a mobile phone when driving by using remote-controlled model cars.

- ✦ Delivering ICT sessions to non-computer users from rurally isolated areas, teaching them how to operate a computer, the basics of common applications, sending emails and surfing the Internet.

- ✦ Delivering leaflets for the parish council.

- ✦ Engaging in a local church project.

Learning that develops balanced learners involves helping them to value relationships. One of the key concepts from the literature that tells us about this is the idea of craftsmanship for the future. Zestful learners *care about people who will come after them to work on something they are learning how to do.* The signature learning experience of learning by volunteering might be useful here too.

Restoration project. This might involve a project to restore something for the school or community. Young learners who are learning to identify trees and plants might help to maintain a seating area in the school's outdoor learning area where future students will sit and make sketches.

Learning in and through worship

Learning that develops purposeful learners involves helping them to find meaning. One of the key concepts from the literature that tells us about this is the idea of grit and the alignment of your goals with a higher purpose. Zestful learners *connect their learning to the well-being of others in some way.* Learning through worship is about connecting learning to faith, wisdom, meaning and vocation.

All education is a moral activity (Claxton and Lucas, 2013). A Church of England report, *The Fruit of the Spirit* (2015, p. 3), observed: 'There is no such thing as a neutral education. As soon as we begin to teach something to someone else, we are inevitably making value judgements about what we are teaching, how we are teaching it and why we are teaching it.'

Pulitzer Prize-winning essayist Marilynne Robinson (2018a, loc. 580) has stated that the latest ideological perspectives are often treated as if they were an evolution in human thinking finally 'sufficient to reality' – 'as if, in excluding all heterogeneous assumptions, of religion particularly, they offered a truer representation of the world'. She laments that such things as beauty, holiness and grace are excluded from any current understanding of objectivity, and yet she observes, 'the celebration of holiness in every form of art has shaped civilizations.'

When thinking about the whole education of children, we need to remember that they are whole beings who need to engage their sense of purpose and wonder as well as their intellect. Robinson (2018a, loc. 603) argues that the removal of the subjective would miss something significant, and that we need to 'create a conceptual space large enough to accommodate human dignity'. This is what worship does. Whether religious or not, and whether they recognise it as such, all people are engaged in worship. Worship means revering what is worthy, and what we view as worthy is seen in what we give our time and energy to, and to what we devote our life's purpose.

Collective worship in schools – which English legislation does not define (Swansbury, 2018) – does not presuppose a particular religious commitment (which would be referred to as 'corporate worship'). There are a number of aims for collective worship. In a Church of England school, many of these relate specifically to biblical beliefs and the Anglican tradition. These might involve celebrating key events in the Christian calendar, reflecting on the teachings of Jesus and expressing praise and thanksgiving to God. More generally, collective worship – which does not assume a shared set of beliefs – is meant to provide opportunities for important things such as engaging in an act of community, exploring the big questions in life, and being still and reflecting (p. 3).

Acts of worship will vary depending on whether the school is a faith school or secular. Inspiring contemplation does not need to be done during formal assembly time or during separate collective worship time.

Contemplation wall. Schools could have an area for reflection where children can write a prayer, an expression of thanks or regret, or where they might just ponder important questions of meaning.

Day-to-day curriculum work also offers plenty of opportunities for inspiring wonder.

Inspiring awe. Teachers could introduce a topic within their subject area by showing an image or video to the class, or reading a description that inspires awe and wonder. How often do young biologists sketch and label the parts of plants without appreciating the intricacy of the real thing? Do English students recognise beautiful prose when they see it? How often to mathematicians get excited about proofs and link their existence to our ability to program technologies? When geographers look at the movement of ice floes, do they appreciate the magnitude of their power? Alfred Lansing's (2014 [1959], p. 3) description of the effect of ice floes on Sir Ernest Shackleton's ship *Endurance* reads:

> She was being crushed. Not all at once, but slowly, a little at a time. The pressure of ten million tons of ice was driving in against her sides. And dying as she was, she cried in agony. Her frames and planking, her immense timbers, many of them almost a foot thick, screamed as the killing pressure mounted. And when her timbers could no longer stand the strain, they broke with a report like artillery fire.

Can teachers take learners to a place of awe and wonder using their senses, as they look closely at phenomena or listen to descriptions of events in a way that describes and conveys their beauty, intricacy or power?

Zestful learners *connect their learning to the well-being of others in some way.* Indeed, Angela Duckworth (2016, p. 91) finds that 'gritty' people have a purpose in common. She believes that interest without a purpose is 'nearly impossible' to sustain over a lifetime. A person's work must be both interesting to them personally, and make some contribution to the well-being of others. She notes that for many, 'the motivation to serve others heightens *after* the development of interest and years of disciplined practice'.

It is important that young people do not leave education without realising that truly motivating purpose which actually leads to satisfaction relates to helping to fulfil the needs of others. We discussed the importance of finding a vocation that recognises something more important than one's own self in Chapter 1.

In *Drive* (2009, p. 133), Daniel Pink tells us that 'The most deeply motivated people – not to mention those who are most productive and satisfied – hitch their desires to a cause larger than themselves.' And the opposite seems to be true as well. Research shows that people motivated in life by profit never actually become happier:

> Those who said they were attaining their goals – accumulating wealth, winning acclaim – reported levels of satisfaction, self-esteem, and positive affect no higher than when they were students. In other words, they'd reached their goals, but it didn't make them any happier. What's more, graduates with profit goals showed *increases* in anxiety, depression, and other negative indicators – again, even though they were achieving their goals. (p. 143; original emphasis)

Pink adds: 'in the end … bringing our understanding of motivation into the twenty-first century is more than an essential move for business. It's an affirmation of our humanity' (p. 146).

> **Core values.** An activity teachers might try is to help learners work out their own core values – the principles that give our life meaning and guide our decisions and actions. Richard Bolles' annually revised bestseller *What Color Is Your Parachute?* helps readers to work out their strengths and mission in life. Readers who work through the exercises carefully are able to rank what is important to them, and gain insight into the sort of work they might want to pursue.

In *The Path to Purpose* (2008, p. 96), William Damon identifies a sequence of steps for 'achieving a path of purpose':

1. Inspiring communication with persons outside the immediate family.
2. Observation of purposeful people at work.

3. First moment of revelation: something important in the world can be corrected or improved.

4. Second moment of revelation: I can contribute something myself and make a difference.

5. Identification of purpose, along with initial attempts to accomplish something.

6. Support from immediate family.

7. Expanded efforts to pursue one's purpose in original and consequential ways.

8. Acquiring the skills needed for this pursuit.

9. Increased practical effectiveness.

10. Enhanced optimism and self-confidence.

11. Long-term commitment to the purpose.

12. Transfer of the skills and character strengths gained in pursuit of one purpose to other areas of life.

Vocational purpose. An activity that could help to identify the meaningfulness of subject and work choices might be to spend time looking at human needs and thinking about how they are met through different jobs. Students might focus on a particular curriculum subject and consider how it can meet human needs.

Learning through sports

Learning that develops purposeful learners involves helping them to find meaning. One of the key concepts from the literature that tells us about this is embodied cognition. *Purposeful learners recognise the inherent value of the body and the intelligence involved in – and dignity that comes from – working with it.*

Good performance requires a degree of bodily intelligence that is not always apparent. The body 'thinks' faster than the eye and conscious mind can process information. Typists, for example, find learning to type much slower if they look down at the keyboard and, indeed, will never master top typing speeds if they rely on this method.

The body gains a 'feel' for correct movement only when it is trained to do so properly, which often means without shortcuts. One method for teaching finger positioning to violinists using tapes fails to work as one might think it should because it 'has not sensitized the fingertip that actually presses down on the string'. As soon as the tapes are removed, 'sour notes appear' (Sennett, 2009, p. 156).

So, looking with the eyes and stretching the body into position is insufficient. The body must feel what it is doing. A signature learning experience that can help learners to recognise their own bodily intelligence is learning through sports.

Netball practice. An example might be in netball, when learners practising for goal shooter or goal attack positions spend time practising scoring in different situations, including under time pressure, and recognise the importance of agility, different muscle groups, hand–eye coordination and balance. They may practise with and without a defender and from different points within the semicircle. They may aim to score a certain number of goals under time pressure as well as focusing slowly on their movements.

Learning dance steps. The sheer intelligence of the body in its ability to learn something quite complex is revealed through practising dance steps. In ballet class, for example, 'centre work' follows focused barre work in which the muscles are trained and strengthened to prepare for dancing. In the 'grand allegro' in the centre, where bigger jumps, more travel, direction changes and speed can be combined, the greatest accuracy of footwork and coordination seems to require a certain type of concentration: one that lets the body do the thinking and does not slow it down with too many silent verbal commands.

The confidence that comes from realising how intelligent the body is helps us to value our bodies.

Learning that develops balanced young people involves helping them to value relationships. Two key concepts from the literature that tell us about this are grit/passion (*balanced learners stick with people who keep going*) and the character strength of social well-being (*balanced learners develop their social awareness and social faculty to foster positive relationships for learning*). The signature learning experience of learning through sports might be useful here too.

In terms of developing grit and passion, the aspect of sport that is a good fit for developing persistence is sporting competition. There are complex motivational factors affecting why young people would continue with or drop out of team sports. In a study exploring why young athletes do or do not persist in organised team sports, Rottensteiner et al. (2015, p. 11) found – contrary to what they had expected – that 'ego orientation was higher for persistent athletes' than for those who dropped out. Even though the emphasis in team sports is usually the team, teachers need to recognise that the ego motive (e.g. beating others) 'may serve as motives for young athletes to maintain participation'.

Team sports with an individual focus. This could be something like ensuring that tasks, exercises and learning opportunities 'foster young athletes' achievement goals, and provide an environment that supports young athletes' autonomous motivation' (Rottensteiner et al., 2015, p. 13). Team sports lessons that take into account and focus on the learning needs of each member may help them to persist.

In terms of developing social well-being, the aspect of sport (or at least physical activity) that might contribute is the idea of team working. Team-building activities can help members of a cohort to communicate and build confidence in their ability to finish a task. Depending on the task, it might focus on building their alternative thought processes, creative thinking, time management skills or ability to evolve tactics and strategise.

Team games. This could be team-building exercises that require taking on team roles, plenty of communication, lots of physical activity (for those who can, and finding meaningful ways to involve those who can't) and working to a team objective. This might include a blindfold obstacle course using standard school games equipment (benches, hoops, traffic cones, etc.).

Learning that develops balanced learners also involves helping them to maintain perspective. One of the key concepts from the literature that tells us about this is optimism and the importance of action: learners *take decisive actions and assume postures that reflect their desired situation.* Learning through sports is also a useful signature learning experience in developing this optimistic perspective.

Jeffrey Hodges, an Australian performance consultant to elite athletes, has developed a questionnaire that is based on – but is more sports specific than – the Attributional Style Questionnaire that psychologists use to assess explanatory style (i.e. whether a person is optimistic or not).

Optimism questionnaire. An activity that teachers might try with learners is Hodges' questionnaire. Or teachers could develop one of their own – or even ask the learners to do this – based on well-cited optimism measurement scales. It can provide a stimulus for learners to 'think about their thinking' and 'establish a dialogue among players and between players and coaching staff as to the types of thinking which lead to good sports performances' (Hodges, 2016). He adds: 'Hand out the questionnaire and encourage your players to complete it quickly, choosing the response that most closely reflects how they would think in the given context.' For example:

Situation: You lose your cool with the referee during a game:

A.   That referee is biased against me.

B.   He/she didn't referee fairly in the game.

Of course, there is a third option: the referee was right and I was wrong! This questionnaire is not diagnostic, but it can certainly open up some thoughtful discussion.

Learning by reading (widely)

Learning that develops purposeful learners involves helping them to find meaning. One of the key concepts from the literature that tells us about this is the idea of a classical education that situates learners in the broader world. Learners with zest for learning *read widely and take a broad interest in the past and present as well as the future. Their learning goals are not purely instrumental and 'career focused', but based on the desire to be educated in a way that is appropriate to free people who hold humanity in high esteem.* As Marilynne Robinson (2018a, loc. 576) says, 'Brilliant voices wait in our books to speak in our minds, if we let them.'

> **Reading challenge.** This might involve something like a reading list challenge that uses a variety of categories from which readers must select in order to broaden their horizons. For example, the list might include the reader's choice of a classic, a book from the nineteenth century, a book about politics, a book from a standpoint they disagree with, a book about philosophy, a biography and so on.

Another concept is the idea of self-actualisation and flow that comes from positive psychology. Zestful learners *spend time doing what they love.* A signature learning experience we think might be useful here is learning by reading (widely). Reading widely in order to get a sense of what the world has to offer is one way by which learners can attempt to find out what they might love doing, what might absorb them and what they should try out for themselves. It can also help to shape our idea of the people we might want to become (Prior, 2018).

To encourage wide reading, teachers need to be more familiar with books than it would seem that many are. Teresa Cremin (2011, p. 2) argues that while research shows that 'successful literacy teachers are knowledgeable about children's literature, [and] prioritise the importance of meaning and teaching through whole texts', this knowledge doesn't always translate into either recruitment practices or expenditure on books. Cremin argues that school librarians have a vital role to play here, although we recognise that this is one place where budgets are so often cut.

Reading can be used to introduce learners to curriculum topics in a way that demonstrates their real-world utility.

> **Subject-based fiction.** An example might be choosing a book to read to the class that introduces curriculum concepts in a memorable way and also serves to develop their love of reading.

Daniel Phelps, the author of *Xientifica SOS* (2018), is a former primary school teacher who began writing when he came to recognise the potential power of narrative as a tool for learning in the classroom. As an experimental psychology graduate, Phelps based his writing on some key observations:

* Children are wired to learn.

* Children learn brilliantly from each other, as Vygotsky noted.

* Context is vital. It provides meaning and helps us understand/remember things.

* Enjoyment and interest are absolutely key. (Taylor, 2019)

Inspired by Ballantyne's *The Coral Island*, Blyton's adventure stories, Golding's *Lord of the Flies* and recollections of hearing his own teacher read powerful narratives to him aged 5, Phelps believes that stories can offer all these elements of learning.

Narrative is a highly effective vehicle for teaching. It provides a web of context that information can 'stick' to. It helps young people to remember details; while they may not enjoy a textbook, they love amazing facts and stories. Stories hold meaning, and meaning gives us a reason to learn things. In his own experience, Phelps has found that the knowledge he has retained tends to relate to concepts set within some kind of context that helped to communicate their meaning and purpose to him.

Xientifica SOS uses the power of narrative to engross children in a story that is primarily about pure enjoyment, but also supports learning by doubling up as a science lesson. Its premise is that each of five children has a science-related gift – for example, the character Luke Close has brilliant observational skills. They must each use their gifts as they encounter dangers along the way. Characters are continually asking questions of themselves and of others – a learning habit the book aims to instil. It also helps children to understand and remember scientific concepts. Memory tricks such as poems are woven throughout the narrative. The story, its mental imagery and the sense of wonder it induces stays with children. Indeed, some years after reading the book to his class, Phelps encountered a former student who was just off to university to study biological sciences, who could remember the story from his early years in school.

Educating is about nurturing curiosity, helping children learn how to learn and encouraging lifelong learning. Books are a wonderful gift that open these doors. Phelps' primary hope is that children enjoy his book as an adventure, but he also wants it to support their learning. It aims to inspire young people to look at the world differently, to notice science all around us and to see the beauty of science.

Learning in and through museums

A powerful learning experience for developing zest in young people is learning in museums (and galleries). A key concept from the literature that speaks to finding purpose is the idea of situating yourself in the world. Learners with a zest for learning *take a broad interest in the past and present as well as the future. Their learning goals are not purely instrumental and 'career focused', but based on the desire to be educated in a way that is appropriate to free people who hold humanity in high esteem.*

The chief executive of Arts Council England, Darren Henley, makes a case for museum learning in terms of the cultural education of children because of 'the inspiration and ambition created from wonderful collections and stories that are embedded in our museums and cultural heritage' (Arts Council England, 2016, p. 4). Henley's independent review for the Department for Education in England emphasised the value of museums in developing curiosity as well as finding meaning and fresh insight in the world (Henley, 2012, p. 8).

According to Semper (1990, p. 50), museums are a kind of 'educational country-fair'. They offer a range of learning experiences in one place but, unlike schools, these are largely informal and the navigation around its spaces are chosen by the visitor rather than dictated by the student's timetable.

There is a significant body of literature on learning in museums and other cultural institutions. Summarising the last decade of research, Andre and colleagues (2017, pp. 47–48) conclude that museums are 'rich with exciting things for individuals to explore and discover through touch and inquiry. Museums direct learning by providing visitors with unique opportunities to explore various concepts of mathematics, art and social science.'

Shari Tishman (2005), research associate at Harvard's Project Zero, tells us that whether 'intentionally or not, museums embody views about what's worth learning'. Further, 'the way that artworks, objects, and historical material are presented – from exhibitions to architecture to wall texts – embody views about how learning happens'. She argues that museums are increasingly aware of the importance of designing visitor experiences to benefit from the features of effective learning which are 'active learning' and 'personal agency'.

Bringing a project to life. Purposeful learning can happen when schools plan museum visits into the academic year which are very closely associated with a particular unit of work or topic. This can help to enthuse children, clarify concepts and bring learning to life.

Purposeful learners find meaning, and an important part of this is connecting to the world through their hands. Christine Taylor, curator of natural history for Portsmouth Museums, told us about family workshops on offer in the city.

Handling real artefacts. Portsmouth Museums run workshops for families including, most recently, 'Marvellous Moths', 'Nocturnal Animals' and 'Woolly Mammoth'. Each workshop introduced the theme with a short illustrated talk, a hands-on experience – touching, looking for key features using hand lenses – and a 'make and take'. Learners had the opportunity to touch artefacts, to feel the sharpness of a hedgehog's quills or the weight of a mammoth's tooth. Looking closely at the antennae of British butterflies and moths helped participants to distinguish one from the other.[5]

The physical site of the museum itself is 'fundamental to their very being' (Kelly, 2011, p. 3), offering a learning experience that is increasingly unique in the digital age. Kelly tells us that one of the earliest models of museum learning is still the most useful. Proposed by Falk and Dierking (1992, 2000; cited in Kelly, 2011, p. 4), it recognises that learning in museums takes place in the physical, personal and social context. Factors relating to each of these contexts affect the way learning takes place for individuals visiting museums.

Learning in museums is a signature learning experience that can also help to develop curious learners as they explore the world. One of the key concepts from the literature that tells us about this is learning through play. Zestful learners *discover rules, connections, patterns and ideas through playful interactions with objects, ideas and people.*

Learning in museums through interactive displays and immersive experiences can help learners to explore the world. Staff at various museums have commented on the link between museums and curiosity:

> Through interactive exhibits and hands-on play, children have the ability to take ownership of their own learning and develop and explore their own curiosities. ...

> As the mother to an almost four-year-old boy and a museum professional, I believe that early exposure to museums fosters curiosity in children. (quoted in Gross, 2014)

According to Gross, curiosity can be developed because museums 'provide memorable, immersive learning experiences, provoke imagination, introduce

---

5   Written correspondence with the authors.

unknown worlds and subject matter, and offer unique environments for quality time'.

Christine Taylor told us how a team of curators, designers and education staff at Portsmouth Museums design interactive exhibits to help learners become curious and purposeful as they learn through play.

> **Recreating an environment.** The butterfly house at Portsmouth Natural History Museum is a green glasshouse that contains large plants, and visitors have to weave their way along the paths. The warmth, humidity, sound of running water and the lemony smell of the lantana leaves create a multisensory experience even before they spot the butterflies. Visitors are encouraged to look high and low for butterflies (some are fast fliers, others rest on leaves), observe the long proboscises of butterflies sucking up juices from the fruit at the feeding stations and look into the puparium – an observation box where developing butterfly pupae and chrysalises on wooden rods turn into butterflies.[6]

Learning by following

Learning that develops purposeful learners involves helping them to find meaning. One of the key concepts from the literature that tells us about this is the idea of a sense of purpose or self-actualisation. Learners *align their performance goals with a purpose outside of themselves*. In Chapter 1 we listed eight characteristics of people who self-actualise, according to Maslow. A couple of these related to social and creative factors, such as concern for humanity, highly creative and strong moral standards.

A signature learning experience that we think might be useful here is, perhaps counter-intuitively, learning by following. For young people, finding something they care about requires them to be informed about issues. Someone who cares about the environment, for instance, needs to educate themselves on complex

---

6   Written correspondence with the authors.

issues and from a range of perspectives. They need to be able to separate the science from the politics. Maslow also cited the ability to look at life objectively, which is partly a function of recognising bias or underlying worldview, and perhaps partly a function of optimism: recognising both the importance of, and the limits to, your own actions.

Learning by following may involve developing an informed interest, concern and passion over a period of time by following websites, blogs, articles, campaigns and interest groups. Followed topics might relate to new technological releases, a political/human/theological/geographic/vocational issue or anything else. Web-based news aggregation apps curate personalised news feeds from selected online sources for users to digest, store and share. They provide learners with relevant topical information, updates and opinions in text, audio and video format. They can strengthen learners' concern for humanity and their sense of ethics. By selecting trusted sources, rather than just browsing the endless content that is pushed through popular social media channels, learners avoid wasting time. Trusted sources will often cite or list their own go-to trustworthy sources, and these can be added to users' news feeds.

> **News feed.** A project in any subject within or beyond the curriculum could involve the curation of news sources via a news feed. Learners could justify their choice of topic and sources, and journal their developing interest in the topic. The use of certain sources could be debated, and learners could become the finders of information rather than relying on teachers to find contemporary examples for each lesson.

Learning by practising

Learning that develops purposeful learners involves helping them to perform well. Four key concepts from the literature that tell us about this are:

1. Deliberate practice that leads to expertise – learners *engage in deliberate practice with a view to improving their knowledge, expertise or performance.*

2. Experiencing flow (the feedback from good performance) – learners *are able, having practised deliberately, to experience an opportunity to enjoy the fruits of their work in a moment of things 'going well', whether alone or performing to others.*

3. Expectation of good performance – learners *have good processes in their practice that they can be confident will lead to successful learning outcomes.*

4. Goals worth pursuing (mastery goals) – learners *set mastery goals for themselves, valuing the learning of something tricky over performing something they can already do.*

A signature learning experience we think might be useful here in helping learners to perform well is learning by practising. Richard Sennett (2009, p. 38) cites the Isaac Stern rule, named for 'the great violinist [who declared] that the better your technique, the longer you can rehearse without becoming bored'.

> **Practice log.** This might be something like practising a skill, perhaps over a fixed period of time. Learners could log and reflect on their practising – what worked particularly well and what led to the most improved performance.

Practising a skill in a way that you are confident will lead to the desired results contributes to the expectation of good performance. If your practice produces the desired result, this also contributes to the feeling of flow – the feedback from a performance or 'doing' that went well. Setting goals for practice that involve getting better than yourself, rather than other people, helps learners to perform well. Peterson (2018, p. 111) states this as: 'Compare yourself to who you were yesterday, not to who someone else is today.'

In addition to developing purposeful learners, learning by engaging in purposeful practice can also help to develop balanced learners as it helps them to maintain perspective. The positive psychology concepts of optimism (and the importance of perception/mindset) speaks to this idea of maintaining perspective. A learner with an optimistic mindset is able to *recognise the degree of agency they have in order to improve in any learning situation. They use their own unique mix of character strengths to challenge thought patterns.* They do not over- or under-emphasise their own agency.

> **Keeping drafts.** This might involve learners actively holding drafts of their current work close to hand. Drafts should be arranged chronologically and could be annotated with their own working thoughts, a teacher's corrections or peer comments. In the midst of a writing project, it is motivating to see a virtual pile of thirty superseded versions, each one an improvement on the last and each one evidencing the time and development in thinking as a testament to the learning that is taking place.

Learning by deliberate searching

Another signature learning experience we think might be useful for helping learners to perform well, drawing from the literature on deliberate practice, is learning by searching deliberately. This can help them to *have good processes in their practice that they can be confident will lead to successful learning outcomes.*

While we are not against young people exercising their curiosity by exploratory, unstructured web searching – provided it is done safely – we notice that young people (and adults) often waste a fair amount of time with ineffective search strategies. They want to find out about something they are interested in, and instead of being purposeful they find themselves in a more passive search, which is really the result of complex algorithms pushing content. The phenomenon of the Internet as an 'echo chamber' is well known. Instead of finding useful information, algorithms steer us towards pages that reflect our ideological preferences (whether we understand what they are or not), such that results echo what we have already seen and what we like.

Zest for learning is encouraged when young people are able to find out what they need to know to further spark their interest. At a simple level, this would suggest that they need to understand about different information sources and ideological bias. Knowledge of search functionality, databases, gauging the quality of sources, how to conduct a Boolean search (using AND, OR, NOT and '...' operators) and looking at reference lists are all helpful.

Dissecting a search. An activity might be something like intentional finding out about a given topic, and taking note of the more fruitful lines of enquiry and those that were just a distraction.

Teachers could write a specific question on the board – for example, 'When is Easter?' They could then ask the learners to find the answer using the Internet and write down what they find out, where their search took them and any thoughts or questions it brought up about the search process.

As a follow-up, teachers could ask the learners what information they needed to know *before* the question could be answered. Did they even understand the question? If they put the question into a search engine, they may have found a website listing public holiday dates for the upcoming year. They may have remembered to check whether it was relevant to their own location. But is this what you wanted to know? They may have found out that the date is decided by a complex set of calculations based on lunar position. They may have found themselves intrigued as to why Eastern and Western churches celebrate Easter according to different calendars. But what if you only wanted them to give you a date?

Ask them to evaluate the way they conducted their search. What did they need to consider before even opening a web browser? What key words did they search for? Did they even use key words? According to Ask.com, as many as one third of queries are entered as questions (Olsen, 2009). Which results did they click on and why? How much could they trust the information? What worked? Did they get distracted? Did anything help to keep them focused?

Learning by performing

Learning that develops purposeful learners involves helping them to perform well. In our section on learning by practising we listed four concepts from the literature that address performing well. The first was deliberate practice. A second key concept is that of flow. Learners *are able, having practised deliberately, to experience an opportunity to enjoy the fruits of their work in a moment of things 'going well', whether alone or performing to others.* In addition, *they allow an experience of flow to feed their motivation for more practice, better learning and more complex performance.* A signature learning experience we think might be useful here is learning by performing. In any given knowledge area this might be something like practising that culminates in a performance of some sort. All subject areas can provide opportunities for performance, not just those classically associated with it, such as music or drama.

Show and tell. Regular opportunities to show the class what they have produced or have been learning can give learners the chance to 'perform', to recognise their own success, to be proud of what they have achieved and to see the value in learning well. For the 6-year-old boy who has made a recycled hedgehog house at home with the guidance of his granddad, an enjoyable project is made more memorable and a source of pride for him if he can show the class a few photographs. It becomes a learning exercise – as well as one that develops his confidence in public speaking – if he explains what he learned from the process about planning and design. The respect he gains from the class from being seen to use 'grown-up' tools stays with him as a highlight of his year. By 'performing' – showing the class the results of his hour spent in the garden and workshop – his attitude to learning new skills and producing something of high quality has begun to be established.

Performance in the sense of acting or 'doing' in front of an audience isn't always a useful tool. In charting changing views of arts education, Fleming (2010, p. 26) cites a comment by Slade (1954) on 'Child Drama' that performance at too young an age turned children into 'bombastic little boasters'! Fleming points out that the Plowden Report (1967) similarly saw 'formal presentation of plays on a stage [as] usually out of place' (p. 30) for primary school children. Fleming concludes that such cautions showed 'considerable wisdom' (p. 43).

That said, there is value in practising something to the point where you can do, show or make use of what you can do. This might mean to yourself or for the purposes of demonstrating to a group of peers. Performing might mean presenting a finished product or piece of work or simply handing it in to the teacher. By performing we really mean doing.

Learning through conversation and listening

Learning that develops curious learners involves helping them to embrace novel experiences. One of the key concepts from the literature that tells us about this is the trait of openness to experience. Learners *keep their minds open to the cognitive exploration of ideas using judgement, critical thinking and rationality. They recognise their own tendencies and push themselves to take on new challenges wherever possible.*

A signature learning experience we think might be useful here is learning by conversation. By having open conversations learners benefit from immersion in the process of logical argumentation, and do not resort to emotional responses. There needs to be an honest recognition of the degree to which beliefs about the way things are, or should be, can claim 'truth' status. Learners need to recognise their own, and others', ideological assumptions. They need to recognise that tolerance does not mean that acceptance of ideas is automatic, but kindness and a respect for a person's right to express an opinion ought to be.

Socratic argumentation. This might be something like engaging in public speaking through debate, dialogue with another student or in a group context through Socratic argumentation. In order to teach for openness to experience it is important that such debates exercise free speech. To think well, a person has to be able to express and weigh up ideas. To debate involves risk; in sharing ideas, thinkers risk being offensive. Each participant gains experience of tolerating the feeling of encountering ideas with which they disagree.

Greg Lukianoff and Jonathan Haidt's *The Coddling of the American Mind* (2018) notes the profound damage done to free speech on campuses by the insidious concept of 'emotional harm'. This stems from three 'terrible ideas', implicit and explicit:

1. Fragility: what doesn't kill you makes you weaker.

2. Emotional reasoning: always trust your feelings.

3. Us versus them: life is a battle between good people and evil people.

The ideas contradict both ancient wisdom (of many cultures) and modern research from psychology on well-being. The authors argue that as these ideas spread from campuses to the public arena and national politics, ideological uniformity follows, and people become compromised in their ability to seek out – and speak out – the truth and learn from a broad range of thinkers.

Learning through conversation is also a signature learning experience that can develop in learners the ability to value relationships. Learners *ask interesting questions that value the other person, and are genuinely interested in the answers.*

Matthew Crawford (2015, p. 179) cites a particular example from the original *Sesame Street* children's television show that would, he argues, be seen as unsuitable for children today. One of the puppet characters responds to a child's statement that celery is a fruit with such gruffness that the young boy seems taken aback: 'But then something in his face becomes more clear. He is smiling. The blue monster takes the boy seriously enough to treat his response as a statement about the world, which can be wrong, not simply as a report about his feelings, which must be protected.' Crawford sees that in this 'bold bit of improvisation we witness a moment of maturation' that would no longer be deemed acceptable at a time when the 'tamping down of face-to-face conflict must be connected to the fragility of the contemporary self'.

Ideas of pedagogy and metacognition that contribute to valuing relationships and honest, open discussion that does not treat other participants as fragile can be seen in Philosophy for Children approaches that develop questioning, dialogue, debate and argumentation skills in children, all within a context of respectful listening and engagement.

School magazine. Learners might try to produce a school magazine article covering an issue on which people hold different viewpoints. The process could involve working out what they want to know and interviewing individuals, who they must listen to and represent fairly. The piece might make ideological assumptions explicit and offer readers a new perspective.

Learning by explicitly developing life skills

Learning that develops balanced learners involves helping them to maintain perspective. One of the key concepts from the literature that tells us about this is the idea of habits for learning. Learners *develop dispositions for learning that enable them to learn well generally in areas like problem-solving, decision-making, self-learning and the ability to collect and use information with discernment.*

John Hattie's (2009) concept of 'visible learning' reminds teachers that a focus on processes is at least as important as focusing on outputs or outcomes. Ranking as the twenty-fifth most effective type of intervention (out of 138 studied), the explicit teaching of study skills has value. Study skills programmes might relate to cognitive skills (e.g. note-taking or summarising), metacognitive skills (e.g. self-management) or affective skills (e.g. motivation). Courses in study skills can be effective, particularly for low-level cognitive tasks. That said, the real benefits and deeper learning come when programmes are 'embedded in the context of the subject to be learnt' (p. 192). Of course, 'life skills' are much more than just 'study skills', and include such things as relationships and personal manners, as we saw in our section on the literature about habits for learning in Chapter 1.

The kinds of examples listed in this chapter and described in the case studies in Chapter 4 offer opportunities for learners to practise something they have learned in one context (e.g. enquiry in science) in another (e.g. researching an issue in a museum). In an analysis of the evidence of learning transfer, Anderson and Beavis (2019, p. 21) point out a key missing element in much teaching of capabilities or life skills: 'Overall, our review suggests a "blind-spot" for transferring learning is the assumption that transfer will take care of itself.'

A helpful strategy that teachers can use is to prompt a student to see connections between something they have learned in one context in order to help them develop it in another: 'it's like ... it's equivalent to ... for example ... it's akin to ... for instance ... it's the same as ... by the same token ... similarly ... in the same way ... it reminds me of ... it resembles ... or, it's analogous to ...' (Haskell, 2001, p. 24).

> **Real-world application.** Learners might regularly be invited to look for opportunities to apply what they are learning in class to something they are exploring in an extra-curricular activity or in their life outside school. Examples include many of the skills we are exploring in this chapter – listening, planning, finding out, explaining, imitating and so on.

It helps if we can make skills teaching much more explicit, prompting students to focus on what it is they are doing or learning in a new context, and helping them to see how similar or different it is from the situation where they learned it.

Learning by travel/being away from home

Learning by travel and being away from home offers a diverse opportunity for gaining zest for learning because it potentially impacts learners' ability to maintain perspective and their curiosity.

Learning that develops balanced learners involves helping them to maintain perspective. One of the key concepts from the literature that tells us about this is the idea of habits for learning. Learners *develop dispositions for learning that enable them to learn well generally in areas like problem-solving, decision-making, self-learning and the ability to collect and use information with discernment.*

Travel can help to develop curious learners (through openness to experience). Zestful learners *keep their minds open to the cognitive exploration of ideas using judgement, critical thinking and rationality. They recognise their own tendencies and push themselves to take on new challenges wherever possible.*

Just as learning through conversation introduces young people to the experience of handling unfamiliar, and even unwelcome, ideas, so travel affords wonderful opportunities for trying new things, coping – and thriving – in unfamiliar circumstances, and uncovering or deepening interests and zest for learning.

Much research has explored the benefits of travel, including independent travel, objectiveless travel and study overseas, where out-of-class experiences are particularly 'impactful' (Stone and Petrick, 2013, p. 731). Stone and Petrick's review of the literature reveals that a number of studies attribute some kind of learning outcome to travel. Outcomes are often obvious ones like 'development of a more complex cultural view', 'cross-cultural skills', 'change of perspective or worldview', 'independence', 'self-confidence', 'dispelling of stereotypes' or similar (p. 736).

Travel can be risky – cognitively even if not always physically – and will naturally expose learners to the unfamiliar. Exposure therapy (a form of cognitive behavioural therapy for people with phobias) recognises that if an individual is able to tolerate mild anxiety for a period of time, anxiety levels reduce. Repeated exposure leads to a measurable drop in peak anxiety – both in intensity and duration. It is reasonable to think that the challenges of travel, and the natural exposure to things that may provoke more than typical levels of anxiety, will lead to learners recognising their ability to take on new challenges, different risks and new situations. The cognitive benefits of travel could lead to a positive feedback loop that sparks a love of embracing novel experiences.

Trip with a simple challenge. Most schools will try to incorporate trips into the learning experiences of their young people. Of course, many of the experiences that truly broaden horizons come with a price tag that makes them attainable by only the more affluent students. But this could be something as simple as planning a bus journey: necessary skills involve interpreting a bus timetable and having some way of identifying where you are when a bus stops at an unnamed stop!

A teenager we know had not travelled a particular bus route before and relied on a friendly bus driver to tell her when she had arrived at the stop nearest her grandmother's house. Despite needing assistance, the experience of success was disproportionately exhilarating; she had made it to where she intended to go and not run out of money! A few years later, on 25 December in Amsterdam, she took the tram the wrong way out of the city, but managed to get off and back on the right line before the service stopped, and is still here to tell the tale. Dogged curiosity led her to wonder: how exactly did that happen, and what on earth do I need to do better next time? The urgency of the situation, and the fact that giving up is less of an option when far from home, provides an imperative to learn quickly.

Travel can help to develop purposeful learners (by helping them to find meaning). At the extreme end of purposeful is the quest for survival. Bold in its embrace of novel experiences, Ernest Shackleton's plan for the first crossing of the Antarctic continent failed, but the expedition's focus quickly shifted from conquering a continent to rescuing the ship's crew through grit and determination (Lansing, 2014 [1959], p. 2).

Literature that speaks to the idea of developing purposeful learners is the area of character development. Zestful learners recognise that development of character is a valuable aspect of their learning journey and are disposed to develop their character strengths in general.

Planning an expedition. An activity that might help learners to embrace novel experiences is planning an expedition. For school students, the Duke of Edinburgh's Award requires completion of an expedition, including the necessary training and preparation. Its requirements provide a prototype for schools thinking about the sorts of conditions that an expedition could involve. For the Duke of Edinburgh's Award, teams have to meet certain conditions, including the need for self-sufficiency and proper planning and organisation around an aim.[7]

---

7   Duke of Edinburgh's Award expedition guidance is available at: https://www.dofe.org/leaders/resources-and-downloads/expedition-downloads.

Travel can help to develop balanced learners (helping them to maintain perspective). Literature that speaks to this idea is the area of tenacity. Zestful learners *are committed to the pursuit of knowledge and expertise.*

Treasure trails. Teachers could take these ideas and make them fit the available terrain: for urban schools, it could be a trip in school hours that involves using two means of public transport and includes a meal within a budget. There are organisations that provide downloadable 'treasure trails' which incorporate self-guided themed walks that require participants to solve clues, find the location of treasure or complete 'missions.'[8]

Geocaching. Another type of outdoor treasure hunt is geocaching, which involves using GPS technology to locate a geocache (a small container) hidden at a specific set of coordinates.[9]

Scavenger hunt. A similar take on geocaching involves participants having to collect items from a list. These can be common items or require initiative and creative thinking. Naturally, teams of schoolchildren in this kind of exercise require creative supervision!

Learning by joining clubs/trying something new

Learning that develops purposeful learners involves helping them to find meaning. One of the key concepts from the literature that tells us about this is self-actualisation and flow; learners in this mode *spend time doing what they love.* A signature learning experience we think might be useful here is learning by joining clubs/trying something new.

---

8   For example, https://www.treasuretrails.co.uk provides over 1,000 trails for all ages across the UK.
9   For example, http://geocachingforschools.co.uk is a project designed by the University of Stirling to develop a new approach to enquiry-based science.

Without trying new things, we won't know what we might love doing. We can't actually imagine what might fully absorb us and satisfy us until we try it. The more opportunities we have for new things to spark our interest, the more likely it is that we will hit on one we want to pursue. In a very important observation in *Grit* – one that parents in particular should bear in mind when guiding children towards certain activities – Angela Duckworth tells us that it is interactions with the outside world, not introspection, that brings to light interests. She describes the process of discovering interests 'messy, serendipitous, and inefficient' (2016, p. 104) because there is no way of predicting accurately what might capture your attention and become an interest.

As well as helping learners to find meaning, joining clubs and trying something new can help them to maintain perspective, thereby developing balanced learners who *engage in extra- and co-curricular activities that meet the goals of a good education.*

> **Activity wildcard.** All schools provide a selection of after-school or lunchtime clubs, sports and activities, and many children will tend to gravitate towards what they know they like, think they might like or see their friends doing. Many teachers will similarly offer what they know. Why not programme in the expectation at the start of every term that each child will pick a wildcard activity to try. This could be chosen by or for children, and completely at random. This could even stretch to the teachers, who might risk running something novel or unfamiliar to them for a term.

A report funded by the Nuffield Foundation (Chanfreau et al., 2016) focused on formal out-of-school activities and 'child outcomes' (including social, emotional and behavioural), although primarily on attainment measures. While the possible relationship between taking part in activities and attainment on standardised tests is interesting (and the authors 'urge the use of caution' (p. 22) in making too many claims), it is the lifelong benefits of finding out what you love doing that is of most concern to us. The report found that inequalities relating to participation in out-of-school activities were largely driven by cost and the need for transport at awkward times. These are hindrances to many children, and the study has implications for policy-makers and practitioners looking to enrich education.

Activity balance. Could schools timetable activities in a way that helps learners to select a mix of extra-curricular activities? Clubs could be organised into 'head', 'heart' and 'hand' groups, such that young people are encouraged to select from a balanced mixture. This could be, for example:

- Head – debating, languages, astronomy, architecture, coding.

- Heart – theatre, ornithology, art club, design, faith societies, political societies, book club.

- Hand – rounders, dance, bike maintenance, tech club, cooking.

Joining clubs can also be a good signature learning experience for helping learners to embrace novel experiences, and thereby develop into curious learners. A concept in the literature that speaks to this is the idea of restlessness or sensation-seeking. *Learners demonstrate a willingness to take risks in order to seek varied, novel, complex and intense learning experiences. They are doggedly curious, with a keenness to understand how things can be made better.*

Novel activity reports. Learners can try out an activity that nobody else in the class has done. It might be helping a neighbour or relative to divide perennials in the spring, propagating geraniums, applying for a job, helping to mix concrete to lay the foundations of a shed, kayaking, helping to plan the week's meals or setting out toys for a toddler group. All of these activities help us work out what we might like to do more of or less of, and what we learned about ourselves. Reporting back to the class can inspire others to try something they might really enjoy.

Learning by planning and following through

Learning that develops curious learners helps them to embrace novel experiences. One of the key concepts from the literature that tells us about this relates to risk-taking. Curious learners *demonstrate a willingness to take risks in order to seek varied, novel, complex and intense learning experiences. They are doggedly curious, with a keenness to understand how things can be made better.* The signature learning experience of learning by planning and following through might be useful for developing risk-taking in learners.

> **Planning a route.** This might be something like learners planning a route they actually have to undertake – for example, the shortest walk through town that enables them to make specific stops to find clues, gather evidence or be checked in at a checkpoint. Criteria might include: pass by three postboxes, don't go north of the library, walk through a green space, cross no more than six roads and so on.

Learning that develops curious learners also helps them to explore the world. David Perkins' (2009) concept of 'playing the whole game' is relevant here. Curious learners *play the whole game as they engage in learning something.* Planning and following through that develops this aspect could involve organising a real, whole event.

> **Organising an event.** Learners might be asked to organise a school event for the public or to undertake a real community project (as Ron Berger's students did, with enormous benefit to their personal growth, in *An Ethic of Excellence* (2003)). Learning activities will involve planning, organising and thinking things through.

Learning that develops balanced learners helps them to maintain perspective. The concept of outdoor learning is relevant here. Balanced learners *relish the challenge of learning in unfamiliar outdoor environments, often in all-age groups.* Planning and following through that develops this aspect will involve the outdoors.

Designing an outdoor space. In terms of maintaining perspective, the concept of outdoor learning could be useful for helping learners to flourish in a holistic way. Learning by planning and following through might involve learners designing a functional external space, perhaps collaboratively, to meet criteria set by school needs.

Learning by researching

Learning that develops curious learners involves helping them to explore the world. One of the key concepts from the literature that tells us about this is the area of creative thinking. Learners *seek out explanations for things happening around them*. The curious individual has 'an impulse to explore novel events and objects' (Engel, 2015, p. 33). A signature learning experience we think might be useful here is learning by researching.

The Children's Research Centre at the UK's Open University summarises the benefits they have identified since the centre was founded in 2004:

- Raised self-esteem and confidence.
- Development of transferable skills.
- Enhanced critical thinking skills.
- Heightened ethical awareness.
- Enhanced problem-solving ability.
- More effective communication.
- Development of independent learning.[10]

While developing research skills is clearly a useful thing in its own right, it also gives a signal to young people that their opinions are valued.

---

10 See https://www.open.edu/openlearn/openlearn-ireland/what-the-childrens-research-centre?in_menu=859000.

> **Setting good questions.** An activity might involve helping learners – in any given lesson – to pose good questions that can be investigated through imaginative approaches to research. It might involve asking students at the end of lessons: 'What are you left wondering today?', 'What else would you like to find out?', 'How might this relate to the real world?' and 'How might you find out about that?'

Learning through reflection

Learning that develops curious learners involves helping them to explore the world. Two concepts from the literature that tell us about this are:

1. Experiential learning. Learners *recognise that fulfilling practical and theoretical work both make cognitive demands, and value each equally. They reflect on their practical experiences in order to learn from them.*

2. Thinking about thinking (metacognition). Learners *monitor their own comprehension, self-regulate and display self-control strategies in order to embed their own learning.*

Both concepts involve reflection. Reflection is a part of learning in that it provides a basis for future action (Ayas and Zeniuk, 2001). It allows individuals to consider and, importantly, to rethink their existing thought and behaviour patterns. Kolb's experiential learning cycle is helpful in connecting theory and practice, research and action. Although reality is not reflected in a neat cycle, teaching for reflection is a way of enabling learning (Lucas et al., 2012). In learning to reflect, and taking the time to do so, the learner becomes more strategic about their own learning. They:

+ Plan: when are you going to take a moment to think about what just happened?

+ Revise: what might you need to do differently next time?

+ Distil: what have you learned about the task/process/area of study?

◆ Engage in meta-learning: what have you learned about learning?

An approach to learning that considers experiential learning might involve helping young people to spend time reflecting on their own or others' experience.

> **Historic decisions.** Learning through reflection could involve thinking about how historical figures arrived at certain findings or decisions. Learners might think about the factors those individuals or groups had to take into account, the information they were privy to, and the consequences of their decisions and actions. Learners could consider how they themselves might make a different decision now, or what they can learn about thinking from others' approaches.

Historic England is a public body that 'helps people care for, enjoy and celebrate England's spectacular historic environment'.[11] It runs a Heritage Schools programme with which 400 schools are involved. On its website it provides a number of open-access teaching activities and accompanying material that encourage learning through reflection.

> **Historic building detectives.** 'What can Victorian buildings tell us about how Victorians thought?' is one of a number of activities that involves looking at and analysing photographs.[12] Teachers are invited to display an image of a building and ask the students to look at it and then describe it in writing and in a class discussion. Teachers ask the learners to think about the question: 'What do you think was in the minds of the Victorians who decided to build their town's police station in this particular style and on this site?' Learners consider what

---

11 See https://historicengland.org.uk/about/what-we-do.
12 See https://historicengland.org.uk/services-skills/education/teaching-activities/
what-can-victorian-buildings-tell-us-about-how-the-victorians-thought.

they see in the image and look for evidence of different motives for building. These might include to encourage trade, to display wealth, to improve conditions, to make life better for people, to improve moral standards, to create a dependable workforce, to promote cleanliness, to leave a legacy, to care for people and so on. Teachers are advised that using buildings close to home may increase motivation and raise local awareness.

Thinking about thinking might involve learners spending time exploring metacognition. In 2018 the UK's Education Endowment Foundation examined more than forty years of research into metacognition and made seven practical recommendations:

1. Teachers should acquire the professional understanding and skills to develop their pupils' metacognitive knowledge.

2. Explicitly teach pupils metacognitive strategies, including how to plan, monitor, and evaluate their learning.

3. Model your own thinking to support pupils to plan, monitor and evaluate their learning.

4. Set an appropriate level of challenge to develop pupils' self-regulation and metacognition.

5. Promote and develop metacognitive talk in the classroom.

6. Explicitly teach pupils how to organise and effectively manage their learning independently.

7. Schools should support teachers to develop their knowledge of these approaches and expect them to be applied appropriately.[13]

While these make obvious sense for teachers seeking to improve learning outcomes for learners more generally, they translate well into the many, often informal, contexts in which students may be developing their zest for learning.

For example, we can see how the impact of (2) could help students to activate whatever prior knowledge they have before starting an activity, then practise the desired skill and reflect on their progress. With (4) it will be important to help

---

13 See https://educationendowmentfoundation.org.uk/tools/guidance-reports/metacognition-and-self-regulated-learning. See also Quigley et al. (2018).

students get better at knowing their strengths and weaknesses and understand where they are on a learning progression towards their desired outcome. Point (5) reminds us how important learner talk is, and (6) is a rallying cry to us all not to assume that students know how to organise their learning, especially how they practise so they become increasingly independent and expert.

> **Learner talk.** Encourage learners to self-talk in class using language like, 'What do I already know about this?', 'Where have I come across it before?' and 'What did I do last time I was faced with this challenge?' This might take the form of the 'coach on their shoulder' – that is, metaphorically whispering to them to, for example, try getting up and going for a walk or asking for help from someone more experienced in the group if they are stuck.

An example of explicit teaching of metacognition comes from North Freemantle Primary School, in Western Australia.[14] At pre-primary level, a teacher and creative practitioner collaborated to introduce the creative habits of mind to young learners in the biological science area of the curriculum. They called this: 'Creative learning challenge: making meaning of big words – what are the creative habits of mind?'

The session aimed to help pupils come up with their own words for the creative habits of mind. Following a mini nature walk during which the children had to select two natural objects, create something with them in a group and then describe it to the class, the children reassessed their preference for particular habits of mind. The teacher found that 'it was lovely to watch these pupils discover their strengths and weaknesses.'[15]

The challenge for teachers is to move beyond labels and help learners to develop in those areas they recognise they do not naturally orient towards. Looking at understanding creative thinking as a life skill (or disposition) in this way helps learners to develop their curiosity.

---

14 See the case study in Chapter 4 on FORM's Creative Schools programme. Teacher Roberta Slattery and creative practitioner Charissa Delima collaborated as part of this programme.
15 Written correspondence with the authors.

Learning through reflection is also a useful signature learning experience for helping learners to maintain perspective and thus become balanced. One of the key concepts from the literature that tells us about this is optimism and the importance of perception/mindset. Learners *recognise the degree of agency they have in order to improve in any learning situation. They use their own unique mix of character strengths to challenge thought patterns.*

> **Honest reflection.** This might be something like a group activity that involves learners fully acknowledging something they did well. This might take the form of an appreciative enquiry which considers the best of what is in order to imagine what could be.

Learning by teaching

Learning that develops curious learners involves helping them to explore the world. One of the key concepts from the literature that tells us about this is thinking about thinking (metacognition), where learners with zest for learning *monitor their own comprehension, self-regulate and display self-control strategies in order to embed their own learning.*

A signature learning experience useful here is learning by teaching. Fiorella and Mayer (2013) conducted a study to explore the claim that learning is enhanced through teaching others. They compared the effects of preparing to teach, and actually teaching, on learning. The authors found that the students who actually taught experienced 'deeper and more persistent understanding of the material' (p. 281). The Education Endowment Foundation (2018) finds extensive evidence for the moderate impact of 'peer tutoring' on learning.

The concept of peer teaching has taken a technological turn in the last couple of decades as researchers at a number of universities have created virtual learners that require teaching input from real students. Scientists at Stanford and Vanderbilt developed the virtual character 'Betty's Brain', which uses the concept map idea to structure and organise, representing students' knowledge based on what they have been able to teach the character.[16]

Daniel Schwartz, one of the researchers involved, explains that learning by teaching is 'a happy confluence of forces' (Berdik, 2015). Students have to think about the underlying concepts and connections, and consider what their tutee already knows. They feel responsible for their tutee's learning (the protégé effect) and spend more time on material, learning it more thoroughly. They are more conscientious because they are motivated to help their tutee to learn.

This social impulse is beneficial for learners because as they prepare to teach, they are organising their own knowledge more carefully, which improves their understanding and ability to recall. A pilot study (Leelawong et al., 2001) showed the effectiveness of the Betty's Brain system in promoting learning and self-assessment among students.

There are plenty of ways to introduce peer teaching. These vary in the degree of exposure of individual students to their peers. On a smaller scale, the students work in pairs.

Think-pair-share. Students are given a selection of questions and each answers one for themselves. They are then paired with a student who has addressed a different question. The learners take it in turns to play the tutor or tutee role. The tutee articulates and explains their answer; the tutor helps them to expand on it, asking questions to check understanding.

---

16 See https://wp0.vanderbilt.edu/oele/bettys-brain.

Low risk but on a larger scale, the students comment individually on the (possibly anonymous) work of others.

> **Gallery critique.** Students have sight of a peer's work. This could be done as a gallery critique, where students move around the room looking at the work of all their peers and using sticky notes to 'compliment' (what they liked), 'suggest' (specific comments on what doesn't work so well/is confusing) and 'correct' (point out errors of a grammatical or factual kind).

> **Jigsaw.** The class is divided into groups of around four to six students, each of whom will teach the other members about a specific part of the lesson topic. One member in each group is assigned responsibility for researching a particular aspect of the knowledge/conceptual content. Their job is to learn their part independently. They then work with an 'expert group' – others who have taken on this same piece of content responsibility from other jigsaw groups. This expert group makes sure they all understand their particular content. Experts then return to their original jigsaw group and take turns to teach what they have become expert on, while listening to others, to ensure they have built up a complete understanding of the lesson content. The whole class then takes an individual quiz to check the learners have been listening to other members of their jigsaw group.

High risk, and on a class-wide scale, are experiences where students are very visible to the whole class. These can be intimidating, but this kind of exposure is important for building confidence and lowering anxiety to this type of exercise. It will stand learners in good stead for further and higher education, as well as for life in general.

> **Assessing understanding by teaching.** Asking learners to explain what they have understood by a concept, and allowing their peers to listen with vigilant attention for any areas where understanding may be partial or

faulty, can have multiple benefits. In this signature experience, learners take on the role of class teacher for a single concept. It is a way of checking understanding and exposing common misconceptions throughout a lesson, and can be done at key points and fairly informally. As learners are making notes in class or answering written questions, they need to keep in mind that these notes might be their preparation for teaching others. The learners doing the teaching practise preparation for the delivery of the material as they make notes. They also practise public speaking, distilling complex ideas into clear language and listening to feedback. Learners doing the listening practise attending carefully, raising counterarguments or contradicting peers clearly and challenging their own understanding. For example:

+ Can Grade 7–8 students in the United States explain how the federal system differs from other forms of government, how the Constitution established a new way to organise government and why the framers of the Constitution created such a system?[17]

+ Can learners in ethical capability at Levels 7–8 in the state of Victoria, Australia, explain the contested meaning of concepts including freedom, justice, rights and responsibilities?[18]

+ In Scotland, the technologies curriculum covers 'technological developments in society and business' (Education Scotland, 2017, p. 5). Can learners explain how and why it is important to conserve energy?

With all these peer learning exercises, teachers need to ensure that learning objectives are clear, that the purpose of peer teaching is explicit, and that 'good' feedback is taught and, of course, always modelled by the teacher.

---

17 In the United States, schools recognise Constitution Day in September each year. See http://www. civiced.org/resources/curriculum/constitution-day-and-citizenship-day.

18 See https://victoriancurriculum.vcaa.vic.edu.au/ethical-capability/curriculum/f-10#level=7-8.

Learning by being mentored

While learning by teaching develops curious learners, learning by mentoring is about developing balanced ones. Learning that develops balanced learners involves helping them to value relationships. One of the key concepts from the literature that tells us about this is communities of practice, where learners with zest for learning *recognise their ever-shifting place within a community of learners, learning from some and guiding others.* This is why we think being mentored might be a useful signature learning experience here.

There has been extensive research on learning by being mentored. The Education Endowment Foundation (2018, p. 23) has weighed up the evidence for mentoring, which 'involves pairing young people with an older peer or volunteer, who acts as a positive role model' and finds that the benefits are not related to attainment but more to attitudes to school, attendance and behaviour. The Education Endowment Foundation also finds that community-based mentoring can be more effective than school-based, perhaps because of the potential for more long-lasting relationships that go beyond school. Clear structure and expectations are needed.

> **Business mentoring.** Successful business people in the community could be involved in mentoring secondary/high school students. The UK's Young Enterprise scheme does this successfully by bringing in volunteers as business advisers to help students set up and run a successful business over the course of an academic year.[19] Learners benefit from mentors' experience in team working, problem-solving, communication, planning and a business-like attitude to work.

As a school-based signature experience, we propose peer mentoring as a practical tool. Mentoring is not aimed at teaching particular skills or knowledge; it is more about behaviour and aspiration. It is primarily aimed at establishing strong, positive relationships and giving participants opportunities to engage in fun, developmental activities 'leading to improvements in mentees' self-image,

---

19 See https://www.young-enterprise.org.uk.

connectedness to school and peers, and self-control' (Garringer and MacRae, 2008, p. 29).

> **Mentoring around a theme.** In a report about developing peer mentoring programmes in schools, Garringer and MacRae (2008) outline how to recruit, screen and train student participants, and advocate for the 'double impact' of peer mentoring because both participants benefit. They also suggest activities and provide links to resources for planning, including:
>
> + Academic activities – e.g. helping with homework, learning how to conduct research, using computer labs.
>
> + Personal growth activities – e.g. setting goals for the relationship, helping mentees respond to bullying/aggression, role playing for conflict resolution, respecting diversity and respecting differences, self-esteem, parent and family issues, anger management, peer pressure, health issues.
>
> + Fun activities – including field trips, picnics, sports and recreational games, arts and crafts, and contests – 'especially ones where the mentor and mentee create something together' (p. 32).

Learning from others' experience

Learning that develops purposeful learners involves helping them to find meaning. One of the key concepts from the literature that tells us about this is lifelong learning, where learners with zest for learning *navigate through life learning what they need in order to serve a higher purpose*, and *recognise that meaning might come from book knowledge or practical knowledge, and don't limit themselves to one or the other to achieve their goals.*

A signature learning experience we think might be useful here is learning from others' experience.

It is well-known, for example, that fewer girls than boys opt for science, technology, engineering and mathematics (STEM) subjects beyond school. In developed countries, this has led to something of a campaign to address the difference. There is increasing evidence that, broadly speaking, more egalitarian societies experience greater sex differences in many traits. There is strong evidence to suggest that 'when men and women have more freedom to pursue their intrinsic interests, the well established sex difference in occupational interests will become more strongly expressed' (Stoet et al., 2016).

While equality of opportunity between the sexes is important, equality of outcomes for its own sake is not a desirable pursuit. That said, if girls are put off studying STEM subjects because of a faulty perception that careers in these fields are not likely to be of interest to them, then that is something that can be addressed by inviting speakers into schools to correct this perception. Students often struggle to make a connection between the subjects they enjoy at school and the careers they might pursue.

Invited speakers. A programme of speaking events might aim to shed light on the varied opportunities in a particular subject area or field. These could be themed by curriculum area, such as biology, technology or textiles.

Teachers and careers advisers could invite ex-pupils who studied particular subjects at school to talk about the choices they made upon leaving school, and where they are now in their career. It would be interesting to compare someone who opted for continuity in their subject choices to higher education with someone who dropped school subjects to study something new (e.g. business or social sciences) beyond school.

Teachers might invite older career changers to talk about what decisions and jobs made them the most fulfilled, and why. This could be conducted as an interview by teachers or learners. How did what they learned at school stand them in good stead for 'real life'? Are there any decisions they would make differently in hindsight?

Parents might be more willing to contribute if they know their experiences offer valuable insight, without having to bring stories of fame, fortune or heroics! In this regard, informative is every bit as useful as inspiring.

Another way of learning from others that has multiple benefits is by debating ideas. School 21 in Stratford, London, sees lack of communication skills as one of the biggest barriers to young people succeeding in life.[20] Oracy is prized as a core pedagogy that is deliberately taught to all students. Debate, discussion and deliberation over ideas contributes to students who are stretched and challenged to form their own opinions in conversation with others.

Talking points. To develop students' oracy, you might give them a talking point or a controversial or provocative statement (e.g. 'Some cultures are better than others') to spark their thinking as they debate in pairs. Learners will need discussion guidelines about what makes for a good discussion.

Tools you might model and use are described below:

- Sentence stems are the first few words of a sentence. They scaffold learners in constructing a sentence using their own ending. They help learners to build a richer vocabulary, to speak in full sentences and to interact with one another.

- Talk tasks are structured activities to help learners talk about their learning with others – to articulate and understand what they are learning.

- Discussion roles help learners to manage talk: they might be an instigator ('I think we should consider …'), a prober ('Can you provide an example of …?'), a challenger ('But have you thought about …?'), a clarifier ('Does that mean …?'), a summariser ('The main ideas we talked about were …') or a builder ('Linking to what X said, I think …').

- Groupings can be varied to support different talk types – for example, trios (where a third person might summarise the discussion) or an 'onion' (where members of an inner circle rotate to speak to a new partner on the outer circle).[21]

---

20 The School 21 Foundation was founded by Voice 21: https://www.voice21.org.
21 Voice 21 provides a number of helpful resources for developing oracy in class. See https://www. voice21.org/our-resources. More information can be found in Minero (2016).

Learning by being coached

Learning that develops purposeful learners involves helping them to find meaning. One of the key concepts from the literature that tells us about this is lifelong learning. Learners *navigate through life learning what they need in order to serve a higher purpose. They recognise that meaning might come from book knowledge or practical knowledge, and don't limit themselves to one or the other to achieve their goals.*

A signature learning experience we think might be useful here is learning by being coached.

> **Coaching community.** This might be something like setting up coaching opportunities between learners and parents connected to the school, local government or business people, trades people or the self-employed. This might relate to careers or interests. We discussed finding meaning in work in Chapter 1, so the coaching relationship would be particularly beneficial if young people interact with coaches who see their role as in some way serving others or the community, either directly or indirectly.

Matthew Syed, the author of *Bounce: The Myth of Talent and the Power of Practice* (2011) wrote a piece in the *Times* (2019) about the success of tennis player Andy Murray, in which he argued that the reason for Murray's breakthrough was not talent, but a 'different quality'. Recognising the 'incalculable benefit' other players were obtaining by practising with world-class partners, Murray relocated in order to face new challenges, 'which he embraced for a simple reason: he was intent on taking a journey to the summit of his potential'.

Murray's use of coaches had a defining feature, which marked what Syed calls the pattern of his career:

> He has never settled. The precise moment that he feels he has learnt everything from his coach, he hires a new one ...

Syed describes an 'inveterate curiosity' visible in the way Murray practises and plays. He is constantly striving to better his performance.

To ensure learners gain the most from coaching activities, we need to think carefully about what we want them to learn, who we assign to them and how long they can best benefit before we revisit their needs.

Learning through play and games

Learning that develops curious learners involves helping them to explore the world. One of the key concepts from the literature that tells us about this is learning through play. Learners *discover rules, connections, patterns and ideas through playful interactions with objects, ideas and people.* A signature learning experience we think might be useful here is providing opportunities for learners to tinker to see what works.

An example of exploring to see what works comes from Glencoe Primary School, Western Australia. At Year 2 level, a teacher and creative practitioner collaborated to introduce a zest for exploratory and collaborative play to young learners across various curriculum areas. In a week of creative learning activities, one challenge encouraged exploration of a range of materials to make echidnas.[22] Mud and paint allowed the children to explore textures and descriptive language. By giving them time for exploratory play, the teachers witnessed them 'come alive' and interact in new ways. Quiet children participated and those who regularly disrupted lessons 'became engaged contributors'. Teachers not involved with the project noticed an enhanced ability in the children to play during breaktimes in a way that was 'elaborate, playful, creative and collaborative'.

Dealing with children who had had a clear 'play deficit' and lacked the 'fundamental play building blocks' required 'much permission, time and space' to be invested in order for the children to play. Teachers needed to learn to be patient and hold back on giving out information until the children asked for it and were ready to receive it.

---

22 See the case study in Chapter 4 on FORM's Creative Schools programme. Teacher Benita Swart and creative practitioner Daniel Burton collaborated as part of this programme. Quotations are from correspondence with FORM. Echidnas are spiny egg-laying mammals which are found in Australia and New Guinea.

> **Free experimentation.** An extension of this experimentation is when learners are given free rein to explore an idea, tool, medium, object or piece of material. Teachers will consider the degree to which playful experimentation is appropriate based on the need for guidance that each medium presents to maximally benefit from it.

The concept of play can involve playing games. A particular benefit of playing games is that they make light of making mistakes. Failure should be expected when learning a game, although for 'gamers' it can be a source of great frustration (Squire, 2005, p. 4).

FutureLab's report on serious games in education cites Patrick Felicia's list of pedagogical considerations for selecting appropriate games (2009; cited in Ulicsak and Wright, 2010, p. 77). Felicia had suggested that (digital) games should have:

- An easy learning curve.
- Relevant educational content – including having clear objectives.
- Clear progression.
- Feedback – verbal guidance or hints to maintain focus.
- Opportunities for collaboration, group work and creativity.
- A help section.

> **Games of skill.** In terms of developing zest for learning, it might be that allowing opportunities for games that require some degree of skill can awaken young people's playfulness. It might give learners space to make connections, link ideas, think laterally, try new approaches, recognise patterns and begin to look for them elsewhere. Play can be through games that involve abstract computational thought, visual observation or physical exertion.

Over the years, the LEGO Foundation has invested in research into the value of play (Zosh et al., 2017). It suggests there are five defining characteristics:

1. Joy – 'pleasure, enjoyment, motivation, thrill, and a positive emotion' (p. 19).

2. Meaningful – 'by connecting it to something they already know' (p. 21).

3. Actively engaging – 'immersed in the act of self-directed effort' (p. 23).

4. Iterative – 'trying out possibilities, revising hypotheses, and discovering the next question' (p. 25).

5. Socially interactive – 'Through the processes of sharing one's own mind, understanding others through direct interaction, and communicating ideas' (p. 27).

All sorts of games. Board games can do this, as can paper-and-pencil word and number games, sports and team games. Consider the power of the 'team-building day' to instil energy in a group of young people! Often these sorts of experiences teach us something profound and linger in the mind long after other lessons are forgotten.

Play can be a useful antidote to the inevitable seriousness of study that comes as students progress through their secondary education.

Learning by exercising

Learning that develops balanced learners involves helping them to maintain perspective. One of the key concepts from the literature that tells us about this is physical activity: learning by exercising. Zestful learners develop *good habits in terms of diet, exercise, rest and sleep.*

Eric Jensen (2011), who finds that research on this association is also mixed, makes a research-based case for exercise in schools, including its important role as an antidepressant. A signature learning experience we think might be useful here is learning by exercising.

Exercise benefits learners with overall physical fitness, a reduction in stress hormones and the release of endorphins.[23] There is also an association between participation in sports and attainment, although 'it is not clear whether this association is a result of positive academic spillovers, or due to the influence of unobservables' (Rees and Sabia, 2010, p. 751).

Daily mile. The sense that maintaining a balance is important can be undermined, or reinforced, by a school's prioritisation of physical activity. The Daily Mile[24] began in a Scottish school in 2012 and is done in addition to PE lessons and playtime. It aims to improve physical and mental health for 2–11-year-olds. Since then, the practice of sending children outdoors to lap the playground for 15 minutes a day, in their normal school clothes and shoes, at their own pace (including those with additional physical needs) and in most weathers has spread to over 9,300 schools and nurseries across sixty-five countries from Nepal to Australia.

It requires no extra workload or training, and has been shown to improve fitness and body composition in primary school children in a study that recommends it be 'considered for inclusion in government policy' (Chesham et al., 2018).

When you are short of inspiration, or unable to connect ideas or solve problems, you need to take a break. A good summary of the pertinent research about the brain and downtime appeared in *Scientific American* (Jabr, 2013), and corroborates the idea that breaks help us to engrain complex learning. Research demonstrates that even a brief diversion from a task can dramatically improve a person's ability to focus on that task. Avoidance of breaks leads to drops in attention as you become habituated to the task (Ariga and Lleras, 2011).

Even better is a break spent in outdoor green space. In fact, even 'visual access' to green spaces can help the mind to focus.[25] Research in the *British Journal of*

23 See, for example, https://www.health.harvard.edu/staying-healthy/exercising-to-relax.
24 See https://thedailymile.co.uk.
25 The University of Washington reports that spending time in nature can boost cognitive functioning – see http://depts.washington.edu/hhwb/Thm_Mental.html.

Sports Medicine (Aspinall et al., 2015) reported the benefits to mental state of moving into green space (such as a park), and to engagement level on moving back out of it. This is because the green environment encourages more effortless engagement. It allows 'involuntary attention' in that it holds our attention while also maintaining scope for reflection. Taking a break is likely to have a 'restorative effect and help with attention fatigue' (Reynolds, 2013).

Sometimes it is a combination of movement and the outdoors that can help with focus and inspiration. A study from Stanford University (Oppezzo and Schwartz, 2014) has demonstrated that for mental tasks needing imagination, such as writing, walking (particularly outdoors) led to more creative thinking than did sitting. A residual creativity boost was also observed when participants were seated after walking. Perhaps this is because walking frees up attentional resources for cognitive processes (Patel et al., 2014).

Brain breaks. Short breaks are invaluable for allowing learners' brains to absorb information, resolve conflicts and solve problems efficiently. Mental processes don't stop when students get up from their desks. When writing, we find it is often extremely helpful to separate physically from the desk and take a walk. A writer might allow their mind to wander to another line of thought altogether. Often, audibly rehearsing a sentence, organising thoughts or 'zooming out' helps you to make creative connections and metaphorically see the wood again instead of just the trees.

Some teachers will have the capacity to make layout changes to their classroom that allow learners to shift location when they get stuck. Other teachers might be able to build in the use of tokens that learners exchange for a quick walk around the block during an intense period of work. Trustworthy behaviour might earn extra tokens.

Although it might take a change of culture, if everyone knows that a walk to the water cooler, the book corner or around the block is not – and should not be – an excuse for a chat, but a real opportunity to reinvigorate their thinking, this discovery can be an important activity that we think all learners need to have in their toolkit.

Learning by being outdoors with nature

Learning that develops purposeful learners involves helping them to find meaning. One of the key concepts from the literature that tells us about this is the idea of teaching for character, moral virtues and values. Purposeful learners *recognise that development of character is a valuable aspect of their learning journey and are disposed to develop their character strengths in general.*

A signature learning experience we think might be useful here is learning by being outdoors with nature. Outdoor learning is a broad term including both formal and informal approaches ranging from environmental education to horticulture, field studies, bushcraft and adventure activities.

The Council for Learning Outside the Classroom (CLOtC) defines this type of learning as 'the use of places other than the classroom for teaching and learning'.[26] CLOtC's vision is for raising achievement by providing direct experiences, and they include indoor non-classroom spaces, like libraries, places of worship, galleries and museums. The Learning Outside the Classroom approach is a 'well-evidenced tool' for developing character, resilience, teamwork and self-awareness. In terms of outdoor locations where these experiences might happen, school grounds, local woods, nature reserves, townscapes, city farms, heritage sites, remote places, zoos and botanic gardens all have a role to play.

---

26 See https://www.lotc.org.uk.

Outdoor character pursuits. This might be something like outdoor pursuits that are traditionally used to develop performance characteristics, such as resilience, positive attitude, self-control, grit and craftsmanship. Examples might be tricky obstacle courses or survival challenges.

Orienteering. An outdoor learning idea that gives a genuine sense of perspective and accustoms young people to uncertainty and unfamiliar surroundings is orienteering. This is a serious sport that is typically competitive, requiring navigational skills, a map and a compass. It has its own International Orienteering Federation. Participants navigate between checkpoints on the map in terrain that is unfamiliar to them. This might be on foot, by bike or even skis. Trail orienteering is suitable for all, including those with limited mobility. There is less choice over the route and it requires accuracy over speed.

In *Incredible Journeys*, David Barrie (2019), who has himself navigated the open seas using a sextant, provokes the reader to consider the dangers of becoming overly reliant on GPS technology for location finding. He has argued (Sanderson, 2019) that GPS may cause the parts of the brain that are exercised through navigation (associated with learning and memory) to be underdeveloped. At a time when mental agility is considered to be preventative in degenerative conditions like Alzheimer's, it may be prudent to encourage young people to develop the skills to prevent their atrophy.

Discovering Orienteering (Charles and Turbyfill, 2013) cites the sport's many benefits, not least of which is that it is fun! In terms of maintaining perspective, orienteering improves learners' problem-solving and decision-making skills. Carried out regularly it helps them to develop good exercise habits. British Orienteering has produced an activity pack for schools that develops orienteering skills.[27] Orienteering can also help to develop curriculum skills. Charles and Turbyfill argue that 'Teachers have found that orienteering relates to every academic discipline, from math to history to environmental awareness to public

---

27 See https://www.britishorienteering.org.uk/images/uploaded/downloads/schools_tri_o_resources.pdf.

policy' (p. 7). This might include counting paces and measuring, keeping personal records to help you improve, writing about your experiences, visiting historic sites or learning to play by the rules.

Being outdoors or with nature can help to develop zest for learning by enhancing learners' ability to maintain perspective. A literature review by Muñoz (2009) finds that there is an emerging body of research into the relationship between outdoor space and well-being, which is an important part of maintaining perspective.

Several concepts from the literature – the habit of mind 'tenacity', the known benefits of practical physical activity and the area of practical learning – suggest to us that the signature learning experience of horticulture/gardening may be useful here. Taking part in gardening activities can help to develop learners who *are committed to the pursuit of knowledge and expertise* (tenacity), as they invest their time in keeping things alive. Gardening is certainly good for fitness and well-being, and the physical exertion involved can also help with sleep (Johnson, 2019).

Horticulture more broadly, with its element of practical learning, develops planning, persistence, tenacity and perspective as learners work with the changing seasons and conditions. It is good for learners who *actively seek balance in their learning by using hands as well as head*. It has broad-ranging, practical applicability for the balanced learner, helping to spark an interest in the natural world through conservation, landscape design, garden planning, construction and arboriculture.

> **Gardening.** Running a gardening club can be a good way to introduce young children to the joys of gardening. They can take part in activities that relate to: biology, such as seed germination or plant identification; chemistry, such as soil analysis; geography, such as the water cycle; technology, such as making hanging strawberry planters, water recycling or tool maintenance; or food technology, such as the selection of pest-resistant vegetable varieties.

Learning by imitation

Learning that develops balanced learners involves helping them to value relationships. Zestful learners *choose to spend time with others who relish learning*. One of the key concepts from the literature that tells us about this is imitation, and learning by imitation might be a helpful signature learning experience here.

Imitation is more than just copying. We imitate others when they do something we are inspired by. If teachers want learners to develop zest for learning and flourish, they need to be demonstrating it to the degree that learners want to imitate them. Teachers need to display enthusiasm, engagement and focus.

Teachers' own work. Teachers who are passionate about what they do are likely to spend their own time on related interests and hobbies. Could an English teacher share their favourite poem or their annual reading list? A historian talk about an archaeological dig or heritage project with which they are involved? A geographer talk about their bucket list for travel locations? A music teacher share their frustrations with a composition or their joys at a concert? These real-world experiences can serve as inspiration for imitation to learners. It should be possible for teachers in most learning situations to imagine opportunities for students to work in pairs or groups and practise observing and imitating one another.

Learners' own enthusiasm for learning can also affect those around them.

Appreciative inquiry. At the end of a lesson, unit or piece of work, learners who teachers identify as having particular zest for learning can share what went well for them. What did they find interesting about the topic? What questions has it left them with? What might they go and investigate now?

Learning by socialising

Learning that develops balanced learners involves helping them to maintain perspective. One of the key concepts from the literature that tells us about this is the study of character strengths. Learners with zest for learning *are disposed to act well in terms of character strengths in general, in areas like creativity, curiosity, open-mindedness, love of learning, bravery, persistence, vitality, appreciation of beauty and excellence, hope, humour and spirituality.*

A signature learning experience we think might be useful here is learning by socialising. Children are naturally egocentric, and it takes training and exposure to the social world to shape character.

> **Community projects.** Learners might develop their concern for, and ability to interact with, diverse groups of people through local programmes. Students might take part in age-appropriate activities, like visiting similar aged children in a school for the deaf, helping at a summer sports camps for younger children, reading to the blind, shopping for the elderly, cleaning up the neighbourhood, volunteering for charities and so on.

A sense of belonging through 'fellowship with peers and teachers' (Dweck et al., 2014, p. 30) is particularly important for students in 'middle and high school'. In our literature section on character strengths, we cited a study that showed the importance of peer support. Dweck et al. report that 'Belonging, in fact, is one factor that schools can build to improve the lives of their students across a host of outcomes ... school connectedness emerged as one of the two most consistent and powerful protective factors against every measured form of adolescent risk and distress' (p. 30) – the other being family connectedness.

Dweck et al. propose that educators connect with students' lives outside of school through simple exercises such as expressive writing.

Expressive writing. Using the medium of expressive writing, a marked improvement can be seen in underprivileged children's engagement when they relate 'their life troubles to social values and literary stories' (Dweck et al., 2014, p. 30).

Of course, cultivating zest is unlikely to happen by just selecting a single approach. Neither is it a recipe to be slavishly followed. Rather, we imagine that these ideas will provide an array of possible approaches from which teachers and those working them might select appropriate ideas.

Chapter 4
Promising Practices

Valuing differences is what really drives synergy. Do you truly value the mental, emotional, and psychological differences among people? Or do you wish everyone would just agree with you so you could all get along? Many people mistake uniformity for unity; sameness for oneness. One word – boring! Differences should be seen as strengths, not weaknesses. They add zest to life.

Stephen Covey[1]

Across the world, schools are beginning to adopt the kinds of ideas described in this book, sometimes surreptitiously as zest is not often considered to be part of the formal agenda of school. By contrast, offering activities which promote curiosity, courage, wellness and passionate engagement is very much what many informal educational organisations do.

In the first two books of our series exploring creative thinking and tenacity we focused primarily on school examples, albeit in many cases schools which actively choose to develop relationships with outside agencies. In this book we go one stage further in our thinking, arguing that it is almost impossible to conceive of schools offering the kind of zestful experiences that we believe matter *unless* they develop partnerships with others.

Arbib Education Trust

The concept of museum learning was inspired by the New York City Museum School in Brooklyn, which uses the wealth of inspiration from museum collections in New York to teach across the curriculum. The Arbib Education Trust was founded with support from the Annabel Arbib Foundation as the first Museum Learning Trust in the UK. The trust is sited in Slough, England, which was identified by the UK government as

---

1   See https://www.franklincovey.com/the-7-habits/habit-6.html.

being the third lowest area in the union for arts engagement, with only 54% of adults having attended an arts event, museum or gallery or participated in an arts activity in the past year.[2] Its slogan 'curiosity, exploration, discovery' reflects its approach to learning. There are three schools in the Arbib Education Trust: the Langley Academy, a secondary school (11–18 years) and two primary schools, the Langley Heritage Primary and the Langley Academy Primary, which opened in 2015. All three schools adopt museum learning: the use of museum objects, stories, skills and partnerships to bring learning to life.

The trust believes that museum learning empowers its children and young people. It gives them vital skills for learning and nurtures cultural confidence to last a lifetime. Jenny Blay, head of museum learning, tells us that its projects 'are often about helping students take the next steps beyond school'. They 'can shape how they see themselves and the world around them. Whatever we do, it is always about helping our children and young people get the best out of life.'

The trust plans projects and partnerships to develop skills, broaden and diversify its curriculum, and bring a vivid immediacy to the learning experience. Its curriculum approach is built around preparing its students for the real world and engaging them in learning that allows them to thrive and achieve. It brings subjects together and challenges learners' metacognitive skills. Its approach includes:

+ Curiosity. The trust aims for pupils to develop their natural curiosity and desire to find out more. Teachers will develop an environment in which pupils share their enthusiasm for learning.

+ Exploration. Children will be encouraged to make use of resources and artefacts around them to explore the possible solutions to their ideas. Staff will ensure that appropriate support and guidance is given to make this child-led exploration purposeful.

+ Discovery. Children will develop their critical thinking and evaluative skills as they explain the possible outcomes of their explorations. Skilful questioning, led by staff, will help children to interpret their experiences and make sense of their new discoveries, thus supporting learning.

---

2   See https://www.artsprofessional.co.uk/news/data-map-reveals-levels-arts-engagement-across-england.

Developing balanced learners

An example of how the trust develops balanced learners comes from the Langley Heritage Primary. Its roundhouse and outdoor learning demonstrate the focus on developing balanced learners: learners who value relationships and maintain perspective.

The Langley Heritage Primary's museum learning overlaps with its focus on outdoor learning. Inspired by the two concepts, and by the pupils' interest in their Year 3 unit on the Iron Age, the museum learning team approached the National Lottery Heritage Fund to support the construction of a replica Iron Age roundhouse in the school grounds. Built using original techniques by the company Conygar Coppice, with help from pupils, parents and teachers, this remains a hugely popular initiative. The pupils learn much more from constructing a real roundhouse than from making one out of cardboard. It is a sensory head and hand experience.

Museum learning can help to develop balanced learners who recognise their place in a succession of learners. In this example, the fact that the roundhouse is constructed of mud, chalk and wood means that it needs additional mending and patching each year. New pupils to the school take part in this mending, which means they can all contribute to something the community will continue to enjoy for many years. As a result of this approach, the pupils in general show great consideration and reflection on natural and environmental issues.

Developing curious learners

Museum learning gives learners opportunities to connect to the world in a way that develops their cultural capital and creates aspiring well-rounded citizens.

One way in which curiosity is developed at the Langley Academy Primary is through its Archaeology Day. Museum learning allows children to ask questions and understand concepts through real-life, hands-on experiences. This is particularly important when teaching children about concepts and ideas. Teachers at the Langley Academy Primary wanted to expose the children to high quality language and experiences to help develop their understanding of prehistory and how people learn about life in the past without written accounts. The children were guided through an excavation dig by an expert and taught how to wash and record their finds. The children also learned about stratigraphy (the branch of geology that studies rock layers), about analysing stomach contents and about the thought process that goes into choosing where to begin an archaeological dig.

Using real artefacts, the children asked questions and sought information about prehistory, and developed an understanding of sources of information about the past. Although the day focused on history and sources, the children also recounted what they had done in written form, measured and weighed the objects they had found, and were exposed to contexts way beyond the primary curriculum. The children wrote accounts of their day and wanted to learn more about how to become an archaeologist in the future.

Developing purposeful learners

Museum learning enhances students' opportunities for comprehending the value of history, science and other subjects in everyday life as well as throughout the history of civilisation. It grounds them in a social and historical context, shaping the way they see themselves as individuals within the wider world, historically as well as geographically.

An example of how purposeful learners are developed is the Langley Academy's cross-curricular project on the nineteenth century. This spanned history, drama and English. Year 10 drama students worked with the museum learning team to make their GCSE unit on 'Devising' more purposeful. The head of creative and performing arts aimed to bring this unit to life for her students. She wanted learners to think about the deeper meaning behind their work, so their dramatic characters would feel genuine and would have a significant inner life and purpose.

The museum learning team sourced five real-life case studies from museums and archives. They chose case studies that built on the students' work in other subjects, particularly history, English and religious and personal studies. For example, one case study focused on the loss of a loved one. Two letters from the

National Archives written during the First World War (the correspondence between Private William Martin and his fiancée Emily Chitticks) provided the background material. Another case study gave learners an insight into forgiveness using the story of Jacob Dunne from the Forgiveness Project. Jacob's story gave them a powerful example of restorative justice.

The students used these real-life histories as a prompt to help them find meaning through deeper and more purposeful research. This in turn stimulated performance, so their final dramas showed a better depiction of what it means to be human. Their grades showed improvement from the previous year, with 45% achieving grades 4 to 9 – up from 38% the prior year.

Not only is museum learning the pedagogical approach to planning the curriculum, but it is also the justification and driving force for wider and co-curricular planning. Museum learning allows the students to develop emotionally and socially through cross-curricular projects, exhibitions and project 'Discovery Days'.

Challenges for leadership

From the trust's inception, this model of museum learning has been at the heart of its pedagogy. The sponsors, trustees and governors all actively support and wish to develop the practice. There is a senior leader in each of the schools within the trust with museum learning as their key focus area.

The trust's keys to success can be summarised as:

+ Say yes! Every level of leadership encourages this pedagogical approach and endeavours to say yes to suggestions.

+ Clear intention. The most successful projects begin with a clear intention about what the pupils need from the project or visit. They focus on how the activity will deliver on this intention.

+ Go local. Find out what cultural and arts organisations there are in your area and reach out to them to develop partnerships.

- Communicate your needs. Work with partners and providers to tailor their offer to your needs; they can adapt workshops and want to work with you.

- Be creative. Think about innovate ways to provide opportunities for your pupils.

Australian Centre for Rural Entrepreneurship

Co-founded in 2012 by Matt Pfahlert, the Australian Centre for Rural Entrepreneurship (ACRE) is a social enterprise with a mission to create a positive, vibrant future for rural and regional Australia by 'lighting a spark' for young people to think creatively, be entrepreneurial, be innovative and be supported by their community. Based at Old Beechworth Gaol (of Ned Kelly fame), ACRE works across the state of Victoria and, increasingly, nationally.

Our human destiny, according to thought leader on global trends Peter Ellyard, is about combining two things: one is what you are passionate about and the other is what you are good at. The connection with zest is clear. ACRE's philosophy is that, if you are not leading your life like that every day then you need to start! If you have not found zest for learning, then ACRE will try to help you find purpose and really value relationships with those around you.

ACRE works with young people to help them turn their ideas into mini enterprises. These are extended and deeply practical examples of problem-based learning that have real purpose and that create benefit for their rural communities.

ACRE's values, while not using the language of zest, resonate strongly with it. As an organisation, ACRE's work is carried out by individuals who:

- Find strength and greater impact through working with others.

- See opportunities in challenges.

- Are role models for entrepreneurial thinking and action.

- Are prepared to fail in order to succeed.

- Don't need to find excuses to enjoy themselves.

- Take their work seriously, not themselves.

- Are the bridge-maker between industries, sectors and generations.

- Measure what matters.

- Are tenacious, fiercely independent and nimble.

In the last five years ACRE has partnered with Social Enterprise Academy Scotland to bring entrepreneurial learning and development programmes to Australia. It has successfully piloted the Social Enterprise in Schools initiative in Victoria's North-East. It has created communities of practice to bring government, business, education providers and the community together to encourage entrepreneurship and social enterprise in rural communities. It has also developed a tool that enables communities to measure and improve their entrepreneurial 'ecosystem'.

CEO Matt Pfahlert reflects:

> What I think is amazing about the social enterprises is that kids are always naturally thinking about what could be different, what could be better, whether they can connect with people in different ways. This is creative problem-solving: being purposefully curious about real-world challenges, and it's just amazing to see the impact it has on young people.

Cultivating balanced, curious and purposeful learners

Principles, not a programme, underpin the Social Enterprise Schools initiative. In terms of the framework for zest, ACRE's activities mesh very closely:

- Balanced. ACRE sees relationships as being at the heart of all it does. Its default position is to encourage learners to experiment, make and experience things first hand. The Social Enterprise Schools initiative promotes students to be champions at practising, to become more active participants in their learning.

In practice, this means offering multiple opportunities and contexts for students to 'prototype and test' their enterprise thinking and tinkering *before* they go 'live' with their trading.

* Curious. All ACRE's work seeks to find and ignite (or reignite) young people's passions to help them explore the world around them and try out new ways of thinking, being and working. Social Enterprise Schools prioritise student voice and agency.

One way this principle comes to life is through students' social enterprises which spring from social or environmental issues the students themselves are passionate about. Students identify a problem they think is worth solving; they are not solving someone else's predetermined problem. It is also evident in the classroom when students apply their social enterprise learning by creating peer- and self-assessments (e.g. quizzes on social enterprise terms).

* Purposeful. ACRE's programmes require problem-solving, character development, practice and the development of goals that are both desired by individual learners and owned by the wider community. Social Enterprise Schools makes explicit and meaningful connections to community and business.

* In practice, this is seen when students need to be investigators and market researchers to find out if the enterprise idea they want to create is indeed innovative, and what their intended target audience needs and is willing to purchase. It is also seen when students invite business and/or community leaders to offer feedback on their social enterprise.

Social Enterprise Schools

ACRE engages with schools formally via the curriculum as it is established by the Victorian Curriculum and Assessment Authority (VCAA). Specifically, it provides practical opportunities for achieving the goals of the Melbourne Declaration on which the Australian curriculum is founded. These opportunities encourage students to become successful learners, confident individuals, responsible citizens and effective contributors.

The Social Enterprise Schools initiative run by ACRE is a collaborative, hands-on experience where young people are in the driving seat of their own learning. Ten journey map stages show the route students will take with their social enterprise. Framing each of the ten journey stages is a key question, from 'What is a social enterprise?', 'How will students lead and collaborate?' and 'What would you like to change in the world or your community?' through to 'How will students share stories?' and 'Have we publicly recognised and celebrated our journey?' Importantly, the students decide what they want to see happen with their social enterprise at the end of the school year (as shown in the journey map on page 168).

Students identifying a social cause they care about (e.g. homelessness, deforestation, animal cruelty) is a core early feature of the journey they will take with their social enterprise. With their cause in mind, students learn how to generate enterprise ideas and then set up and manage their own social enterprise – a business with a social purpose. Most of all, the Social Enterprise Schools initiative helps young people to build skills, confidence and links with the community. Students develop an understanding of the social enterprise business model and gain hands-on experience of setting up and running it. They learn how to lead and become good team players, acquiring enterprise, leadership, numeracy, literacy and creative thinking skills.

ACRE commissioned an independent evaluation of its Social Enterprise Schools pilot in rural North-East Victorian schools (Anderson and Beavis, 2017). The evaluation found the initiative to be deeply practical, engaging and suitable for any age or ability. The programme builds on strengths and develops confidence. It supports students to develop, practise, demonstrate and deploy their entrepreneurial knowing, doing and being, while simultaneously becoming responsible citizens with more understanding of the world around them.

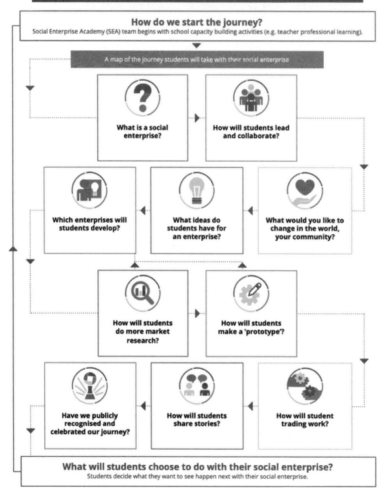

Social enterprise schools journey map

Developing activities with stakeholders

Working with independent researcher Michelle Anderson, the evaluation of Social Enterprise in Schools led to the creation of a detailed online resource called the Social Enterprise Schools Teacher Toolkit.[3] This is a guide for teachers to use with their students rather than a prescriptive manual. The toolkit's content takes each social enterprise journey map stage and makes relevant and meaningful curriculum links to it; notable among these are critical and creative thinking capability and personal and social capability. At every journey stage a teacher will find three sets of information:

1. Journey stage expectations: clarifying what students will be doing, learning and creating, and key vocabulary.

2. Curriculum mapping (which is done by curriculum levels): matching the 'knowing' and 'doing' stages of the journey to key and relevant achievement standards and content information in the Victorian curriculum.

3. Establishing and understanding progression: using the achievement standards and content for every journey stage to help inform what steps along a learning continuum might signal evidence that students are progressing in their learning.

Rounding out the toolkit is a suite of learning activities which teachers can mix and match according to students' interests and needs. Teachers have the opportunity to use the learning activity structure to create and populate the toolkit with their own lesson activities or units of enquiry.

A distinct feature of the toolkit was who did the creating. Alongside lead developer Michelle Anderson was a co-design team of primary and secondary students and their teachers, a specialist critical and creative thinking teacher from the VCAA and a businessman-turned-social entrepreneur from ACRE's team. For twelve months the co-design team went about developing, testing and retesting a suite of learning activities with each other. Some students even took the prototype learning activities back to school and tested them by teaching their peers. Importantly,

---

3   See https://www.socialenterprise.academy/aus/teacher-toolkit.

this co-design process aimed to ensure that teachers and students have materials which are relevant, useful, engaging and of high quality.

Leading by example, ACRE's approach to developing the toolkit exemplifies how it seizes diverse opportunities to cultivate zestful learning experiences with its partners in learning. Signals of this include:

+ Balanced: a co-design team of students and their teachers, with a visible way to value contributions.

+ Curious: students and teachers being open-minded and curious enough to embrace seeing one other as learners and designers side by side. This was a first for all involved.

+ Purposeful: persisting together as a co-design team to scope, test, ditch, improve and expand on ideas for the toolkit, even when they were not quite sure what the final product might look like.

In a sense, ACRE's goal is to get zest for learning back into school settings, and especially (although not only) into those students who, by dint of their detachment and demotivation, have lost it. Almost all children are born with a zest for learning, and for these students in particular, leading their own social enterprise seems to reboot it. Matt says: 'Building economic and social capital in rural communities produces an amazing sense of pride, belonging and resilience among people who start to feel fiercely proud of where they live.'

When the broader community starts to hear about students who are running social enterprises – real businesses with a moral purpose, not just school fundraising activities with a financial goal – their reactions are quite different. As a small businessperson in a small town, it is exciting to witness young people taking an interest in areas of community need. It is easy for such people to see how they might play a mentoring or coaching role.

Leadership lessons

ACRE has learned much since 2012. Matt thinks there are five key messages:

1. Start young.

2. Be experimental and experiential.

3. Work with collaborators across all sectors.

4. Always think about learning *beyond* school.

5. Help the community to own the assets wherever possible.

With regard to the last of these, ACRE's home, the Old Beechworth Gaol, has been bought for, and by, the community and provides a physical centre of a challengingly different kind from the school.

ACRE found that when it started Social Enterprise Schools four years previously, it approached school principals and talked about the importance of developing in young people enterprise capabilities for the future. At the time principals had little interest in capabilities, but were instead preoccupied with the concept of student engagement. Off the record, principals told ACRE that the greatest impact on job prospects for young people was the loss of motivation – you could say zest for learning – at age 10 or 11. At this point, Matt told us, they 'drop out of education in droves'. Even those who turn up aren't necessarily engaging with learning.

ACRE has found that the kinds of learning experience it can offer with its many partners seem to have the impact of re-energising the very same young people on whom dispersed rural communities come to depend.

Bedales

Bedales School is a progressive, co-educational boarding school in Hampshire founded by John Badley. Established in 1893 to be radically different from its founder's own experience at a traditional English public school, it was among the very first to accept boys and girls, has had an influential school council for over 100 years, and abandoned uniforms and 'sir' long ago in favour of first names and sartorial autonomy. The school's desire to give students a genuinely balanced experience is reflected in its motto: 'Head, hand and heart'. The earliest curriculum was delivered through intellectual 'head' pursuits in the morning, outdoor 'hand' work on the farm in the afternoon and broader, cultural, community-based 'heart' activities in the evening.

Recovering zest for learning

Since its establishment, Bedales has changed with the times, maintaining its distinctiveness in many areas. It found itself dismayed, however, by the dismal diet of GCSEs and grinding exam preparation into which it had fallen in the early 2000s. A plot was hatched to balance out the school experience again. Teachers felt that although there is nothing wrong with the odd exam, there are other ways of valuing and assessing students' work and of developing the sorts of capabilities they will need after school.

As the school contemplated its first school aim – 'to develop inquisitive thinkers with a love of learning who cherish independent thought' – it felt there were ways it could inject considerably more zeal and engagement than by continuing with the drab, off-the-peg, GCSE mono-experience. In its own aspirations it was aiming very much for the combination of balance, curiosity and purpose embodied in the notion of zest.

A focus on curriculum

After three years of careful planning and consultation with universities, parents and students, the Bedales Assessed Courses (BACs) were launched in 2005 in lieu of many – but not all – GCSEs. Written by its own teachers with 'love of learning' at the heart of their design, Bedales developed courses which weren't all about timed terminal assessment. Presentation, portfolio work, group projects, performance, vivas and creative responses were woven into the curriculum and assessment schema.

Real-life purpose pervades much of the curriculum design. Outdoor work students renovate tractors and Land Rovers, set up pizza-making businesses, construct roundhouses and halter-train animals for county shows, while documenting and reflecting on what they are learning. A small shop has been set up to sell the food and craft products the students make, and a renewable energy project saw solar panels installed on the plant nursery. Performance and practical subjects spend more of their time on the dance, the play, the product or the dress, and less time box-ticking. A 'Utopia Project' enables students to synthesise their learning creatively in producing their own multifaceted blueprint for a better society, following the ambition of Plato and Thomas More – and learning about their models on the way. Unsurprisingly, its outputs have improved in ambition and quality, since more time can be spent on 'the thing itself' rather than accountability exercises.

Across the board, the school allows significant scope for students to shape the direction of their own learning. Drafting plays an important part in many of the school's project processes. Its close relationships with students enable constructive progress through drafts prior to final pieces. The school's ownership of the curriculum means it can make changes from year to year in a process of continuous improvement, with student motivation very much at the heart of its thinking.

Evidence for success

How does Bedales know that its approach works and that its students are more zestful as a result of the steps it has taken? To those on the ground it has just been 'glaringly obvious' that the students enjoy the autonomy and variety that has been injected into their educational diet. The school had aimed to make BACs better preparation for A levels too, and results improved measurably as the first cohorts rolled through.

Truthfully, the school didn't launch into its project after a careful literature review and randomised controlled trial. Nor did it pilot the approach with one or two subjects. Teachers just went for it wholeheartedly on the basis of their collective educational convictions, informed by their combined experience: nine new subjects at once, growing to twelve later. (Bedalians still complete a core of five GCSEs – in English, maths, double science and a language, and then most take four BACs alongside those.)

Several years after the launch, the school undertook a research exercise with Research Schools International, which is affiliated to Harvard's Graduate School of Education, focusing primarily on student motivation. The school was pleased, if unsurprised, to find that Bedales students' levels of engagement and enjoyment of their subjects were significantly higher than the average, and particularly high in the BAC subjects. Equally, it felt affirmed to find, retrospectively, that there was so much in the research literature to support its intuitive emphases on choice, hands-on, outdoor-based learning, and scope to follow the particular curiosities of the students.

Challenges for leadership

Many schools have visited Bedales over the years as they seek to inject more zest into their own students' experience, wondering how Bedales 'gets away with it'. A key part of its success has been its positive relationship with the Universities and Colleges Admissions Service (UCAS). At an early stage UCAS generously agreed to list Bedales' courses on their drop-down menu within the university application process. They are not explicitly accrediting what the school does, but enabling universities to see clearly what its students have done. The school is its own accreditor, although it does use external moderators to ensure that it is grading in line with GCSEs, as far as it is possible to make comparisons. It writes from time to time to admissions departments to remind them about the nature of its offering but, by and large, they simply trust Bedales to deliver an inspiring education and report honestly on it.

For Bedales, zest for learning is an apt synonym for the long-held educational goal which has led to its love-of-learning-led BACs programme. While the school feels it has been more or less an unmitigated success educationally, its approach does provide management challenges.

Attempting to ensure parity between its courses in terms of challenge is difficult given the very different nature of, say, outdoor work from ancient civilisations. Another complication is getting the balance right between the different kinds of learning activities across a dozen subjects. Trying to ensure comparability of grading with dissimilar GCSEs is another. Holding enthusiastic heads of department back from including too much in the courses, and so over-burdening students, is yet another challenge. Persuading sixth-form colleges – which are more sceptical than universities – that BACs are of equivalent currency to GCSEs for entry can be tricky. On top of that, the school must keep up sufficient external scrutiny to feel confident that the system is robust, so to keep it sharp it invites the Independent Schools Inspectorate to come and put it under the magnifying glass periodically on a consultancy basis. The school also has a nominated head of BACs who oversees these issues, steering heads of department in sharing practice and agreeing common policy.

The school's experiment has been a highly fertile one; of that it is convinced. It is an approach that Bedales would recommend to any school wearily ploughing a GCSE-shaped furrow. They invite readers to go and visit! They love showing people around.

Explorer Scouts

Twenty years ago, Explorer Scouts didn't exist. Today they are a key part of the UK Scout movement with over 44,000 of these 14–18-year-olds gaining leadership and team work skills, developing confidence, resilience and a habit for learning.

To Matt Hyde, chief executive of the Scouts, zest for learning is about nurturing a lifelong love of learning; it is about encouraging members to be open-minded to new people, ideas and experiences. Being an Explorer Scout helps them to develop the skills and perspective to consider different ways of thinking:

> The experience helps young people to develop the empathy, values and judgement to balance different viewpoints and reach their own conclusions. It is about creating that initial spark that lights up a young person's interest and then supports them on a journey of growth, discovery and, we hope, self-realisation. In Scouts, there is a belief that you never stop learning.

It is also about creating an environment where young people can ask questions and talk freely, but respectfully, in a safe space. Across different communities and settings – including in deprived communities and in schools – Explorer Scouts *want* to learn rather than feel they have to.

Learning by doing

The Scouts believe that young people learn best when they learn from each other, and most importantly when they learn by doing. Explorers are encouraged to investigate an issue not simply by reading a blog but by meeting people and taking action in the community. It is also about connecting them with great role models. People learn from people; that is what lights the spark. Scouts is about preparing young people with skills for life. It has inspired generations of dreamers and doers, and has been doing this for over 100 years.

Explorer Scouts have been with us since 2002. It was born out of a now defunct scheme called Venture Scouts (for 16–21-year-olds) which thrived from the 1970s to 1990s. Explorer numbers quickly outstripped those in the Venture Scouts, and Explorer membership has been steadily growing ever since. It is part of the UK Scout movement's 6–25 programme which inspires learning at every stage of a young person's development.

A culture of curiosity

Part of the Scouts' unique offer is a balanced programme of activities, introducing Explorers to a range of themes, issues and activities. To achieve the top awards Explorers need to tackle several within each area – and, of course, along the way they often discover a particular activity or issue they feel close to and want to specialise in. That is how curiosity is piqued – by offering a wide choice of activities. And it is by providing freedom within a framework (to choose their own community impact projects and expedition destinations, for example) that Explorers are encouraged to take ownership of their learning, and in so doing become more purposeful.

Learning and making a difference – the double benefit

A vital part of the 6–25 Scout programme is making a positive impact in local communities. It has created opportunities for over 250,000 Scouts to take social action and engage in a range of themes (from assisting those with dementia to mental well-being), supported by the organisation's charity partners.

At the same time as helping others (part of the DNA of Scouts), members also get to develop key character and employability skills. A 2018 YouGov poll of the UK public revealed that nine out of ten people believe Scouts develop active listening skills, while over 90% believed Scouts help young people to develop empathy.[4]

As a case in point, Chapelhall Explorers chose to take social action on mental well-being (something that felt very real to them around exam time). Working with a local charity, the Explorers gained an understanding of the factors that

---

4   See https://www.scouts.org.uk/news/2019/may/scouts-helps-young-people-develop-active-
     listening-skills.

contribute to both good and poor mental health. They also took practical action by participating in a Darkness Into Light charity walk.[5]

Meanwhile, in Cumbria, Xenolith Explorers chose to take action on a disability theme, carrying out an accessibility audit in their local community, as well as inviting guide dogs and their owners along to their unit evening. 'The Explorers enjoy the adventure and fun on offer,' said their leader, Bryan Caine, 'but feel that being an active citizen is the key for them as young people – they feel it is important to be seen at the heart of their community.'

Offering a balanced programme

Every aspect of Explorer Scouts is designed to promote non-formal learning and help develop a young person's skills and character, while instilling its core values of care, respect, belief, integrity and cooperation.

With the promise, law and federated structure, Scouts are a familiar part of the landscape, but as a movement it changes with the times too. It provides opportunities to gain a huge range of skills – from life-saving and emergency aid, to leadership and the performing arts. It even helps young people learn to code. Explorer Scouts work towards the Platinum and Diamond Chief Scout's Award, as well as the coveted Queen's Scout Award, covering a range of community-, values- and international-based activities.

In summer 2019, over 2,000 Explorers attended the twenty-fourth World Scout Jamboree in the United States, jointly hosted by Canada, Mexico and the USA. They met young people from over 100 countries, lived and worked alongside each other for ten days, swapping ideas and experiences. Such opportunities leave an indelible impression on young people. The friendships formed and cultural exchanges make for an intensive learning and life experience.

---

5   See https://www.darknessintolight.ie.

Learning and leadership

One of the most exciting opportunities open to Explorers is to become a Young Leader. These are young people aged 14–18 who volunteer to help run Scouts for younger children, planning and delivering programmes. The movement is incredibly proud that over 18,000 of its Explorers choose to take on this challenge.

Being a Young Leader runs alongside (and often contributes to) their own development, awards and activities. Often this is an Explorer's first taste of volunteering and leadership. It takes the fear factor out of leadership and gives them the confidence and experience they need. Every Young Leader is supported with a mentor and a modular training scheme which covers every aspect, from safeguarding to coping with challenging behaviour. Being a Young Leader is a key part of an Explorer's learning journey, developing skills while giving back at the same time.

All this leads to happy, resilient citizens who are engaged in more civic participation, improved social mobility for the individual and better social cohesion as a whole.

Explorer Scouts in schools

Nottingham High School is just one example of a school that has embraced Explorer Scouts as a way to develop young people's essential skills. Meeting every Friday during term time after the academic day has finished, they have found it a brilliant way to promote wider learning and give greater opportunities within a ready-made framework. 'Scouts make up some of the happiest memories of my time at this school,' said Callum, a student and Explorer Scout. 'The leaders are great fun and the atmosphere is amazing.'

The students also take on a greater role in the planning of their ambitious programme, which has included trips to Norway and Switzerland, scaling 4,000-metre peaks, descending deep limestone gorges and crossing vast glaciers. Explorers also get the chance to work towards their Scout awards and Duke of Edinburgh's Award.

In 2015, Explorers conducted an intensive study of Scouts in schools (Scott et al., 2016), running pilots in a number of schools. The students who took part exhibited an increase on five character measures: empathy, community, leadership, communication and problem-solving. Overall, students who took part were overwhelmingly positive. They agreed strongly that they had enjoyed the programme (91%) – particularly the mix of indoor, outdoor, active and creative activities and opportunities to make friends and work together – and wanted to continue in Scouting (88%). Scouts made them want to come to school (86%) and they looked forward to Scouts (84%).

Scouts in schools: what works?

A study on Scouts in schools conducted by Demos (Birdwell et al., 2015) identified a number of key success factors. The biggest of these was buy-in from senior leadership at the school, specifically the head teacher. Where this wasn't in place the pilot often failed.

The study identified the difference between the more formal role of teacher and the less formal role of Scout leader. It concluded that the different roles the teacher plays in the less formal setting of a Scout meeting can 'improve relationships between students and teachers, and improve the discipline of some pupils' (p. 76).

Another key finding was that teachers and head teacher have to *want to* set up Scouts. Where they are told to do it, the initiative invariably struggles. Talking up the key benefits, giving teachers opportunities to try Scout activities and visit other groups to see what success looked like were vital. Good training, the effective management of challenging behaviour, support from the local Scout infrastructure and volunteer management is also critical. Finally, teachers need to be comfortable with the time commitment required and how they balance this with their existing workload.

Explorer Scouts helps young people to develop a habit of learning. This makes them happier, more employable, more active in their communities and have better relationships. Explorers helps them to get a sense of themselves and find their place in the world.

Forest School Association

The Forest School Association is the UK's professional body promoting best practice for the Forest School model of education delivery. This model gives learners hands-on experience in the natural environment. There are many approaches to outdoor learning, which is a broad term encompassing both formal and informal education. Forest School can be distinguished from other outdoor learning models (e.g. bushcraft, horticulture, forestry) by its six principles:

1. *It is long term, frequent and regular, encompassing all of the seasons. Rather than being a one-off visit, its delivery involves planning, adaptation, observations and reviews.*

2. *It takes place in a woodland or natural wooded (to a greater or lesser degree) environment.*

3. *It aims to promote holistic development of participants, fostering resilient, confident, independent and creative learners. It aims to link experiences to home, work and school education, where appropriate.*

4. *It offers opportunity for appropriate risk.*

5. *It is run by qualified Forest School practitioners.*

6. *It uses a range of learner-centred processes to create a community for learning and development. Play, choice and reflective practice are integral elements.*

In terms of what is taught through Forest School, its programme can be embedded into the school curriculum or even replace it. Aspects of England's national curriculum can be taught from an outdoor location, using the forest environment as a place from which to explore the natural world, while also learning more holistically.

Zest for learning

The Forest School approach is, by definition, learner-centred. Schools using this approach seek to provide multiple opportunities for young people to develop their zest for learning. As an antidote to the inevitable formality of indoor, subject-based learning, they offer outdoor spaces where healthy activities can be enjoyed, new relationships developed and a different perspective on the world experienced.

Curiosity is of central importance, with an emphasis on the active exploration of the natural world and the embracing of new, mainly practical experiences. By providing children with sustained exposure to woodland, schools using Forest School programmes explicitly seek to help learners find meaning as they develop a deeper understanding of the world around them.

A focus on character

Forest School is a holistic, nurturing approach built on the rich heritage of outdoor learning from across cultures and throughout history. Over the last quarter of a century these ideas have grown as a grass-roots movement until the ethos and principles, first agreed by the Forest School community in 2002, were adopted by the fledgling Forest School Association in autumn 2012.

Forest School programmes offer a radical return to ancient ways of being and an innovative response to the serious decline in the health and well-being of children, their teachers and families. The important contribution of Forest School to the nation's ecological awareness and well-being of children and young people is recognised in the UK government's (2018) twenty-five-year environment plan. The value of long-term nature connection for mental health and well-being has also been reported on by Forestry Commission England (O'Brien and Murray, 2006).

When Forest School programmes are embedded in the school curriculum, or in some cases replace it, they are able to provide deeply engaging weekly sessions, often over a whole year. Children are exploring the natural world and covering many aspects of the national curriculum without being explicitly taught, while learning how to navigate the ups and downs of life.

The Forest School approach has an explicit focus on the development of character. Participants in Forest School programmes are empowered to manage their own emotional risks, resolving conflicts and learning the give and take of healthy relationship-building. A child who knows what 'good risky' feels like will be far more able to navigate peer pressure in their teenage years. If you have lit fires safely since you were 3, you are less likely to need to burn a car when you are 14.

At the heart of Forest School is the belief that children and young people are hugely capable beings who, when trusted and supported in the right ways, will exceed the expectations many adults have of them. They often surprise themselves with how physically strong they can be and how many brilliant ideas they come up with when left to it. They learn with and from each other when skilled Forest School practitioners are able to stand back, observing and scaffolding the learning with open-ended questions. Having an adult joining in with the wondering encourages children to think bigger and bigger questions; if they are used to adults having the answers it may sometimes take a while for them to adjust. When adults model trust alongside curiosity, learning spreads very rapidly. Forest School training is often about liberating adults from having to 'teach' and being the expert all the time.

Cultivating balanced learners

Forest School programmes are natural laboratories for cultivating zestful learners, and help to develop balanced learners who can maintain perspective and value relationships. In terms of maintaining perspective, an opportunity for 'epic adventure', sometimes requiring bravery and a willingness to try something new or physically challenging, is an important element of children learning that discomfort may be OK, and sometimes it reaps huge rewards. Very young children exhibit grit and determination when learning to walk. Forest School offers a multitude of ways to rekindle this quality, even in the most reluctant teenager.

In terms of valuing relationships, this role of the 'significant other' is sometimes missed by adults in the throes of a busy school day. Forest School leaders cultivate relationships that are respectful. They are able to give children and young people time because they are working with smaller groups and higher ratios of adults to participants. Training offers practitioners time to reflect on pedagogy; of the five units studied, 'Learning and Development' is the weightiest. They consider the power of relinquishing their 'expert status' and then try it out when leading their six-week introductory programme to Forest School.

Problem-solving in the real world – working out how to throw a rope over a branch, setting up a tarpaulin to provide shelter, or getting a fire lit to make a drink – requires lateral thinking and team work. Learning to value each other's strengths in a non-competitive environment is a powerful lesson that arises from the Forest School approach.

Cultivating curious learners

Forest School helps to develop curious learners who explore the world. Fire is synonymous with Forest School for many. This is particularly true for older children, who relish the sense of power and danger at the same time as valuing the sense of community engendered by staring into the flames together. Cooking on a fire meets basic human needs for warmth, safety and sustenance. At the hearth something happens to the most boisterous individuals. Calm descends and deep reflection happens. Stories are told and songs are sung.

While relishing discovering new worlds under logs, climbing trees or building with natural materials, young people are learning how to manage their sites for biodiversity. Forest School leaders develop woodland management plans and work with their groups to minimise the ecological impact. Carrying heavy branches, building dens and swinging from rope swings helps them to learn about forces, choose natural materials, measure for purpose, discover how to join materials together and make beautiful art – all while caring for nature. Woodlands are not seen as adventure playgrounds to trash; they are wildly exciting places, teeming with life that needs to be protected. Children learn the properties of different plants and trees, discover how history has been shaped by timber and how healing happens because of plants.

Older children understand the incredible function of trees as sequesters of carbon once they have burned wood from a tree, to release the energy as heat and to make charcoal. Comparing a piece of coal to a charred log gave a Key Stage 2 Forest School group the prompt they needed to start investigating fossil fuels. It can inspire weeks of investigation into questions of sustainability, morality and environmental justice.

Cultivating purposeful learners

Forest School provides opportunities for learners to find meaning. Time around the fire is an opportunity for grateful reflection, either as a whole group or through smaller conversations, as learners and leaders sit together at the close of a session. Developing a respectful, reflective culture – a moment where those present listen to one other – is a cornerstone of Forest School sessions. Being present and 'in the moment' is talked about a lot. Mindfulness happens in the woods. Young people find a favourite spot to return to; they are encouraged to take time to just 'be'. Some head teachers are ensuring that young people in Year 6, facing SATs, have a full year of Forest School.

Learners can experience flow through Forest School. Leaders witness teenagers diagnosed with ADHD, who are unable to focus in the classroom, spend whole afternoons persevering to use a flint and steel. They identify the most effective natural tinder, learn from each other how to create a spark and get it to catch. They may not succeed in achieving the instant fire they want for several weeks, but they will feel satisfaction when they master the skills needed. They have not given up. Bread has never tasted as good as when cooked on a fire you have built and lit yourself.

One of the many ways in which Forest School is distinctive is its focus on making the experiences core to school, rather than extra-curricular. Forest School *is* the curriculum.

Challenges for leadership

One of the main challenges for school leaders is society's current obsession with risk and the ways in which schools have begun to deal with this. The Health and Safety Executive chair Judith Hackitt has said: 'Health and safety laws are often wrongly cited as a reason to deny children opportunities, contributing to a cotton wool culture' (*Telegraph*, 2012). Play England, the Royal Society for the Prevention of Accidents and many other watchdogs have championed the basic need of children for adventurous play.

FORM

FORM is an independent non-profit organisation based in Perth, Western Australia. It develops creativity, and aims to make a difference to people's lives though a broad portfolio of artistic activities, thought leadership, creative learning projects, cultural infrastructure and residency programmes. FORM explores how:

- *Creativity sparks art and culture, inspires learning and social well-being, and generates opportunity.*

- *Creative capacity can be built through culture, visual arts, learning, industry development and community engagement.*

- *Creativity drives positive change, enhancing quality of life and livelihoods, transforming environments and cultivating more fulfilling relationships.*

FORM aims to stimulate curiosity and engagement, attentiveness and questioning, enjoyment and reflection, critical thinking and growth. In FORM's lexicon, a zest for art and culture equates to a zest for learning and experience – and these equate to a zest for life.

Equipped for today and tomorrow

It is FORM's belief that creative learning is a powerful means of creating a 'win-win-win' approach to education that aligns academic attainment, the development of the skills required to thrive in contemporary society, and the fostering of a zest for learning that cultivates an appetite and capacity to learn. FORM sees this combination as essential to more effective learning, both in schools and onwards throughout life. This approach can also help to build a community and culture around young people that supports learning in and out of schools, and is effective in engaging teachers, school leaders, parents and the wider community to this end.

> What I love most about this programme is the belief these children hold that they can make a difference and make change with us backing them up 100%. (Rikke, special needs education assistant, North Fremantle Primary School)

Creative Schools

The Creative Schools programme pairs up teachers and creative practitioners for sixteen weeks to co-design and co-deliver an aspect of the school curriculum in a creative way. The programme responded to identified needs in Western Australia to re-energise the 38% of pupils disengaged from learning, to help teachers deal with disparities in ability levels in classes, and to better equip pupils with creative and critical thinking and other essential future-focused capabilities.

The programme was developed in partnership with Paul Collard, chief executive of Creativity, Culture and Education (CCE), an international foundation dedicated to unlocking the creativity of children and young people in and out of formal education, and Paul Gorman, founder of Hidden Giants. This education consultancy agency supports schools to reimagine their curriculum by placing disruptive, creative and critical thinking at its heart.

The programme was piloted in five schools in 2018. During 2019, co-funded by the Department of Education for Western Australia and the Department of Local Government, Sport and Cultural Industries, the programme expanded to sixteen primary and secondary schools in both metropolitan and rural areas across Western Australia, working with children across the age range of 3–16.

Creative Schools explores the value of bringing artists and creative practitioners directly into school environments through a sustained engagement. Zest for learning has been demonstrated in all parties as a result of the creative learning engagements. Sourcing and training local creative practitioners has been essential, with creatives now energised, skilled and motivated to rise to the challenge and inspired by the results being achieved. Teachers have reported being re-engaged with a focus on learning, rather than just teaching. They are more actively trialling new solutions in their classes. Pupils have been highly engaged, are showing academic improvement and, moreover, are displaying considerable improvement in actively applying the five creative habits of mind: being inquisitive, collaborative, persistent, imaginative and disciplined:

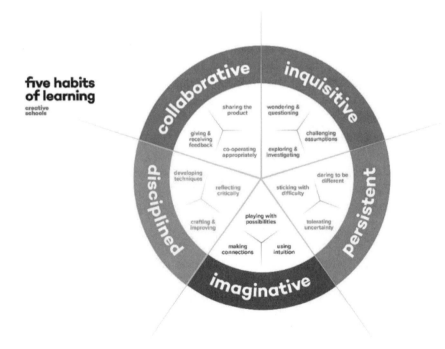

The five creative habits of mind developed by the Centre for Real-World Learning

Deep learning

The Creative Schools programme aims to instil deep learning in young people. It has four key components:

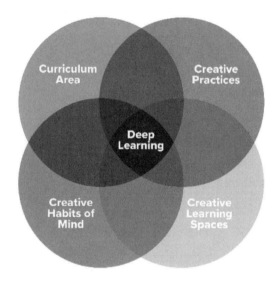

FORM's deep learning model

Some of the key decisions that make the Creative Schools programme successful can be linked to these four components:

1. Curriculum area

+ Addressing a priority learning area in each class (e.g. mathematics, history, science) and exploring novel, creative ways of teaching this curriculum area.

2. Creative practices

+ Partnering teachers (experts in curriculum) with artists/creatives/creative practitioners (experts in creative practices, e.g. painters, game designers, musicians, actors, chefs, writers) to devise and deliver classroom activities to teach the curriculum in ways that are physically, socially, emotionally and intellectually engaging. FORM's Creative Learning programme manager Lamis Sabra tells us:

> Teachers are experts in pedagogy and knowledge of the curriculum. Creative practitioners are skilled in thinking creatively and engaging young people. FORM can bring them together and train them to partner effectively in the classroom. Utilising creativity to help children to engage with learning; to collaborate and listen, challenge and discover, fail and grow, think and reflect; to solve problems by combining imagination and materials with technology, performance, executive functions, motor skills and play.

+ Engaging the whole of the school community (including principals and parents) in the support, delivery and outcomes of the programme.

+ Engaging rigorous evaluation of the programme by external academic and creative learning consultant Mathilda Joubert.

+ Demonstrating powerful impact on student, teacher and creative practitioner learning. Lamis adds:

> We're finding that nurturing creative thinking in schools really can help children's learning and social skills to flourish, especially in schools in low socio-economic areas. It's very exciting to witness deep learning, and with the research and evaluation running concurrently we hope to show some really solid outcomes that can support an ongoing engagement with many more schools.

3. Creative habits of mind

+ Providing intensive professional development for teachers, creatives and school leaders on creative learning and effective strategies for nurturing the creative habits of mind in the classroom.

+ Acknowledging that if some pupils have difficulty learning or even just being in class, creative learning can help to ease or eliminate that difficulty *and* increase achievement for those pupils who can already cope well. One student at Merriwa Primary School asked: 'Is thinking like football – does it take practice to get good at it?'

+ Starting each session with a physical warm-up to prepare pupils for learning, followed by a main creative learning challenge and concluding with a reflection around the development of creative habits of mind and capabilities.

4. Creative learning spaces

+ Considering the characteristics of a creative learning space. Teachers and creative practitioners use an adaptation of the Lucas et al. (2013) framework, which was developed for CCE to help them make pedagogic decisions (see page 192).

The impact of Creative Schools

Evaluation of the programme demonstrates significant positive impact on young people, including increased agency, enhanced creative thinking skills, increased confidence and self-belief, improved attitudes to learning, deeper learning and thinking, improved behaviour, improved academic learning outcomes, changed learning environments, and enhanced connectedness to school and family. The collaboration also contributes to enhanced creative teaching practice for both teachers and creative practitioners.

The findings of the Creative Schools pilot evaluation report are summarised in the figure on page 194. This shows that input of specific resources (like creative practitioners) results in a diverse set of classroom interventions. These lead to a set of (largely) behavioural outputs (such as improved collaboration). These, in turn, generate performance and understanding outcomes in participants (including pupils, teachers and creative practitioners). Finally, the sustainable impact of the

The High Functioning Space

creative schools

Low Functioning		High Functioning
GUIDED	ROLE OF THE TEACHER	CHALLENGING
CONTRIVED	NATURE OF THE ACTIVITIES	AUTHENTIC
BELL-BOUND	ORGANISATION OF TIME	FLEXIBLE
CLASSROOM	ORGANISATION OF SPACE	WORKSHOP
INDIVIDUAL	APPROACH OF TASKS	GROUP
HIDDEN	VISIBILITY OF PROCESSES	HIGH
STATIC	LOCATION OF ACTIVITIES	MOBILE
IGNORED	SELF AS LEARNING RESOURCE	CENTRAL
IGNORED	EMOTION	ACKNOWLEDGED
SOME	INCLUSIVENESS	ALL
DIRECTED	ROLE OF LEARNER	SELF MANAGING
LIMITED	REFLECTION	CONTINUOUS

The high functioning space

Source: CCE, adapted from Lucas et al. (2013, p. 136)

programme is achieved through embedding a set of changes in the pupils, teachers and creative practitioners.

How does Creative Schools translate into a zest for learning?

The use of creativity to engage pupils in multisensory ways at all levels – physical, social, emotional and intellectual – and give them more agency is particularly effective for engendering a zest for learning.

There is no set curriculum for the learning activities co-created by teachers, creative practitioners and students in each Creative Schools classroom. Each week, new learning activities are designed, trialled and reviewed through a continuous experimentation cycle of plan-do-review.

Despite the unique nature of the learning activities in each classroom, research data from the past two years indicates how all the characteristics of zestful learners are being fostered in Creative Schools classrooms.

Zestful learners are balanced

* Valuing relationships. Creative Schools sessions continually engage learners in collaborative learning activities. They may be challenged to look at the world from the perspective of their peers, learners from a different age group, or refugees. Interactive arts-based learning strategies are employed to encourage students to become vulnerable and thus develop trust, empathy and other-centeredness.

  I didn't just learn about the topic, I also learned how to be more caring and more open-minded to others' ideas. (Pupil, Highgate Primary School)

* Maintaining perspective. Learner agency is developed by giving students voice and choice within Creative Schools sessions. For instance, they might choose different ways to express their learning to an audience. Examples might be

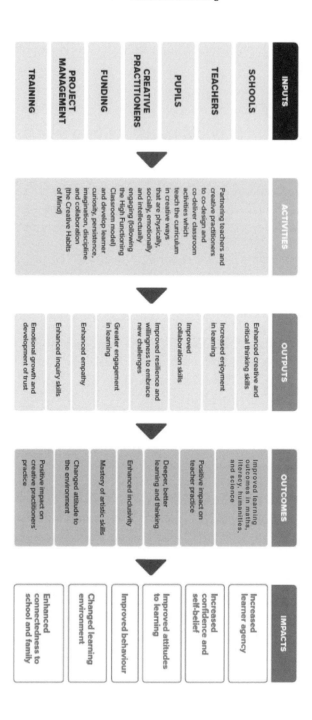

Impact model depicting the intended impact of the Creative Schools programme on stakeholders

a cooking display, teaching fractions to class mates, a sock puppet show to teach the school values, a younger buddy class, composing and recording an original song to teach Australian geography to parents, or the design and production of marble runs to teach science concepts like gravity, friction and gears to other high school students.

These hands-on, interactive learning activities provide opportunities for learners to develop dispositions like problem-solving and decision-making. Weekly reflection on the creative habits of mind enables learners to gain perspective on personal strengths and areas for development. Different physical learning spaces are also activated – for example, the development of outdoor learning and the use of nature pedagogy.

I think we are learning to step outside of our own shadows and stop trying to be like others. I like how we are learning the five senses and we have to say if the lesson was imaginative and collaborative. That is a part of our own thoughts and not just following what everyone else thinks. (Pupil, Melville Primary School)

Zestful learners are curious

+ Exploring the world. Reflection and the development of self-awareness and self-regulation skills are key components of every Creative Schools session. Learners are encouraged to think about their thinking and to make connections between different ideas and contexts.

  A variety of reflection tools are used to facilitate personal and collective reflection, including journals, sticky notes, drawings, freeze-frames, photos, classroom discussions and a poster of the creative habits of mind.

  I'm learning to think in a different way. I recognise things around me in a new way, to interact with nature, to pick ordinary things up and notice special things about it. I am learning in a whole new way. (Pupil, Melville Primary School)

+ Embracing novel experiences. On a weekly basis learners in the Creative Schools programme are challenged to move beyond their comfort zone, to try new experiences, to take risks and to challenge assumptions and preconceived ideas. This could be by learning English skills through making mud, filming adverts to develop understanding of a different culture or team-building challenges.

> We learn new stuff. We do different things. People are trying harder. They are trying new things and believing in themselves more. (Pupil, Kinross Primary School)

The ability to embrace novel experiences is something that has developed in children throughout the programme:

> The gift that Creative Schools is giving me as a teacher and our classroom is invaluable as the personal growth we are all experiencing is phenomenal. What I found incredibly rewarding was those children who rarely orally contribute to discussions were voicing their ideas and really felt heard. The children started to feel empowered that they were taking ownership of their outdoor learning environment. (Roberta, pre-primary teacher, North Fremantle Primary School)

Zestful learners are purposeful

* Finding meaning. Learners find meaning in Creative Schools learning activities that encourage them to solve problems in creative ways. This may involve developing solutions to engage children in other countries in healthy lifestyles or spending time doing what they love by immersing themselves in nature or a deeply creative pursuit. Inquisitiveness is fostered through non-routine thinking challenges, and aspirations are being fuelled through the regular contact with professional creatives, opening up glimpses of opportunities.

> He learned to look at problems in a more creative sense – not to try and provide an answer he thought the teacher wanted. (Parent, Scotch College)

* Performing well. Creative Schools sessions are highly engaging. Learners experience flow as they immerse themselves in deep learning experiences with high levels of personal ownership – for example, designing games, writing scripts, creating cartoons, building models or writing songs. Even the most reluctant learners find the practical nature of the activities enjoyable, leading to improved attitudes and behaviour, enhanced motivation, increased confidence, deeper learning and thinking and, ultimately, improved academic learning outcomes.

It has been a pleasure to observe students change and grow in confidence in their maths. They also know they are doing better and have proudly said, 'I get this! I am getting the answers right!' (Teacher, Bentley Primary School)

Challenges

While the Creative Schools programme creates rich opportunities to develop learner zestfulness, it is not without challenges. Finding time for teacher–creative practitioner collaboration to co-plan and co-reflect is always difficult, which is why school leadership support is key to the success of the programme to provide sufficient planning time for teachers.

Another potential challenge is that teachers could feel threatened (or inspired) by the presence of a creative practitioner in their classroom, particularly if they are not clear why they were selected for the programme. FORM addresses this challenge by creating early opportunities for the teacher–creative practitioner pairs to develop a relationship of trust. Off-site training sessions are attended together before teams start the work in schools. FORM guides school leadership teams in their selection of teachers for the programme.

Finally, securing funding to employ creative practitioners to work in this intensive way in schools remains a challenge, which is why the emphasis of the programme is on transforming teacher practice. This means that the programme's impact can be sustained for future generations of children, even if the level of collaborative activity cannot be maintained in each classroom. This is complemented with a partnership approach that brings together creative sector and education sector interests, so that funding for arts in schools can also be rethought more effectively through the example of this programme.

It has forever changed the way I plan my lessons. (Teacher, Kinross Primary School)

Holyport College

Holyport College is a state boarding school in Berkshire, England. Opened in 2014, it has a strong commitment to developing young people's attributes as learners, ensuring that rich and varied opportunities abound both within and beyond the curriculum to foster a culture whereby young people have the opportunity to develop their zest for learning. Ben McCarey has played a key role in embedding this ethos during his five years leading the school, initially as deputy and now as head teacher.

When Holyport College opened in September 2014, it did so promising to provide a different – and in its view, better – model of education than the majority of maintained sector schools. The school set out its stall as combining a focused academic curriculum – which would be followed by all students, regardless of background or ability – and an expansive approach to extra-curricular learning. Holyport deliberately avoided adopting any particular pedagogical approach; it was neither hard line nor particularly liberal in its approach to behaviour management. In short, it disregarded many of the headline approaches to education that have defined so many schools which have opened under the government's flagship free schools programme in England.[6]

Holyport was fortunate to have two idiosyncrasies that have come to form the cornerstone of its approach to developing zest in students. First, Eton College was its educational sponsor. Second, as a state boarding school, the school day was modelled around that of a traditional, independent school with the students in school until half past five and ninety minutes set aside for the co-curriculum each day.

---

6   There are a number of types of academy school in England, and a 'free school' is one type. Free schools were established under the government's free schools programme. They are self-governing, non-profit charitable trusts, and can be created by charities, businesses, parents or teachers. Free schools are funded by central government and are independent of local government control, but they are subject to England's regime (Ofsted). They are not obliged to follow the national curriculum, but they must offer a broad and balanced curriculum, including the core subjects of maths and English.

Building a culture of zest in a new school

As with so many new schools, the founding cohort arrived with very high expectations. The impact of the association with Eton College was immediately apparent. Students and their families believed that because Holyport College was sponsored by Eton, it followed automatically that they would be academically successful. However, the reality was that in such a young organisation, with no established culture among its student body, very few, if any, of these students initially possessed the attributes associated with successful learning. They could certainly be purposeful, but two key elements of zest — balance and curiosity — were in short supply. Their academic aspirations manifested themselves in a desire to be led to a fixed end point (essentially defined by good test scores), but without any of the resilience or, indeed, zest that might be expected in young people in the most academically successful organisations.

The predominant culture among the student body at the time was risk aversion; they had already taken a big risk in choosing a brand new school. The school's desire for them to be settled and happy led to a decision-making process that did all it could to avoid rocking the boat. For example, the compulsory weekly choir practice for all students, introduced in September 2014, was a riotous, joyous and, admittedly, musically challenging occasion. In January 2015 it was abandoned based on feedback from students and parents that the time might be better spent studying towards their academic targets. Holyport was in danger of inadvertently creating a culture where its students relished academic success but had little zest for learning whatsoever (or, indeed, any understanding of what this meant).

Zest in the curriculum

Holyport's vision is unambiguous, stating: 'We will give our students the tools they need to go on to lead independent, purposeful and fulfilled adult lives.' Early in its journey the school decided to focus on some key attributes for learning in all its students. Drawing on thinking in *Educating Ruby* (Claxton and Lucas, 2015), Holyport developed a programme to embed attributes such as confidence, curiosity, collaboration, communication, creativity, commitment and craftsmanship within the formal curriculum.

It has involved provision of professional learning for staff where they have the opportunity to suggest approaches for pedagogy as they try out approaches and feed back to colleagues. It has also seen a simple tracking system put in place to record student progress in the valued attributes (confidence, curiosity and so on), which now sits alongside more conventional academic tracking. This has involved creating 'icons' representing each of the attributes so they are widely understood by staff and students.

A focus on breadth of experiences

At the heart of the Holyport offer is the breadth and range of opportunities outside the classroom. More than 75% of students complete at least the Bronze Duke of Edinburgh's Award. Younger students take part in up to ten hours of compulsory sports per week, and all students are required to participate in a sporting activity at least once a week until the end of sixth form. Compulsory choir is back (for those who pass the obligatory auditions!), and the co-curriculum offers upwards of 200 clubs, societies, interventions and activities on a weekly basis. External speakers visit the school regularly, and all staff are actively encouraged to run trips and off-site activities.

Holyport deliberately extends students' learning opportunities far beyond the classroom. It explicitly seeks to inspire them to be curious and passionate about the world and encourages them to extend their horizons through foreign travel, exchanges, field trips, day trips, conferences and museum visits. A unique local opportunity for students is that they are able to attend societies at Eton College on weekday evenings.

None of these activities explicitly uses the label 'zest', but year-on-year an increasing proportion of Holyport students do engage in the co-curriculum programme with enthusiasm and purpose. Slowly but surely, a culture of engagement and zest for learning – purpose, curiosity, a balance between academic and real-world activity – is developing.

Embedding zest within the school day

A specific focus of the Holyport experience is the co-curriculum, which takes place for all students on Monday to Thursday for ninety minutes. By explicitly sandwiching these experiences within the formal learning, the school gives a powerful message about the value it attaches to them. Activities fall into six broad types:

1. Physical: sports and activities which promote physical fitness and well-being.

2. Intellectual: activities that challenge students to think, often in different ways from the traditional curriculum.

3. Cultural: activities that encourage students to engage with, and contribute to, cultural heritage including music, art, drama, film, literature and philosophy.

4. Service: activities that encourage students to become active citizens of the modern world and to contribute both to the college community and to the wider community as a whole.

5. Mindfulness: activities that allow students to slow down, de-stress and take a break from the busyness of their lives.

6. Intervention: activities designed to provide additional academic support to students over and above their timetabled lessons.

An A–Z of these activities indicates their wide range: Africa club, American football, art, badminton, board games, chamber music, chess, computing, craft, creative writing, debating, drama, Duke of Edinburgh's Award, fashion, knitting, magic, mindfulness, movie club, multi-sports, pétanque, philosophy society, poetry corner, robotics, role-playing games, rowing, Royal Geographic club, running, singing, ultimate Frisbee, volunteering and Young Enterprise.

Challenges for leadership

The greatest challenge from the perspective of Holyport College's leaders has been overcoming the fear of risk and finding ways to say yes to things that would not previously have been possible. For a state school head teacher, in an era of accountability where an unfavourable Ofsted outcome could mean the end of a career, the use of opportunities outside of the classroom as a vehicle to improve grades inside the classroom seems counter-intuitive. Holyport's head teacher has needed the confidence to remain firm in his resolve to focus on giving students these opportunities.

Likewise, persuading tired and overstretched staff that forty-five minutes spent running American football club on a rainy Thursday afternoon is a better use of their time than any one of the myriad tasks on their to-do lists is a challenge. Sustaining this priority can't be achieved without a whole-team approach where everybody does their bit and shares in the rewards.

Developing young people's zest for learning is about the culture of a school, not simply the shopping list of opportunities and interventions on offer. The past five years at Holyport College show that developing that culture is a slow process which, inherently, requires perseverance on the part of the leadership team.

The first time students were offered the opportunity to take part in Combined Cadet Force (CCF) 75% of those who signed up dropped out within three months.[7] Rather than writing this off as a failure and giving up, Holyport is taking action to ensure a greater commitment to participation. It is introducing more compulsory outdoor activities further down the school in order to develop a culture of purposeful participation and to ensure that there is a greater balance in young people's lives than was afforded to them by the previous singular focus on academic outcomes. These outcomes, it should be said, continue to improve.

---

7   The UK's Ministry of Defence (MoD) sponsors the youth organisation Combined Cadet Force. CCF operates in over 400 secondary schools across the UK as an educational partnership between the school and the MoD. It may include Royal Navy, Royal Marines, Army or Royal Air Force sections, and aims to develop young people's personal responsibility, leadership and self-discipline. See https://combinedcadetforce.org.uk.

Kopernikus

Colegio Kopernikus is a school in Frutillar, Chile. Established in 2014, it expanded its twelve classrooms to thirteen to incorporate secondary schooling in 2019; previously it had served only nursery to Grade 8 pupils. The school aims for its pupils to develop self-awareness and to exercise autonomy, to care about global challenges, and to approach them creatively and through collaboration. The school's model for pedagogy distinguishes itself by bringing together and valuing equally academic content and skills. It develops simultaneously the children's personal interests and demonstrates a special sensitivity to the arts and the natural environment. Its slogan 'creativity, autonomy, collaboration' reflects its approach to learning.

The Kopernikus pedagogical model

Kopernikus was established with the purpose of being different. A number of beliefs about education have been present from the school's genesis, and have contributed to the development of its pedagogic model:

+ The opportunities for learning are everywhere and not restricted to the classroom.

+ Significant learning comes from strong pedagogical processes.

+ A focus on collaboration and autonomy is key.

+ Today's students are tomorrow's global citizens.

+ Excellence should be sought in all aspects of education.

+ The school's thinking and action should be creative.

+ The children are at the centre of the process, and each child is unique.

Kopernikus already uses the five-dimensional model of creativity developed by the Centre for Real-World Learning (see Lucas and Spencer, 2017), and its model aligns very closely with the three aspects of zest – balance, curiosity and purpose.

The model sees classical content and broader areas of learner development as wholly complementary. Staff energy is focused on four specific areas, a lens through which teachers can make decisions about how school life should operate (see page 205).

The director of Kopernikus, Trinidad Aguilar Izquierdo, has been in charge of the process for five years and has had the privilege to work with a highly motivated team. One of the things that she values most is 'the possibility that we give each other: to try; to look for new alternatives; and to put our passion for education over results, over rankings, over achievement. Students and learning come first.'

Getting to this place has not been an easy journey for the team because, as Trinidad explains, 'We were not taught like this at school. We didn't learn this way, so today, as adults, we are asking things from our students that we don't usually practise or have ourselves, such as large amounts of autonomy.'

Specific time is assigned in the school's schedule and calendar for each one of the four approaches. This means that children should experience each of the four, every week, in classes or workshops. The school's calendar contains dates for outdoor activities, for celebration, for personal development and so on. It has become the school's way to see education as a process that is multidimensional. Each of the four areas is equally important, and the school works to maintain a balance between each.

1. Development of capabilities

The school's approach aims to develop three key dispositions in its learners:

1.   Creativity: using the Centre for Real-World Learning's five habits –
     inquisitive, imaginative, persistent, collaborative and disciplined.

     As a community, all of the school's efforts go towards bringing the
     development of these dispositions into everyday school life, not just in the
     context of specific events. Lessons are taught in a way that fosters creativity.
     Learners can learn to persevere and to be imaginative in all learning

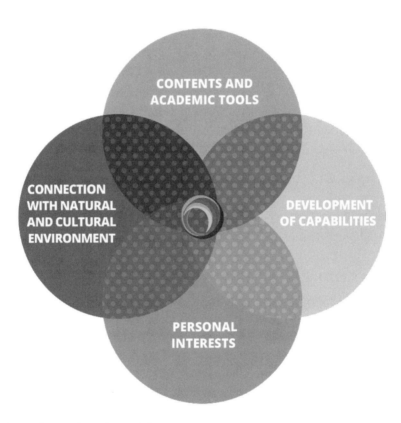

The Kopernikus pedagogic model

contexts, thereby developing their ability to think creatively and enjoy the learning process.

2.   Autonomy: being responsible for themselves and others, and exercising an active role in decision-making.

The school's secondary students are owners of many of their learning decisions, which puts them in the driving seat of their learning process. Not child-centred for its own sake, the school aims to teach learners that freedom and responsibility go hand in hand. Their rights should not come at the expense of others' freedoms.

3.   Collaboration: working with others in pursuit of a common purpose; valuing the contribution of others in order to address the challenges of today's society.

The school aims to educate children in a way that develops their ability to listen to others and treat all people with dignity. Teachers model this by listening to children and demonstrating how to value others' ideas by taking their ideas seriously enough to air them in discussion.

2. Personal interests

Six years after it was founded, Kopernikus can see zest for learning in its learners. Young people enjoy being at the school and it feels like a family. Learners see learning as a motivating process. They have space for healthy, balanced development because there is room for different kinds of things; not just typical school lessons, but different learning experiences. For example, each semester the children can choose from a variety of workshops that are not linked to the curriculum. This helps to develop their curiosity as they explore and come to understand the areas in which they thrive.

Learners are particularly motivated because space is allocated for the development of their own curiosity by following personal interests, and they are given responsibility for many decisions concerning their learning. For example, each morning, learners have time set aside where they choose what they need to focus on from the previous week. They spend some time practising whatever they think needs to be improved on.

3. Connection with natural and cultural environment

One of the ways in which Kopernikus develops the curiosity of its learners and helps them to maintain a balanced perspective on the world is its recognition that learning is not confined to the classroom. The school is located in a particularly special environment. The children are privileged by their proximity to both natural and cultural opportunities, such as a lake, volcano, national parks, and the theatre and musical history of Frutillar. They visit all of these places regularly. Teachers seek to create opportunities to expose learners to the physical environment and to the learning afforded by engaging with members of the community. Interactions with the cultural environment provide opportunities for cooperation and learning responsibility towards others.

Knowledge of the contemporary world is one of the school's priorities. Children must learn to deal with nature and people. They do this by listening to other children's stories, to the teacher, to external visitors, by observing and asking questions, and by looking for answers in places such as the library. Visitors might include parents with particular expertise, musicians and artists who are working at the local theatre. Visitors might work directly with teachers, who then apply what they have learned with the children.

4. Content and academic tools

The school uses vertical grouping in its structuring of classes to reflect the way that the world involves communities of heterogeneous individuals. The message here is clear: that developing and maintaining relationships across ages matters in the real world. It is not the typical approach and it has required many adjustments, but it has led to numerous benefits. One of the most powerful of these arises as children interact with peers of different ages. Each year, their perspective and respective social roles change as they progress from being the youngest, to the middle, to the eldest. This changing viewpoint impacts on the way they relate to others in the class, and to the way they approach their learning. For example, younger children are tutored by older students, and they come to expect help from them. When they become the eldest, children learn to take on an active leadership role as they help to incorporate the youngest new members.

The mixed-age grouping, with its challenge of diverse ages and interests of learners, also affords opportunities for teachers to be highly flexible and creative with both content and curriculum, although it can also be a real challenge in terms of class design, evaluation and teaching methods. Under this structure, learning through projects becomes very stimulating, and almost the natural way of approaching content, particularly because it connects learners with skill development as well as content.

In order to prepare children for the future that awaits them, academic training is not enough for their development. In terms of schedule and timetabling, the school has selected subjects within the broader Chilean curriculum based on the degree to which they afford interesting opportunities to help fulfil the school's pedagogical model. These include subjects like global citizenship, theatre, individual work, circle for dialogue and workshops of all kinds, which learners can take freely in the afternoons. Circle for dialogue is a formal activity in which the older children take an active leadership role. It is a secure place where group members share things that happen to them. Workshops might include sports, debate, music, visual arts, dance, programming, theatrical make-up, learning about herbal properties, climbing, outdoor activities or swimming in the lake.

The school offers multiple opportunities for outdoor experiences in the natural and cultural world as well as community experiences. These might include working with other schools, beach cleaning or local sports championships.

Trinidad believes the school has managed to mix curricular and extra-curricular activities in such a way that they feel like one continuous process for the students. For example, they might learn about the different states of matter while visiting the volcano or they might use what they learn in workshops at a school presentation. It might involve parents and students working on projects together. One result of this way of working is that learners are very motivated. She believes this is because when learners' personal interests are involved, they are seen as a whole person, not just a student receiving content.

Another positive motivational tool has been the removal of grading, which has communicated the value that all learning is important, not just the end test result. The school took the decision to get rid of grading in Years 1 to 6 because the teachers saw no need for it in the early years. Teachers evaluate constantly, but the marks are not made available to the children or their parents, in order to remove any sense of competition between them. Removing the ability to make these sorts of summative comparisons can lead a student to feel unable in a particular area, which is a great shame at such an early stage of their development.

Learning through play is important at Kopernikus. It is through play that everything that has been learned comes together and experiences are internalised. Games incorporate dramatisations, including those that explore emotions and the management of feelings, and free play.

Challenges for leadership

One of the main challenges Kopernikus has had to overcome in recent years was to establish a balanced relationship between parents and school in terms of the important decisions. Parents need to be fully involved, but also to truly trust in the school's work with their children. Parents need to be absolutely convinced that this is the way they want their children educated, so that parents and the school can work together and not against each other.

Once that consensus was reached, parents and the school started learning from each other. Parents play a very active role in everything related to school life, and how the school can make sure it is caring for its surroundings and the wider environment. Parents propose ideas through a formal parent–school committee and the school puts them into action. The school also involves parents through a 'school for parents' system, which parents can attend two or three times a year. This is an opportunity for the school to inform parents about the upcoming curriculum and how they can help their children's learning with appropriate activities at home.

A second challenge is finding the right sort of teachers to work at the school. The school's approach to teaching is not taught at universities, and nor is it being practised in many other schools in Chile. The pool of candidates was small, so the school decided that it would train teachers internally. Teachers do not always find this easy in the first year, but after that, if they allow themselves to be flexible and passionate, they enjoy their job, which is naturally contagious for the children. This approach needs close attention by leaders, however, because adults find engrained habits hard to change. This is an ongoing challenge.

Professional development

Trinidad tells us that one of the key adjustments that must be made in a school is in its organisation to allow for the learning process. An example of this adjustment might be the practice of giving teachers as many chances as possible to make decisions. Trusting teachers with responsibility gives them zest for their own jobs, and is actually a very powerful way of enabling teachers to model zest for learning to their pupils.

Another key part of the process for the teaching team is that they all learn together. This strengthens their sense of community and unites them in purpose, because they are all part of a very motivating project. They are members of a learning community where each individual can participate in the process of building something that works by sharing their ideas.

Leading well

Advice to educational leaders from Kopernikus includes:

+ Trust each other. Give responsibility and space for decision-making to other members of the team, not just the leadership team.

+ Work as a community that learns together – not having one person with all the answers, or even just the adults. Listen to the children and make them lead part of the process as well, not just as passive listeners.

+ Dare to propose change and different ways of doing something. Be persistent with that intention so you can see it materialise.

+ As a leader, be open and receptive to the ideas of your team and others. If you normally say yes, new and better ideas start to appear.

+ Don't get distracted with every new discovery in education. Choose a path and be persistent with it, because it is not about the big things. It is about being able to work out the details, and for that you need time.

Royal Yachting Association

The Royal Yachting Association is Britain's national governing body for all forms of boating sport. Since the introduction of National Lottery funding in 1997, it has consistently produced the most successful sailing team at the Olympics since 2000. This includes winning fifty-eight Olympic medals (twenty-eight of them gold) plus many other accolades at top-level international competition.

Developing purposeful and curious learners

Over the past twenty years or more, the Royal Yachting Association has worked hard to instil a healthy zest for learning and problem-solving within its sailors and associated support staff. It has focused particularly on developing a process-focused mindset that values learning over the outcome or result. This pedagogic approach has been proven to drive success, particularly in the long term. It is an approach that flows through the whole programme and is consistently reiterated and repeated. All staff receive education and training on having a process-focused mindset, all the way through from managers to administrators and from coaches to sailors.

The process-focused mindset approach is centred on a purposeful and positive approach to problem-solving. An example might be sailors using competition as a way of evaluating their strengths and weaknesses and, on completion of the event, creating detailed action plans to develop their weaknesses, while also building on their strengths.

Learners must pursue high levels of curiosity and creativity when seeking out solutions and evaluating outcomes. For example, learners experiment to find the optimum rig or boat tuning settings. They need to be curious and not satisfied with the norm, or what is widely believed to be the fastest settings. Instead they will use high levels of data to inform their decisions.

The association's sailors clearly understand how they learn, highly value a positive learning environment, and seek out dynamic and challenging situations to test their ability to adapt a solution to match the situation.

Learning for coaches

Coach and instructor education is critical, and the association has invested significant resources in ensuring that their network of coaches are appropriately educated and developed. This includes a mixture of knowledge sharing and education through conferences and workshops, all the way through to bespoke one-to-one continuing professional development (CPD) programmes which allow for a more tailored and flexible approach to coach development.

During this time, the programme has evolved dramatically and has reached the point where many coaches now report their development experience as both inspirational and having fundamentally changed their coaching practice for the better. In a recent peer review, Professor Vincent Walsh of University College London commented: 'Open-minded, open learning and a thoughtful approach to constant improvement are how I would describe the coaches, coach developers and programme managers at the Royal Yachting Association. Their coaches present a real challenge. They are accomplished, serious experts who want to extend and disrupt their practice in order to improve.'

Deliberate practice for purposeful learning

The coaches are developed and supported to learn how to expose their sailors to learning environments that vary the conditions of practice and learning skills which are in the long-term developmental interests of the sailors, rather than short-term quick wins. Coaches set problems for their sailors to solve, often slowing the rate of learning, but in doing so, allowing them to learn how to test an approach to match the situation, learn from the outcome and produce an overall higher level of performance.

At the under-18s stage of the Pathway, the coaches' practice is best defined by an approach called 'deliberate play'. This means the coaches carefully create experiences that intentionally give opportunities for their sailors to explore, test and adjust different solutions to relevant and realistic performance problems. While the solution may be obvious to the coach, they resist the temptation just to give answers, preferring to scaffold learning experiences and allow their sailors to generate rather than imitate.

Zest for learning follows on from this good, deliberate practice because learners become less dependent and more self-sufficient and confident. They consequently enjoy the process of learning and seek out more learning opportunities, often on their own and without the support provided by a coach.

Developing curious learners

The whole team are also supported by a strong culture which is based on a clear set of values and standards which, while running throughout the entire programme, are tailored for each step in the journey. As an example, and with respect to curiosity, sailors are supported to be 'curious and willing to try new things' at the entry level of the Pathway, while they are expected to 'learn from mistakes and embrace learning opportunities' by the time they leave and move into the Olympic programme. Coaches have their own values and standards too, and with respect to curiosity they are expected to be 'fascinated with how people learn and make decisions.'

Challenges for leadership

Sometimes, this approach can be a challenge to implement, particularly with respect to the parents of the sailor. They are often very results focused, which is perhaps driven by their own experiences at school and a results-driven education system. Therefore, the Royal Yachting Association spends a great deal of time and effort educating and communicating with parents, particularly with respect to the learning process and associated theories such as Carol Dweck's growth mindset. They use the term 'performance parent' to summarise the behaviours which the organisation looks to endorse in the parents linked to the programme, particularly with respect to valuing long-term learning over short-term and easily lost performance. This part of their programme involves a sequence of workshops and online learning, with ongoing support via a digital platform.

Connecting with school

Increasingly, the Royal Yachting Association looks to work with educational establishments, both to demonstrate the complementary advantages that sailing can provide, but also to work together to provide a level of continuity across the two environments. For example, the association's OnBoard programme covers many areas of England's Key Stage 2 curriculum, including geography, maths and science. Examples might be: working with angles when turning a boat, identifying the effects of air and water resistance, or understanding forces in relation to working with pulleys and levers on a boat. Sailing and windsurfing can also help to fulfil some of the goals of personal, social, health and economic (PSHE) education. This might be through the way it develops good communication and builds relationships, boosts self-confidence and fosters determination. Of course, sailing covers many aspects of physical education within the curriculum.

The Royal Yachting Association is very aware of the additional advantages this can provide to a young person and help them to benefit from a rich and varied set of experiences, which in time help them to become more effective learners. Sailing teaches students how to read situations and solve problems from an early age. It gives them a zest for learning.

By taking a risk and pushing themselves physically, young people experience intense learning experiences. They develop a keenness to improve their technique and they understand what it means to be a curious learner. By practising a skill deliberately, and experiencing the fruits of their labour as things go well – even momentarily – they understand what it means to learn purposefully. By persisting with problem-solving and having to make quick decisions on the water, they develop their learning dispositions and gain a sense of what it means to be a balanced learner.

The association's achievements are impressive given the uncontrollable and challenging nature of sailing, in which participants must continually assess the variable wind, weather and tide and make accurate predictions to out-sail the competition. No situation a sailor faces is ever the same, and successful sailors are those who are best able to understand quickly the environment in which they are operating and adapt a solution to match.

Shireland Collegiate Academy

Shireland is a secondary school in Smethwick in the West Midlands, England. The school has developed an innovative competence-based curriculum for students, organised into themes, each lasting about half a term. Shireland believes in all students receiving a rounded education where they are at the centre of their own learning.

In 2014, England's accountability body, Ofsted, published an important report, *Key Stage 3: The Wasted Years?*, detailing that in traditional Key Stage 3 curricula students were a low priority for most secondary schools, often not seen as a priority by staff and whose transition from primary was frequently poorly managed. Unsurprisingly the performance of many students dips, as does their zest for learning more generally.

Rethinking Key Stage 3 to develop balanced, curious and purposeful learners

The Ofsted report stuck a chord with the head teacher, Sir Mark Grundy.[8] It confirmed a line of thinking he had begun much earlier – that a more substantial rethink was required. He would need to draw on primary practices, on connecting with learners' interests and on the role of technology. Shireland had decided to develop a wholly different approach to teaching those aged 11–14 in 2007, and this report confirmed why. The school pulled together a team and started to plan.

Instead of a fragmented curriculum taught by many teachers, they recruited teachers prepared to teach the majority of subjects to their Year 7 students, radically improving the quality of the relationships between teachers and learners. They reorganised subjects into themes, each likely to engage students' curiosity and encourage them to explore the world. They changed the way students were assessed by putting far greater emphasis on purposeful activities leading to exhibitions, displays and presentations capable of showing their learning in far greater depth and rigour than an essay or classroom exercise.

Shireland called their new curriculum Literacy for Life. It has many of the hallmarks of our model of zest, explicitly seeking to create balanced, curious and purposeful learners who are able to thrive in the real world.

Literacy for Life

Literacy for Life (L4L) is founded on four key ideas (see page 218):

+ The safe and secure base enables students to value and build deep relationships.

+ Engaging and exciting themes stimulate students' curiosity, requiring them to explore the world and try new things. It also develops purposeful learners who seek authentic connections with their world.

---

8   Sir Mark was honoured with a knighthood for his work in helping to turn around a second school as well as leading Shireland.

- The focus on competencies enables students to take a more balanced view of their learning, valuing knowledge, skills and capabilities.

- The emphasis on team ethos contributes to the overall sense that Shireland cares about relationships. This process is accelerated by an extended summer school for new Year 7 students at the end of Year 6.

Students have seventeen hours per week with the same teacher in Year 7, thirteen hours in Year 8 and eight hours in the first half of Year 9. Instantly, students and families have a single point of contact within the academy who has a focus on the academic and pastoral well-being of the students in their class. This kind of timetabling enables the emphasis to be put on the quality of relationships between staff, students and parents. Students are taught in a Year 7 and Year 8 base which also eases the transition process to a large secondary school.

The curriculum integrates all the subjects required in Key Stage 3 into a series of engaging themes designed to pique their interest and curiosity. A theme is a topic, usually around six weeks long, which the students use as a hook on which to base their learning. The underpinning philosophy is that students learn better in context than in isolation. Themes cover all areas of the national curriculum, but not every theme contains a full balance of every subject – some might be more geography based, while another may contain more drama. Designing the curriculum in this way allows for deeper experiences and more extended blocks of time to produce high quality outcomes.

Examples of themes in Year 7 include: Citizen Me, Silent Movies, Plants and Journeys, Pantomime, Fairy Tales, Growing, Going Green, I Robot, In Days of Old, Water and What If. Themes have within them certain key characteristics: a long piece of extended writing, time set aside for developing reading, and a number of competencies that the students will develop. Each theme starts with a highly immersive experience in a room with a projection on three walls, more akin to museum learning than to the more typical instructional modes associated with schools.

Competencies are broken into ten areas – numeric, scientific, reading, social and environmental, technological, communication, personal learning, personal social, creativity and professional development. For example, a student can perform

The Shireland Literacy for Life model

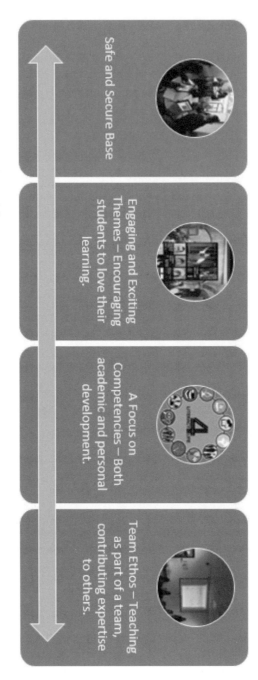

Safe and Secure Base

Engaging and Exciting Themes – Encouraging students to love their learning.

A Focus on Competencies – Both academic and personal development.

Team Ethos – Teaching as part of a team, contributing expertise to others.

a piece of diary writing in a Great Fire of London-based theme or create an instructional manual in a theme based on robotics.

One way that Shireland develops learners who are balanced (they value relationships and maintain perspective) is through the L4L theme called 'Citizen Me', which works hard on developing students' sense of community – their sense of family, local, national and international perspectives – and what they can do to make a difference. In this theme, which lasts for four weeks at the beginning of the students' journey, they explore with teachers what it means to be a decent person, to be a good member of society and how they can impact the world.

Students come from sharply divergent backgrounds, and a series of structured activities help to blend their strengths by looking at family histories, school experiences and considering shared problems in the community. Shireland brings in local politicians to talk about how they look to make change happen. Students take part in a shared community project. A series of personal social competencies are explored, which help them to consider how they will develop as both people and learners.

Curiosity and creativity are hallmarks of the L4L programme. The thematic approach to learning, through Shireland's 'connected curriculum', allows students to make strong connections between subjects in a way which can become lost when they are jumping from subject to subject in a silo-based system.

One theme is 'Grand Designs'. Here, students are undertaking their learning through a three-week architectural project. They are encouraged to explore architecture throughout the world and locally through trips and visits. They begin to learn materials science, physics, geometry, measurement and construction techniques by exploring some of the greatest constructions in the world. Closer to home, they explore the economics of house design, aesthetics in art, the practical skills of buying a house in real life, advertising and financial literacy.

This is then brought together through group-based design projects where students design their own buildings and present their work to a panel of judges. Working in an area of high deprivation, the academy strives to give students a broader view of the world in projects like this, and where possible it will engage industry professionals to talk about their experiences of working on real-life examples.

An example of how Shireland develops learners who are purposeful (they find meaning and perform well) is through a strong application of audienced learning. When students write a letter, the academy looks to have opportunities for them to send it. When they do a presentation, they do so within national competitions or by bringing in external judges. Learners see that their work is valued in the real world. Professionals are appointed to work with students from different sectors, such as a partnership with the Birmingham Hippodrome.

Pride in students' work comes from the desire to produce items of real quality. As such, Shireland has looked to minimise posters, worksheets and similar tasks in favour of larger pieces of work which are supported by extended blocks of time. Each theme is supported by Big Writes, Big Reads and Big Problems which build into this ethos.

L4L teachers work as teams, blending their subject specialisms and joint planning, and training each other. They have more of a pastoral link to the students than traditional teachers might, and this model allows them to truly understand the needs of the young people in their care. Music, languages, physical education, dance and design technology are taught outside of the integrated curriculum, although they will occasionally have a presence in the themes.

Evidence of success

There are a number of indications that Shireland is successful. Ofsted has twice graded Shireland outstanding, noting its innovative and imaginative range of courses, and the way they are extremely carefully planned to meet the precise needs and interests of learners.

Students gained a quarter of a grade better than government expectations in 2014/2015, rising to a third in 2016. In 2017 Shireland achieved a 0.53 Progress 8 score (a measure of value-added growth in England), meaning that the students are achieving well above their expected level.

The school has been recognised by a number of external bodies and given significant funding by the Mercers' Company to help it to transfer its model of learning to other schools. It has also developed an extensive bank of online teaching and learning materials which are much in demand from other schools keen to adopt its approaches.

Challenges for leadership

It was hard to recruit new teachers at first, who were faced with much collaborative planning to enable them to teach more than the one subject a secondary teacher would traditionally teach. But once staff realised they would see twenty-five students, not 400, and could focus on the individual needs of those students, they realised the attractiveness of the offer. Today, Key Stage 3 posts are oversubscribed.

Initially, instilling a culture of collaborative professional learning and lesson planning was counter-cultural to those who had worked at secondary level, although it came more naturally to those with a primary background. The creation of a 'planning bank' has provided a great solution that everyone contributes to and benefits from. It has been of enormous benefit for workload reduction.

Steyning Grammar School

Steyning Grammar School in West Sussex, England, has, at its heart, an ethos of developing character, including zest for learning. Head teacher Nick Wergan has embedded this ethos during his six years leading the school. The school aims for students to flourish both in and out, and post school. Martin Seligman's research has informed the school's understanding of flourishing to mean that students develop to be happy and engaged people who maintain positive relationships, feel they have meaning in their lives and achieve what they want to achieve.

In order to foster its desired ethos, the school specifically aims to develop the seven characteristics of grit, growth mindset, self-control, emotional intelligence, gratitude, curiosity and zest. Each characteristic is clearly defined to the children, teachers and parents, so that everyone understands what is meant when 'character conversations' are held at parents' evenings, in tutor time or in lessons.

The school defines zest as 'an approach to life and learning filled with excitement and energy'. In terms of what it looks like, assistant head teacher Andrew Wood tells us that teachers observe zesty learners in lessons and the wider curriculum being enthusiastic, helping to motivate others and getting involved in the varied opportunities that school and wider life has to offer.

To help facilitate discussions about, and analyse, the seven characteristics, student self-reflection questionnaires are used. When the data is processed the characteristics are placed into groups. For example, grit, growth mindset and self-control are called 'achievement characteristics' because it can be shown that when students have strengths in these areas, they are also likely to be making strong progress. Zest and curiosity are grouped as 'healthy mind characteristics'. When these are measured it can be seen that not only do they affect academic progress but, in addition, students with high healthy mind characteristics are less likely to suffer from mental health or well-being issues.

Leading well

Andrew tells us that the school has found zest to be developed by:

+ A strong school ethos: with the school's character programme at its heart.

+ Exposure: students need to experience a wide range of character-building activities.

+ Enthusiasm: teachers 'ooze enthusiasm' for their subject which infects the school's students.

+ Optimism: courses and activities are deliberately designed to build optimistic approaches in students.

Leading a school to develop characteristics such as zest is a challenge when set against academic pressures, Ofsted and the lack of teacher training in character education. Steyning Grammar is five years into the leadership journey and recognises it is still making mistakes, re-evaluating and improving. However, three things it knows to be critical are: a leadership team that is fully and visibly on board, a CPD programme that inducts teachers into the school's character ethos, and an integrated approach to a balanced curriculum and co-curriculum.

A focus on curriculum and co-curriculum

Steyning's curriculum and co-curriculum aim to develop zest by exposing students to as many experiences and opportunities as possible. Students need to find their zest and learn the joy of curiosity. Some students, particularly those from disadvantaged backgrounds, have had limited opportunities, and the school's curriculum encourages participation in a wide variety of activities in and out of lessons.

Key Stage 3 students have five hours each fortnight of specific character learning. Through this character education course they are given the chance to write and read a book for local primary school children, raise money for charity through a 'tenner challenge', work with the school's alumni and, crucially, develop a project on something about which they are curious. Andrew believes that through these sorts of activities, students develop zest because:

+ They become balanced members of the school's community with buy-in to its values and ethos.

+ They experience a wide variety of activities, which they have considerable control over, and this gives them a chance to find or develop their passion.

+ They are asked constantly to reflect on their experiences through a 'reflection log'. They celebrate their character strengths and consider how they can transfer these to their traditional subjects.

+ They understand the beneficial effect that their actions can have on others and themselves, often leading to a positive spiral of purposeful actions.

+ They often gain a clearer idea of the pathway they are interested in following in their life, and this helps to give them a sense of purpose.

+ The character education course links in with Steyning's involvement in the National Baccalaureate programme, which encourages a wide, integrated, co- and core curriculum, and helps students to see a purpose to their character learning.

Key Stage 4 continues the emphasis on character with initiatives such as Steyning Grammar School's SGS10. Students are encouraged to try ten activities a year alongside their academic programme. The school aims to use these activities to keep its character ethos visible, to offer more opportunities for students to find their zest and to develop cultural capital.

Tutors can see whether their tutees have done the activities through the school's online classroom, and can set shorter term targets as they mentor their young people. Activities are carefully balanced and include going to the theatre, going on a hike, volunteering at a school event and joining a club. The school's faculties and year teams are asked to provide these opportunities through their yearly development plans.

Alongside the school's growth mindset approach to teaching, and plenty of character-based mentorship, the SGS10 demonstrates to students that the school values their attitudinal progress equally with their academic progress. It gives them positive characteristics, such as zest, to work on instead of target grades. It is great to see that they demonstrate these characteristics in both their co-curricular and academic lives.

Challenges for teachers and leaders

Steyning Grammar relies heavily on research, evidence-based teaching and pedagogy. It believes in its own power to improve progress and to turn students into lifelong learners. Effective evidence-based pedagogy is at the core of effective classroom teaching. That said, the school is mindful that planning for evidence-based learning pathways should not detract from teachers' ability to enthuse learners about the wonders of their subject. A teacher's own zest is a critical tool in their toolkit, and one that rubs off on their students. It motivates learners, making them curious and helping them to understand the purpose of their learning. The school does not insist on any lesson planning structure. It encourages teachers to go off-piste if they think it will benefit the students, and it makes sure that individual faculties have sufficient time to develop interesting subject knowledge in their CPD programmes.

Teachers also need to think about the feedback they give and the effect it has on students' zest for learning. As part of their character education induction training, Steyning's teachers learn how to create positive 'micro-moments' of feedback for the students. This training is an evidenced way of encouraging a positive ethos in the classroom. The CPD is practical and emphasises the importance of teachers demonstrating a growth mindset, using character language and responding positively. This helps to motivate students, thereby building zest and curiosity.

Cultivating optimistic learners

The school has found zest for learning to be linked to learners' optimism. Optimism means students understand that if they do the right things, it will pay off and they will achieve what they set out to do. Optimism helps them to believe that if they engage in purposeful practice, it will reward them with better outcomes.

Through the work of Martin Seligman and colleagues in *The Optimistic Child* (1995), the school has developed a Year 8 course that helps its students to understand what optimism is, why it is important and how they can develop it. Students' optimism is measured using the self-reporting Children's Attributional Style Questionnaire (CASQ). Students who are low in optimism are further mentored by the school's learning support team, and the school has been able to show its success in raising optimism levels by doing so. Optimism is one of the school's three key indicators of a student's development that teachers see in their electronic mark books and which enables them to tailor lessons that might help to develop zest in those who are less optimistic.

The benefits of character education

The wonderful thing about Steyning's work on character is that it seems to be a win-win. The vast majority of its teachers agree that the school's emphasis on character works and should continue. Students enjoy their character-building curriculum and understand the importance of character growth, and this is, in itself, zestful.

As a result, the students are more focused in what they want from school, because they have linked their learning to a pathway and understand the positive effect it has on them and others. In addition, their wider exposure to activities and experiences has helped to make them more curious in their lessons. The growth mindset they develop through this process gives them hope for the future and, as a result, they are happier.

West Rise Junior School

With well over twice the national average for free school meals, West Rise is situated next to an Eastbourne council estate as well as an area of floodplain that it leases from the local council. A recipient of the 2015 TES Primary School of the Year title, the school benefits from supportive parents whose most common reaction is, 'I wish I could have been to a school like this,' according to head teacher Mike Fairclough in a Telegraph *feature (Wallop, 2016).*

Having a zest for learning is a natural childhood trait which, if cultivated, can be sustained throughout an individual's entire lifetime. Attributes such as playfulness, having a spirit of adventure and risk-taking are also naturally occurring childhood characteristics.

Head teacher Mike Fairclough explains how zest for learning benefits a child's life:

> Cultivating a zest for learning and maintaining this level of enthusiasm and engagement in life is vitally important. Without it, existence is lacklustre and feels like a chore. Clearly, zestful living and learning support positive mental health. If a person is excited and engaged, they generally feel happy and content. In turn, positive mental health promotes good physical and emotional health. This cocktail of well-being, on every level, makes a person more effective and efficient when performing an activity, creating a sense of purpose and focus. Whether it be during a child's education or as an adult in the workplace, having a zest for learning can only be a positive attribute.

Balance and curiosity through learning outdoors

A key part of the provision at West Rise, designed to encourage these traits in the pupils, is its outdoor learning offerings. The school is located opposite Langney Marsh, an area of 120 acres of marshland, including two large lakes. This area, designated 'the marsh', is leased from the local authority. It has become an environment for very deep experiential learning and the inspiration for a number of innovative projects.

As teachers know, children love to have adventures, to experience new things and to explore. West Rise's activities, which take place on the marsh, facilitate this by allowing the children to roam freely across the land and to connect with the natural environment. All of the children learn to light a fire and to cook over flames. They forage for edible plants, use knives, bow saws and bill hooks to make objects out of wood, and learn about the marsh's diverse fauna and flora. During these times, the children are self-directed in their learning and the adults support them, if required. This cultivates a genuine sense of freedom which inevitably leads to the feeling of zest.

Teachers are very clear from observations and discussions with their pupils that the outdoor learning environment, and specifically the natural world, offers them immense inspiration. Everything from the tiniest insect discovered within the reeds to the larger migrating water birds as they take flight across the lakes will ignite enquiry and spark the imagination.

Teachers are encouraged to integrate the natural world, and specifically the school's marshland habitat, into their curriculum planning. There are numerous opportunities through the science curriculum (plants and living things), geography (hills, streams, rivers and settlements) and history (everything from the Stone Age through to the Second World War) which can be explored while learning outside. The children also regularly write stories and poems about the marsh and its wildlife, and make artwork inspired by the environment.

The school manages a herd of Asian water buffalo on the site, a bee and reptile sanctuary, as well as farm animals including sheep, ducks and chickens. Each individual species inspires a sense of awe and wonder in the children. They ask questions about them, make observations or simply 'be' in the presence of nature

– the latter being something which few children do these days, and yet is so very powerful.

Openness to experiences

The concept of 'moving out of the comfort zone' as a way of expanding children's minds and building resilience is another important educational tool embraced by the school. When a child has moved out of their comfort zone, through enduring extreme weather conditions, engaging in a challenging activity or facing their fears (such as creepy crawlies or large farm animals), they will expand. The first thing that will expand is the child's sense of possibility and their perception of what they are capable of achieving. For example, a child who has managed successfully to light a fire in sub-zero temperatures or torrential rain will have battled against the elements and won. They will never believe again that this is an impossible task, beyond their skill and capabilities. Equally, the enhanced resilience and feeling of empowerment transfers to the classroom.

Resilience cultivated through outdoor learning supports academic and emotional resilience. This can happen in numerous ways. One opportunity for this is offered by the school's own bees. Dressed in protective clothing, the pupils inspect the beehives with trained beekeepers. A child who may have had a tendency to run away from a single bee in the playground will be covered in thousands of them when opening the hives. Each time they do this, the children will emerge from the experience wide-eyed and feeling electrified. They will have stepped out of their comfort zone and expanded their awareness and understanding of the bees.

Similarly, when there are adverse weather conditions, such as sub-zero temperatures or driving rain, the children will continue to work outside on the marsh. Again, they will move out of their comfort zones and accomplish things that they would previously have thought impossible. Lighting fires in the rain and keeping physically active in icy conditions, while also cooking, craft-making and foraging for food, is difficult. Overcoming these challenges builds resilience in the children and empowers them to believe that they can achieve against the odds.

Each time these events take place, the children are visibly transformed and will have expanded on many levels.

These learning experiences relate to and support what is taught in the classroom. For example, it was recently discovered that the dykes which criss-cross the marsh are of medieval and prehistoric origin. A group of biologists have also revealed that the marsh is home to some very rare species of insect, such as the raft spider, and that these are the descendants of an unbroken lineage of their kind since prehistory. Immediately, this becomes wildly inspiring to a child when they are learning about the Bronze Age and other periods of history.

An annual event on the marsh, known as Bee Fest, involves the children beekeeping, finding snakes and lizards, hearing Celtic folk stories about the land and tree planting. West Rise has integrated these new revelations about animal species and the physical landscape into this event, so the children feel like they are stepping into a lost world full of magic and wonder. This then promotes further enquiry and investigation back in the classroom and at home.

Challenges for leadership

Mike Fairclough became the school's head teacher over fifteen years ago. The school itself is located on a council estate in an area of social and economic deprivation. Expectations of the children were low when he arrived, and there was no outdoor learning or creative curriculum in place. Since then, the marsh, the animals and the approach the school adopts have grown organically.

As a school leader, Mike does not believe in micromanaging others. His leadership style involves setting an ethos and trusting that others will be inspired to subscribe to it. He is also entirely open to, and excited by, other people's strengths and visions. If someone has a great idea which will benefit the pupils, then he will support it.

Today the school is a thriving and successful place, where all the staff have high expectations of the pupils and of themselves. It is constantly learning and growing as an organisation. Mike believes that it is this positive outlook, coupled with outdoor learning experiences, which creates the perfect conditions for zest for learning to be harnessed.

This zest for learning is then witnessed back in the classroom, and strongly supports the enthusiasm teachers want to see in all aspects of the curriculum. The energy of the children's outdoor learning permeates the work of the entire school. West Rise Junior wants its pupils to perceive their educational experience as holistic and integrated. This then allows for a child's zest for learning to become transferable between learning environments and across all subjects.

Chapter 5
Brave Leadership

Engaging Partnerships with Bold Vision

To be able to meet all our students' diverse needs, we need to invest in ourselves. We need to be fired up, enthusiastic, engaged and positive about our work if we have any hope that our students will be.

Tom Sherrington, Great Lessons 10: Joy (2013)

Across the world schools tend to gain and retain approval by dint of how well their students do in examinations and how their country's external accountability body rates them. Of course, it is not that simple; performance in sports and the arts counts too, as does that elusive commodity – reputation.

Zest, like the other two capabilities on which we have focused in this series, creativity and tenacity, does not appear on school timetables. Neither does it get noticed in formal judgements of schools. In fact, the idea of zest is virtually invisible in schools across the world.

In this chapter we look at the leadership challenges for head teachers who nevertheless see zest for learning as a core goal of education. We look in particular at the ways in which they engage with the many external organisations that can help them and their students. We also look at schools from the outside in: what are the leadership challenges for those who try to work with them? Let's look again at our three-dimensional model of zest (see the figure on page 82) through the eyes of leaders both within schools and from those organisations seeking to work with schools. What are the challenges they might face?

In a global educational climate in which performance in examinations and national self-interest assume great importance, what can leaders do to ensure that all relationships are valued and students keep a sense of perspective? When many examinations seek one right answer, and in a culture which can all too easily be risk-averse, how do leaders continue to stimulate the curiosity of young people to explore the world and try new things? And when many subjects can seem abstract and removed from some young people's life experiences, how do leaders ensure that learners keep their eyes on the true meaning of the knowledge and experiences they are presented with?

Partnerships for learning

As can be seen from the case study examples in Chapter 4, a common feature of almost all of this kind of education is that it requires schools and outside organisations to work together to achieve the range of experiences which are likely to cultivate zest.

From a school's perspective, this requires a leader to know which community or regional organisations might best help them to enrich the experiences they can offer students. To make these kinds of connections leaders may find it helpful to undertake three kinds of mapping in parallel.

The first is to think in general terms about the opportunities for learning which exist locally (as indicated in the figure on page 233).

This map is written from a humanities perspective and is designed to be indicative of an approach, rather than descriptive of what you might produce if you were thinking explicitly about opportunities for developing zest.

The second mapping activity involves the identification of potential partners within a reasonable distance from the school – for example, organisations with interests in culture, heritage, sport, the environment, global understanding and so on.

The third is to map out from the formal and informal curriculum to see where current provision at school is not yet rich enough.

From the perspective of organisations wishing to work with schools, a similar mapping process is necessary. Initially this involves identifying schools which are located within a realistic distance – a relatively easy task. More generally it

Built environment

Castles and historic houses

Farms and botanic gardens

Monuments and parks

Industrial and commercial buildings

Schools

Canals, railways and roads

Places of worship

Natural environment

Seashore and coastline

Fields, trees and woods

Marshes, bogs and rivers

Hills, peaks and mountains

Dales and valleys

The locality

Social and cultural environment

Groups and societies

Art exhibitions and galleries

Libraries, museums and archives

Festivals, customs and folklore

People

Shopkeepers, factory and store managers

Curators, archaeologists and local historians

Field officers and rangers

Ministers, missionaries and preachers

Librarians and archivists

Charity workers

Councillors

Emergency service personnel

Mapping the locality

Source: Grigg and Hughes (2013, p. 114)

requires any organisation wishing to work with a school to be able to articulate their offer, being clear as to whether it is designed to complement and enrich the formal curriculum and/or to provide extension or extra-curricular experiences.

A much more challenging process for an external organisation is finding the right teacher contact within a school. Secondary schools are notoriously difficult to fathom for outsiders and require persistence, often questioning a receptionist to establish the name of the teacher whose role might be best suited to the planned visit or partnership. At primary schools the head teacher or deputy head teacher is often much more accessible and willing to have an initial conversation. School secretaries at both primary and secondary level can often seem off-putting to outside organisations, perhaps because they see it as their role to protect busy teachers from potential salespeople.

From an analysis of guidance produced by many bodies working with schools, and our discussions with the case study organisations featured in this book, the tasks shown below occur frequently.

School	Both	Organisation
Define the need		Define the offer
Invite/nominate teacher(s)		Identify key teacher(s)
	Make the case for the benefits of partnership working	
	Inform parents	
	Get to know each other	
	Agree clear objectives	
	Agree roles and responsibilities	

Agree type and
frequency of
communications

Plan together (or
actively accept an
existing programme)

Learn and reflect as
you go

Agree a simple
means of evaluating
the impact of your
partnership working

Be flexible

Respect each other's
strengths and
weaknesses

Take photographs
and share widely with
appropriate credits

Share experiences
with other schools

Invite school to
dissemination events

Key steps in partnership working

These important aspects of partnership working remind us that it takes time and commitment to make it work effectively.

A starting point for a school might be to use the mapping tool on page 236 to see where there are opportunities for developing zest and share this with potential partner organisations.

Year ____	Opportunities to develop zest			
Habits of zest		Formal curriculum	Co-curriculum/ extra-curriculum	In the community	Trips, festivals and special events
Balanced Maintaining perspective					
Valuing relationships					
Curious Embracing novel experiences					
Exploring the world					
Purposeful Finding meaning					
Performing well					

Creating a supportive ecology

A huge amount of what leaders need to do is cultural – that is, creating a climate in which zest for learning can flourish. From our earlier exploration of the literature and a reading of our case studies, a number of key environmental factors become clear. These include:

- Having adults who model their own love of learning and their interest in the learning passions of other people.

- Being genuinely outward facing.

- Valuing learning of all kinds – head, heart and hand.

- Encouraging deep questioning, research and scholarship of all kinds.

- Embracing students as co-designers.

- Making space for activities which are authentic and extended in length.

- Perceiving learning outside the classroom as valuable.

- Actively seeking to build and maintain relationships.

- Embracing novelty.

- Leaving space for the unexpected.

It might be useful to consider the extent to which your own school currently provides these kinds of opportunities. Take a moment to go through each of these factors and think about whether – and if so, how often and how well – you do these things. You could rate each one on a continuum:

| Never | Sometimes | Mostly | Always |

For those about which you are confident of your provision: what is it you are doing, and what is the leadership role?

Where good provision is not yet in place: what might you do as a leader to create the kind of culture you want to see?

Understanding and communicating a vision for zest

We hope that the extensive exploration of the idea of zest in this book has begun to make the case for an education which is balanced, curious and purposeful in the ways we have outlined. But in a world in which zest may sometimes seem like an extra or a luxury, it is a core role of school leaders at all levels to explain explicitly why it matters. This might be largely motivated by an emphasis on improving students' experience of the formal curriculum or more widely on the motivation and re-engagement of students (as in the case of the ACRE case study, for example).

In different parts of the world the focus of leadership arguments will necessarily need to be different, picking up on opportunities suggested by national curriculum documents and/or the kinds of issues being examined by external accountability bodies. In the UK, for example, there may be different arguments depending on where your school is located.

In England, the Office for Standards in Education has recently introduced a new framework for inspection (Ofsted, 2019), describing its intent, implementation and impact. This provides a particular opportunity for school leaders to frame their decision to focus on zest in these terms, potentially drawing on the arguments in this book.

In Wales, a new curriculum invites schools to think more widely about the scope of their curriculum: 'Curriculum for Wales 2022 seeks to allow for a broadening of learning, supporting settings and schools to be more flexible in their approaches, and provides education leaders and practitioners with greater agency, enabling them to be innovative and creative' (Welsh Government, 2019, p. 3).

The Scottish Government's *Curriculum for Excellence* (2008, p. 7) focuses on the development of four capacities – 'successful learners, confident individuals, effective contributors and responsible citizens' – which provide a helpful language to describe many of the features of zest we have been exploring. In other countries it will be helpful to identify formal opportunities within national curricula.

More specific arguments may be called upon to build a bigger vision for the value of cultivating zest, drawing on the evidence we presented in Chapter 2. For students this will include:

+ Developing an openness to new experiences.

+ Bringing practical and academic learning together in ways that are meaningful.

+ Enhancing motivation.

+ Learning how to practise more effectively.

+ Developing powers of attention and concentration.

+ Improving well-being.

+ Developing a sense of perspective.

+ Building a range of character strengths.

+ Learning the value of outdoor and physical activity.

Rethinking the curriculum – expanding the formal curriculum and valuing co-curricular and extra-curricular learning

In practical terms there are some issues that school leaders may need to consider in order to embed opportunities to develop zest. Perhaps the most important of these is a reappraisal of the way in which the curriculum is experienced. For students, passionate engagement in their learning knows no subject boundaries. One way to promote interdisciplinary learning is to reorganise the curriculum at lower secondary level, as Shireland has done, teaching knowledge and skills through well-planned enquiries and ensuring that the experience of Years 7 and 8 are more integrated by having one teacher take on a coordinating role.

Similarly it may be helpful, as Holyport College has shown, to locate the co-curriculum within a longer school day. If this is not possible, then it may help to focus more on providing high quality extra-curricular activities, as well as motivating students to take up these opportunities.

New roles for staff

All of our case study examples are either encouraging or actively hosting trips out of school, and this inevitably necessitates fresh thinking about the roles teachers are required to play. In some cases this may simply require a slight shift in the activities a member of staff undertakes. In others it may be helpful to signal a commitment to zest by dint of a job title, such as head of museum learning, director of outreach or head of partnerships.

Often these roles can be very temporary. For example, you might choose to have an artist in residence for a short period of time, something that schools have experimented with for several decades. It is an opportunity for schools to exercise their creativity in deciding which other roles they might wish to use as a means of focusing attention – for example, ecologist, historian or philosopher in residence – bringing with them an interest in the topic even before any activity is undertaken.

Tracking the development of zest in young people

In both of the previous books in this series we have had a whole chapter exploring approaches to the assessment of each capability. With zest we offer a much softer approach given that the concept is in its infancy.

Let's return to our model again:

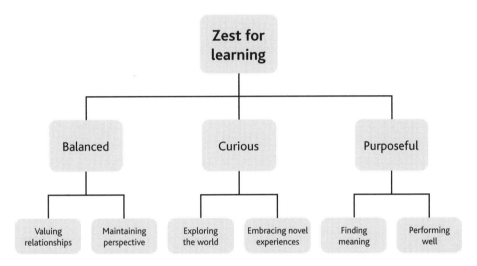

A three-dimensional model of zest for learning

How would you show that students were becoming more balanced in valuing relationships and maintaining perspective? How would you track the development of their curiosity in exploring the world and embracing novel experiences? What evidence might you use to indicate that they were becoming more purposeful in finding meaning and performing well?

It is worth perhaps looking outside schools for inspiration here. The Duke of Edinburgh's Award has an eDofE portfolio through which participants keep track of their progress by using activity logs and uploading photographic evidence of their experiences and skills development.[1]

The Scout Association uses badges to show that Scouts have undergone specific experiences and acquired certain capabilities as a consequence. These are wide-ranging in their interests, including such diverse activities as angling, astronomy, climbing, conservation, global issues, faith development, photography and many more. Other organisations are beginning to take the Scouting idea of badging and combine these with the Internet to create digital badges.

---

1   See https://www.dofe.org/do/edofe.

Across the world there is growing interest in the potential for young people to 'curate' the development of their wider capabilities of the kind that are covered in our framework for zest by means of some kind of electronic portfolio. Two good examples of this are Skillsbuilder[2] in the UK and CharacterLab[3] in the United States.

For schools in England and Wales, one specific opportunity presents itself in terms of a post-16 qualification, the Extended Project Qualification (EPQ). The EPQ, equivalent to half of an A level, encourages students to undertake a largely self-directed and self-motivated project. Students choose a topic, plan, research and develop their ideas, and decide on an appropriate medium for a finished product. Creativity and curiosity are actively encouraged. The finished piece can be a research-based written report, a production (such as charity event, fashion show or sports event) or an artefact (like a piece of art, computer game or designed product). For instance, the exam board AQA gives one example title, 'To build a "High Performance" Desktop PC and evaluate it against commercial pre-built alternatives', noting its clear aim and measure of success.[4]

Of all the examined opportunities available to schools in England and Wales, the EPQ offers perhaps the best opportunity for students to exercise their curiosity and develop a sense of purpose through passion-led study. The means by which such projects are assessed will depend on whether it takes the form of an extended dissertation, a performance or an artefact. Whichever format is chosen, it will require a combination of internal assessment and external moderation.

There is some variation between individual exam boards, but the criteria by which projects are assessed include: the significance of the student's input into the choice and design of an extended piece of work; the ways in which they have applied decision-making and problem-solving skills; how they have shown initiative and enterprise; their planning, research, critical thinking, analytical, synthesis, evaluation and presentation skills; and the degree to which they have used their learning experiences to develop their personal aspirations or interests.

---

2   See https://www.skillsbuilder.org/my-skills.
3   See https://characterlab.org.
4   See https://filestore.aqa.org.uk/subjects/AQA-7993-W-TG-GA.PDF.

Globally the International Baccalaureate (IB) is a similarly helpful approach. It is organised around the IB learner profile,[5] which includes ten attributes or capabilities:

1. Inquirers. Learners aim to develop skills in curiosity, enquiry, research, learning and zest for learning.

2. Knowledgeable. Learners strive to develop conceptual understanding across disciplines and engage with global issues.

3. Thinkers. Learners aim to develop critical and creative thinking, analysis, complex problem-solving, initiative-taking and decision-making.

4. Communicators. Learners strive to develop self-expression, collaboration, language and listening skills.

5. Principled. Learners set out to develop integrity, honesty, respect for the dignity of others, responsibility and a sense of what is fair and just.

6. Open-minded. Learners aim to grow in understanding and appreciation of their own culture and history, as well as to seek and evaluate other viewpoints.

7. Caring. Learners aim to develop empathy, compassion and commitment to make a positive difference.

8. Risk-takers. Learners strive to be courageous and independent, to act with forethought, and to be resilient and resourceful when faced with new or challenging situations.

9. Balanced. Learners discover how to achieve balance in intellectual, physical and emotional dimensions.

10. Reflective. Learners aim to consider their own learning strengths and limitations.

---

5   See https://www.ibo.org/contentassets/fd82f70643ef4086b7d3f292cc214962/learner-profile-en.pdf.

There is obvious synergy between our idea of balanced and the IB's balanced and reflective attributes. There is clear overlap between our focus on being curious with the IB's inquirers, thinkers, open-minded and risk-taking. And our idea of being purposeful maps onto the IB's principled, caring and knowledgeable. In everything we are exploring there is the need to be a good communicator.

One particular aspect of the IB – creativity, activity, service (CAS) projects – offers considerable potential for students to explore many of the aspects of zest we have been describing. The three strands of CAS are:

1. Creativity: experiences that involve creative thinking, including the arts.

2. Activity: experiences that involve physical exertion, contributing to a healthy lifestyle.

3. Service: a learning experience that is unpaid and voluntary.

The CAS project must involve:

+ Real, purposeful activities with significant outcomes.

+ Personal challenge.

+ Thoughtful consideration, such as planning, reviewing progress and reporting.

+ Reflection on outcomes and personal learning.[6]

CAS projects challenge students to show initiative, demonstrate perseverance and develop skills such as collaboration, problem-solving and decision-making.

The IB website gives a number of examples of what this might look like in practice. For a creativity project, a talented musician could learn a particularly difficult piece or a different style of playing. In New York, a group of students produced and performed a play to raise awareness of a real-world issue.

Activity projects do not have to be sports-related or competitive. A valuable activity project could help a student to overcome a personal fear, such as rock

---

6   See https://www.ibo.org/programmes/diploma-programme/curriculum/creativity-activity-and-service/cas-projects.

climbing. An example given is of a student in Australia who achieved his dream of becoming a youth soccer coach through CAS.

Service projects must be beneficial for the community as well as providing a learning opportunity for the student. For example, students in Indiana organised a huge recycling drive to help an IB World School in Flint, Michigan.

Zest for learning – celebrating success

Schools that actively seek to promote zest, keep young people's love of learning alive and help them to find and explore their passions rapidly realise that current curricula and their examinations rarely offer such opportunities.

Consequently, Bedales created its own Bedales Assessed Curriculum. Shireland rethought its 11–14 curriculum to present it in a way that would engage students and developed an online tracking system to record progress. Schools working with Explorer Scouts in the UK used the badge system for which the Scouts are well-known. Schools in Perth working with creative practitioners used the five creative learning habits model we have developed to record progress. And schools in rural Victoria adopted approaches such as exhibitions and presentations to share their work and have it critiqued by real-world entrepreneurs.

We aren't sure about the wisdom of formally assessing zest; it might just dampen it! But by using our framework as a prompt for gathering evidence about students and their zest and as a focus to structure conversations, you may be able to help staff, students, parents and members of the community better appreciate the importance of zest.

The table on page 246 adapts some of the thinking we developed in our two earlier books to indicate some of the ways in which progress could be celebrated. At the very least there will be many opportunities for mentions in assemblies and individual commendations of students by teachers and others. Against the row heading 'Different kinds of evidence' are some possible sources of evidence that can be considered.

Approaches to assessing zest for learning

Habits of zest		Different kinds of evidence to consider using to demonstrate growth in the habits of zest below	Teacher-led	Pupil-led	Real-world ways of evidencing zest	Online assessment
			Photos and learning journeys Rating of products and processes Structured interviews Reports	Self-report questionnaires Real-time peer feedback Photos Logs/diaries/ journals Peer review Extended projects	Authentic tests Displays Presentations Podcasts Films Exhibitions	Digital badges E-portfolios
Balanced Valuing relationships Maintaining perspective						
Curious Exploring the world Embracing novel experiences						
Purposeful Finding meaning Performing well						

In each of these examples, it is not possible for school leaders to go with the status quo. If they want to embed zest within the curriculum and have some means of tracking progress, even in a light-touch way, they need to be bold.

To paraphrase Martin Luther King, Jr.: courageous school leaders never lose the zest for living even if their national education systems are zestless.[7]

---

7   King (2013, p. 120) originally wrote: 'Courageous men never lose the zest for living even though their life situation is zestless.'

Chapter 6
An A–Z of Ideas for Developing Zest

True happiness comes from the joy of deeds well done, the zest of creating things new.

attributed to Antoine de Saint-Exupéry

In developing each of zest's six sub-habits, a range of literatures have informed our thinking and given rise to ideas for signature experiences that could help to develop zest for learning. In Chapter 3 we illustrated each signature experience with practical examples for teachers. These are reproduced below under each of the six sub-habits for ease of reference. In reality, these examples can be used however you like, with many having scope for impact on more than one sub-habit.

Balanced learners value relationships

Appreciative inquiry. Zestful learners sharing what went well in a topic.

Business mentoring. Business people from the community acting as advisers to students running enterprises.

Mentoring around a theme. Peer mentoring around specific needs.

Restoration project. Restoring something for the school or community.

School magazine. Representing the views of others fairly while also uncovering ideological assumptions.

Teachers' own work. Teachers sharing the highs and lows of their own hobbies.

Team games. Team building that requires team roles and a team objective.

Team sports with an individual focus. Team sports that focus on the goals and needs of individual players.

Balanced learners maintain perspective

Activity balance. Clubs organised into balanced categories from which students can select.

Activity wildcard. Each student tries a wildcard club or activity each term.

Brain breaks. Learners reinvigorate their thinking by physically walking away from their desk.

Community projects. Programmes that involve learners with their community.

Daily mile. Scheduling in opportunities for physical activity.

Designing an outdoor space. Planning a functional outdoor space.

Expressive writing. Relating troubles and social values to literary stories.

Gardening. Making use of the school grounds for food and flower production.

Geocaching. An outdoor treasure hunt using GPS.

Honest reflection. Recognising what students did well.

Keeping drafts. Keeping annotated drafts close to hand for motivation.

Optimism questionnaire. Attributional-style questionnaire that invites learners to consider their attitude in sporting scenarios.

Real-world application. Routinely and explicitly practising skills learned in the classroom in other settings.

Scavenger hunt. Finding and bringing back a complete set of items from a list.

Treasure trails. Self-guided walks that involve finding clues.

Curious learners explore the world

All sorts of games. Group team-building, board games, word games and so on.

Assessing understanding by teaching. Learners describe and explain a curriculum concept to the class, who correct any misunderstandings.

Free experimentation. Learners explore an idea, tool, medium, object or material.

Gallery critique. Students all display a piece of work, then everyone sticks a 'compliment', 'suggestion' and 'correction' to everyone else's work.

Games of skill. Games that involve complex thought, observation or action.

Historic building detectives. Looking for clues about the purpose of old buildings.

Historic decisions. Consider how a particular important decision was made in the past.

Jigsaw. Learners work in groups to piece together their learning about different aspects of a topic.

Learner talk. Encourage self-talk for metacognition.

Organising an event. Planning and running an event from start to finish.

Recreating an environment. A multisensory experience.

Setting good questions. Home learning that stems from interesting thoughts in class.

Think-pair-share. Pairing up learners who take it in turns to be the 'tutor' or 'tutee' as they tackle a question.

Curious learners embrace novel experiences

Creating art with the body. Using the body as an extension of the canvas or to express a connection with the natural world.

Novel activity reports. Reporting back to the class about an activity the students have tried out.

Planning an expedition. Preparing for an overnight rural expedition with an aim.

Planning a route. Planning and timing a route that meets certain criteria.

Socratic argumentation. Group debate that allows free speech.

Trip with a simple challenge. Planning a bus journey.

Purposeful learners find meaning

Artefact project. Creation of a specific artefact challenge.

Bringing a project to life. A well-timed and relevant museum trip to accompany a specific unit of work.

Coaching community. Involving community/parents in careers and activity/interest coaching.

Contemplation wall. An area for reflection.

Core values. Students thinking about what motivates them and the principles they operate by in life.

Duke of Edinburgh's Award. Giving up time for others.

Elected positions. Standing for election to a school-based role responsibility.

Handling real artefacts. Workshops that bring in relevant and real artefacts.

Inspiring awe. Finding amazing facts, images and prose to inspire students with the wonder of nature and humanity.

Invited speakers. A programme of themed speaking events.

Learning dance steps. Recognising the body's ability to learn something complex.

Multifunctional practical project. A product for the community that serves various functions.

Netball practice. Recognising the body's role in learning and perfecting a skill.

News feed. Curation of news sources around a theme – critiquing sources.

Orienteering. Competitive sport requiring navigational skills, a map and a compass.

Outdoor character pursuits. Activities that develop performance character such as obstacle courses.

Public art. Creating an artwork for the community to enjoy.

Reading challenge. Selecting books from a variety of categories to broaden understanding.

Sculpture and the body. Creation of sculptures inspired by the theme of prosthetics at the centenary of the end of the First World War.

Subject-based fiction. Reading a book to the class that introduces concepts in a fictional context.

Talking points. Debate a provocative statement in pairs.

Vocational purpose. Considering how different subjects and jobs meet human needs.

Purposeful learners perform well

Dissecting a search. Practising good online searching.

Practice log. Logging and reflecting on practice.

Show and tell. Showing a piece of work and explaining the learning behind it to the class.

Appendix
Signature Learning Experiences

Each of our three habits for zestful learners can be developed by teachers with an eye to a particular learning experience.

Balanced

Habit (and sub-habits)	Key concepts	Literature informing our understanding of key concepts	Signature learning experiences category name	Signature learning experiences
	BALANCED			
Valuing relationships	Craftsmanship for the future	Real-world learning	Learning by volunteering	Volunteering in a project that restores something for the community
	Communities of practice		Learning by being mentored	Being mentored
	Imitation		Learning by imitation	Working in pairs or groups and practising observing and copying one another
	Grit and passion		Learning through sports	Sporting competition using team sports that also have an individual focus
	Social well-being (a strength of character)	Positive psychology	Learning through sports	Sports team for developing shared sense of persistence
	Asking good questions	Metacognition	Learning through conversation and listening	Philosophy for Children, questioning, listening, dialogue, debate and argumentation

Maintaining perspective		Habits for learning / Positive psychology	Learning approach	Example
	Dispositions for learning/epistemic outcomes	Habits for learning	Learning by explicitly developing life skills	Teaching for transfer
	Tenacity		Learning by being outdoors with nature	Gardening/horticulture
			Learning by travel/being away from home	Residentials; taking young people out of their 'comfort zone'
	Character strengths – hope, zest, curiosity, gratitude and love	Positive psychology	Learning by socialising	Working directly with people in the community
	Optimism and the importance of perception/mindset		Learning by practising	Engaging in purposeful practice. Keeping track of how much improvement is happening by looking at drafts. Being realistic about how much improvement to expect
			Learning through reflection	Group activity that involves fully acknowledging something you did well

Optimism and the importance of action		Learning through sports	Reflection on performance, and the way thinking impacts upon it
Physical activity		Learning by being outdoors with nature	Gardening/horticulture
		Learning by exercising	Keeping fit, endorphins, sense of perspective by using the body as well as the mind
Practical learning	Real-world learning	Learning by being outdoors with nature	Gardening/horticulture
Outdoor learning		Learning by planning and following through	Design of external space
Co- and extra-curricular activities		Learning by joining clubs/trying something new	Attempting to find what we love doing/ what absorbs us by trying new things. Participating in different after-school or lunchtime clubs

Curious

Curious

Habit (and sub-habits)	Key concepts	Literature informing our understanding of key concepts	Signature learning experiences category name	Signature learning experiences
	CURIOUS			
Exploring the world	Creative thinking	Habits for learning	Learning by researching	Research – and learning how to go about doing good research
	Experiential learning	Theories of intelligence	Learning through reflection	Spending time reflecting on experience
	Thinking about thinking	Metacognition		Spending time thinking about metacognition
	'Playing the whole game'		Learning by planning and following through	Organising a school event for the public or a real community project; planning, organising and thinking things through
			Learning by teaching	Teaching others how you did something

Learning through play	Real-world learning	Learning in and through museums	Visiting museums with interactive displays and immersive experiences
		Learning through play and games	Tinkering to see what works; playing games
	Psychological traits	Learning through the arts	Looking at the world with interest or from a different angle
Embracing novel experiences	Openness to experience	Learning through conversation and listening	Public speaking, debate, conversation, dialogue, Socratic argumentation; debate that exercises free speech (with no trigger warnings, safe spaces or mention of 'emotional harm'); logical argumentation not emotional responses
		Learning by travel/being away from home	Travel and school trips

Restlessness and sensation-seeking	Learning by joining clubs/trying something new	Trying an activity nobody in the class has ever done
Risk-taking	Learning by planning and following through	Planning a journey or a route

Purposeful

Habit (and sub-habits)	Key concepts	Literature informing our understanding of key concepts	Signature learning experiences category name	Signature learning experiences
	PURPOSEFUL			
Finding meaning	Connecting to the world through your hands	Real-world learning	Learning by making (and the promise of making)	Making something tangible with your hands and with tools; making something the school/organisation needs and will use and keep for a long time; making a piece of public art as the outcome of a community project; recognising the future practical application of more abstract learning
			Learning in and through museums	Handling artefacts
			Learning through the arts	Creating something that leads to a tangible product that reflects the use of the hands or body in creating

Grit and purpose (aligning your goals with a higher purpose)		Learning by volunteering	Volunteering for something that holds importance or personal significance
		Learning in and through worship	Taking part in acts of worship or theological study with your faith community; developing worldview awareness
Embodied cognition	Theories of intelligence	Learning through sports	An act that involves driving or controlling something with your body and developing muscle memory (e.g. horse, simulator, golf clubs, dance steps)
Situating yourself in the world	Purpose (education for flourishing)	Learning by reading (widely)	Reading list challenge that uses categories (e.g. a classic, a book from the nineteenth century, a book about politics, a book from a standpoint you disagree with); reading subject-based fiction stories that develop subject matter understanding
		Learning in and through museums	Linking a museum visit to a school topic

Teaching for character, moral virtues and values		Learning by being outdoors with nature / Learning by travel/being away from home	Outdoor pursuits like orienteering, obstacle courses and survival challenges
Self-actualisation and flow	Positive psychology	Learning by joining clubs/trying something new / Learning by reading (widely)	Attempting to find what we love doing/what absorbs us by trying new things; reading widely to get a sense of what the world has to offer
A sense of purpose and/or self-actualisation	Psychology of motivation	Learning by following	News feed or interest channels
Lifelong learning	Purpose (education for flourishing)	Learning from others' experiences	Meeting older career changers through careers advice sessions

Performing (well)	Deliberate practice (expertise)	Theories of intelligence	Learning by being coached	Assigning learners to appropriately chosen others for a period of time to meet a particular learning need
			Learning by practising	Practising a skill; being mindful to recognise when practice is more and less effective, and why
			Learning by deliberate searching	Intentional finding out using high quality sources
	Experiencing flow		Learning by performing	Practice that culminates in a performance or a 'doing' of the thing you have mastered
	Experiencing flow (the feedback from good performance)	Psychology of motivation	Learning by practising	Practice that produces a result, culminating in the opportunity to perform (whether to others or alone) in a moment of flow
	Motivation by expectation of good performance		Learning by practising	Setting specific goals that enable realistic but genuine personal achievement
	Goals worth pursuing (mastery goals)		Learning by practising	Setting goals that involve getting better than yourself

References

Ackerman, J. and Bargh, J. (2010). The Purpose-Driven Life: Commentary on Kenrick et al. (2010). *Perspectives on Psychological Science* 5(3), 323–326.

Alexander, R. (2017). The Arts in Schools: Making the Case, Heeding the Evidence. In *Curious Minds in Conjunction with RECP Conference on Intercultural Dimensions of Cultural Education*. Chester: University of Chester. Available at: https://www.robinalexander.org.uk/wp-content/uploads/2017/07/Alexander_Curious_Minds_July17.pdf.

Anderson, M. and Beavis, A. (2017). *Evaluation Report: Social Enterprise in Schools Pilot Program in North-East Victoria, Australia*. Beechworth, VIC: Australian Centre for Rural Entrepreneurship.

Anderson, M. and Beavis, A. (2019). *Teaching for Transfer*. Melbourne, VIC: Victorian Curriculum and Assessment Authority.

Andre, L., Durksen, T. and Volman, M. (2017). Museums as Avenues of Learning for Children: A Decade of Research. *Learning Environments Research*, 20, 47–76.

Ariga, A. and Lleras, A. (2011). Brief and Rare Mental 'Breaks' Keep You Focused: Deactivation and Reactivation of Task Goals Preempt Vigilance Decrements. *Cognition*, 118(3), 439–443.

Arthur, J. (2014). To Be of Good Character. *Independence*, 39(1), 4–8.

Arts Council England (2016). *Now and the Future: A Review of Museum Learning*. London: Arts Council England. Available at: https://www.artscouncil.org.uk/sites/default/files/download-file/Now_and_the_future_formal_learning_in_museums_NOV2016.pdf.

Aspinall, P., Mavros, P., Coyne, R. and Roe, J. (2015). The Urban Brain: Analysing Outdoor Physical Activity with Mobile EEG. *British Journal of Sports Medicine*, 49, 272–276.

Ayas, K. and Zeniuk, N. (2001). Project-Based Learning: Building Communities of Reflective Practitioners. *Management Learning*, 32(1), 61–76.

Bandura, A. (1977). *Social Learning Theory*. Englewood Cliffs, NJ: Prentice Hall.

Barrie, D. (2019). *Incredible Journeys: Exploring the Wonders of Animal Navigation*. London: Hodder & Stoughton.

Berdik, C. (2015). Pay Attention, Robot: Having Students Teach an Avatar Helps Them Learn. *Slate* (29 April). Available at: https://slate.com/technology/2015/04/teachable-agents-making-kids-teach-a-robot-can-help-them-learn.html.

Berger, R. (2003). *An Ethic of Excellence: Building a Culture of Craftsmanship with Students*. Portsmouth, NH: Heinemann.

Berger, W. (2018). *The Book of Beautiful Questions: The Powerful Questions That Will Help You Decide, Create, Connect, and Lead.* New York: Bloomsbury.

Berger, W. (2019). The Best Networking Advice I've Seen Yet. *Quiet Revolution.* Available at: https://www.quietrev.com/the-best-networking-advice-ive-seen-yet.

Birdwell, J., Scott, R. and Koninckx, D. (2015). *Learning by Doing.* London: Demos. Available at: https://demosuk.wpengine.com/files/Learning_by_Doing.pdf.

Bolles, R. N. (2019). *What Color Is Your Parachute? 2019: A Practical Manual for Job-Hunters and Career-Changers.* New York: Ten Speed Press.

Bronk, K. C., Finch, H. and Talib, T. L. (2010). Purpose in Life Among High Ability Adolescents. *High Ability Studies,* 21(2), 133–145.

Bronowski, J. (2011 [1973]). *The Ascent of Man.* London: BBC Books.

Buschor, C., Proyer, R. T. and Ruch, W. (2013). Self- and Peer-Rated Character Strengths: How Do They Relate to Satisfaction with Life and Orientations to Happiness? *Journal of Positive Psychology,* 8(2), 116–127.

Cain, S. (2012). *Quiet: The Power of Introverts in a World That Can't Stop Talking.* London: Penguin.

Chanfreau, J., Tanner, E., Callanan, M., Laing, K., Skipp, A. and Todd, L. (2016). *Out of School Activities During Primary School and KS2 Attainment.* Centre for Longitudinal Studies Working Paper 2016/1. London: UCL Institute of Education.

Charles, F. and Turbyfill, R. (2013). *Discovering Orienteering.* Champaign, IL: Human Kinetics.

Chesham, R., Booth, J., Sweeney, E., Ryde, G., Gorely, T., Brooks, N. and Moran, C. (2018). The Daily Mile Makes Primary School Children More Active, Less Sedentary and Improves Their Fitness and Body Composition: A Quasi-Experimental Pilot Study. *BMC Medicine,* 16(64), 1–13.

Church of England (2015). *The Fruit of the Spirit: A Church of England Discussion Paper on Character Education.* London: Church of England Education Office.

Claxton, G. (2015). *Intelligence in the Flesh: Why Your Mind Needs Your Body Much More Than It Thinks.* London: Yale University Press.

Claxton, G. and Lucas, B. (2013). *Redesigning Schooling 2: What Kind of Teaching for What Kind of Learning?* London: SSAT (The Schools Network).

Claxton, G. and Lucas, B. (2015). *Educating Ruby: What Our Children Really Need to Learn.* Carmarthen: Crown House Publishing.

Claxton, G., Lucas, B. and Webster, R. (2010). *Bodies of Knowledge: How the Learning Sciences Could Transform Practical and Vocational Education.* Winchester: Edge/Centre for Real-World Learning.

Confederation of British Industry (2012). *First Steps: A New Approach for Schools.* London: CBI.

Costa, A. and Kallick, B. (2000). *Discovering and Exploring Habits of Mind.* Alexandria, VA: ASCD.

Covey, S. (2004). *The 7 Habits of Highly Effective People: Restoring the Character Ethic*, rev. edn. New York: Free Press.

Crawford, M. (2009). *The Case for Working with Your Hands: Or Why Office Work Is Bad for Us and Fixing Things Feels Good*. London: Penguin.

Crawford, M. (2015). *The World Beyond Your Head: How to Flourish in an Age of Distraction*. London: Penguin.

Cremin, T. (2011). *Reading for Pleasure and Wider Reading*. Leicester: UKLA Resources.

Csikszentmihalyi, M. (1997). *Finding Flow: The Psychology of Engagement with Everyday Life*. New York: Basic Books.

Cullinane, C. and Montacute, R. (2017). *Life Lessons: Improving Essential Life Skills for Young People*. London: Sutton Trust. Available at: https://www.suttontrust.com/wp-content/uploads/2017/10/Life-Lessons-Report_FINAL.pdf.

Damon, W. (2008). *The Path to Purpose: Helping Children Find Their Calling in Life*. New York: Free Press.

Department for Education (2016a). *DfE Strategy 2015–2020: World-Class Education and Care*. London: DfE. Available at: https://www.gov.uk/government/publications/dfe-strategy-2015-to-2020-world-class-education-and-care.

Department for Education (2016b). *Educational Excellence Everywhere: Assessment of Impact*. London: DfE. Available at: https://assets.publishing.service.gov.uk/government/uploads/system/uploads/attachment_data/file/508427/Educational_excellence_everywhere_-_Impact_Assessment.pdf.

Department for Education and Employment (1998). *The Learning Age: A Renaissance for a New Britain*. London: DfEE.

DeYoung, C., Quilty, L., Peterson, J. and Gray, J. (2014). Openness to Experience, Intellect, and Cognitive Ability. *Journal of Personality Assessment* 96(1), 46–52.

DuBrin, A. (1978). *Fundamentals of Organizational Behaviour: An Applied Perspective*. New York: Pergamon Press.

Duckworth, A. (2016). *Grit: Passion, Perseverance, and the Science of Success*. New York: Scribner.

Duckworth, A., Peterson, C., Matthews, M. and Kelly, D. (2007). Grit: Perseverance and Passion for Long-Term Goals. *Journal of Personality and Social Psychology*, 92(6), 1087–1101.

Dweck, C. (1999). *Self-Theories: Their Role in Motivation, Personality, and Development* (Essays in Social Psychology). Hove: Psychology Press.

Dweck, C. (2006). *Mindset: The New Psychology of Success*. New York: Ballantyne Books.

Dweck, C., Walton, G. and Cohen, G. (2014). *Academic Tenacity: Mindsets and Skills That Promote Long-Term Learning*. Seattle, WA: Bill & Melinda Gates Foundation.

Education Endowment Foundation (2018). *Teaching & Learning Toolkit* (10 October). Available at: https://educationendowmentfoundation.org.uk/public/files/Toolkit/complete/EEF-Teaching-Learning-Toolkit-October-2018.pdf.

Education Scotland (2017). *Benchmark Technologies* (March). Livingston: Education Scotland. Available at: https://education.gov.scot/improvement/documents/technologiesbenchmarkspdf.pdf.

Edwards, J. (2018 [1746]). *The Religious Affections* [Kindle edn]. N.p.: Musaicum Books.

Engel, S. (2015). *The Hungry Mind: The Origins of Curiosity in Childhood*. Cambridge, MA: Harvard University Press.

Ericsson, A. and Pool, R. (2016). *Peak: Secrets from the New Science of Expertise*. New York: Houghton Mifflin Harcourt.

Falk, J. and Dierking, L. (1992). *The Museum Experience*. Washington, DC: Whalesback Books.

Falk, J. and Dierking, L. (2000). *Learning from Museums: Visitor Experiences and the Making of Meaning*. Walnut Creek, CA: AltaMira Press.

Felicia, P. (2009). *Digital Games in Schools: A Handbook for Teachers*. Brussels: European Schoolnet – EUN Partnership AISBL. Available at: http://games.eun.org/upload/GIS_HANDBOOK_EN.PDF.

Field, J. (2012). Is Lifelong Learning Making a Difference: Research-Based Evidence on the Impact of Adult Learning. In D. Aspin, J. Chapman, K. Evans and R. Bagnall (eds), *Second International Handbook of Lifelong Learning*. Dordrecht: Springer, pp. 887–898.

Fiorella, L. and Mayer, R. E. (2013). The Relative Benefits of Learning by Teaching and Teaching Expectancy. *Contemporary Educational Psychology*, 38, 281–288.

Flavell, J. H. (1976). Metacognitive Aspects of Problem Solving. In L. B. Resnick (ed.), *The Nature of Intelligence*. Hillsdale, NJ: Erlbaum, pp. 231–236.

Fleming, M. (2010). *Arts in Education and Creativity: A Literature Review*, 2nd edn. London: Creativity, Culture and Education.

Garringer, M. and MacRae, P. (2008). *Building Effective Peer Mentoring Programs in Schools: An Introductory Guide*. Folsom, CA: Mentoring Resource Center.

Gratton, L. and Scott A. (2016). *The 100-Year Life: Living and Working in an Age of Longevity*. London: Bloomsbury.

Grigg, R. and Hughes, S. (2013). *Teaching Primary Humanities*. Harlow: Pearson.

Gross, R. (2014). The Importance of Taking Children to Museums [blog]. *National Endowment for the Arts* (20 June). Available at: https://www.arts.gov/art-works/2014/importance-taking-children-museums.

Gutman, L. and Schoon, I. (2013). *The Impact of Non-Cognitive Skills on Outcomes for Young People: Literature Review*. London: Institute of Education, University of London.

Haskell, R. E. (2001). *Transfer of Learning: Cognition and Instruction*. New York: Academic Press.

Hattie, J. (2009). *Visible Learning: A Synthesis of Over 800 Meta-Analyses Relating to Achievement*. Abingdon: Routledge.

Hattie, J., Biggs, J. and Purdie, N. (1996). Effects of Learning Skills Interventions on Student Learning: A Meta-analysis. *Review of Educational Research*, 66(2), 99–136.

Heckman, J. and Kautz, T. (2013). *Fostering and Measuring Skills: Interventions That Improve Character and Cognition*. Bonn: Institute for the Study of Labor.

Henley, D. (2012). *Cultural Education in England: An Independent Review by Darren Henley for the Department for Culture, Media and Sport and the Department for Education*. London: Department for Education.

Herzberg, F. (1968). One More Time: How Do You Motivate Employees? *Harvard Business Review*, 46(1), 53–62.

Hinds, D. (2019). Vision for Character and Resilience. Speech delivered at the Church of England Foundation for Educational Leadership Conference, London, 7 February.

Hinrichs, J. R. and Mischkind, L. A. (1967). Empirical and Theoretical Limitations of the Two-Factor Hypothesis of Job Satisfaction. *Journal of Applied Psychology*, 51(2), 191–200.

Hinton, C. and Hendrick, C. (2015). *Getting Gritty with It: Gritty Students Cultivate Effective Learning Strategies and Dispositions*. Cambridge, MA: Harvard Graduate School of Education.

HM Government (2018). *A Green Future: Our 25 Year Plan to Improve the Environment*. London: HMSO.

Hodges, J. (2016). Sports Optimism: Building a Positive Mental Attitude in Sport, *Sportsmind* (4 February). Available at: https://www.sportsmind.com.au/index.php/article/positive-thinking-improved-performance/entry/sports-optimism-building-a-positive-mental-attitude-in-sport.

Holt, J. (1967). *How Children Learn*. New York: Pitman.

Ivcevic, Z., Hoffman, J. and Brackett, M. (2014). *Arts and Emotions: Nurturing Our Creative Potential*. Santander: Botin Foundation.

Jabr, F. (2013). Why Your Brain Needs More Downtime. *Scientific American* (15 October).

Jensen, E. (2011). How Important Is Exercise at Schools? [blog]. *The Whole Child* (11 November). Available at: http://www.wholechildeducation.org/blog/how-important-is-exercise-at-schools.

Johnson, S. (2019). Grow Yourself Healthy: Improving Sleep. *Gardeners' World* (May), 55–58.

Jubilee Centre for Character and Virtues (2017). *A Framework for Character Education in Schools*. Birmingham: University of Birmingham.

Kann, L., Kinchen, S., Shanklin, S. L., Flint, K. H., Kawkins, J., Harris, W. et al. (2014). *Youth Risk Behavior Surveillance: United States 2013*. Washington, DC: Centers for Disease Control and Prevention.

Keller, T. (2012). *Every Good Endeavour: Connecting Your Work to God's Purpose for the World*. London: Hodder & Stoughton.

Kelly, L. (2011). *Student Learning in Museums: What Do We Know?* Ballarat, VIC: Sovereign Hill Museums Association.

Kenrick, D., Griskevicius, V., Neiberg, S. and Schaller, M. (2010). Renovating the Pyramid of Needs: Contemporary Extensions Built Upon Ancient Foundations. *Perspectives on Psychological Science*, 5(3), 292–314.

Kesebir, S., Graham, J. and Oishi, S. (2010). A Theory of Human Needs Should Be Human-Centered, Not Animal-Centered: Commentary on Kenrick et al. (2010). *Perspectives on Psychological Science*, 5(3), 315–319.

Kijinski, J. (2018). On 'Experiential' Learning. *Inside Higher Ed* (8 January). Available at: https://www.insidehighered.com/views/2018/01/08/why-experiential-learning-often-isnt-good-classroom-learning-opinion.

King, Jr., M. L. (2013). *A Gift of Love: Sermons from Strength to Love and Other Preachings*, rev edn. Boston, MA: Beacon Press.

Kleinke, C. L., Peterson, T. R. and Rutledge, T. R. (1998). Effects of Self-Generated Facial Expressions on Mood. *Journal of Personality and Social Psychology*, 74, 272–279.

Kobayashi, M., Gushiken, T., Ganaha, Y., Sasazawa, Y., Iwata, S., Takemura, A. et al. (2013). Reliability and Validity of the Multidimensional Scale of Life Skills in Late Childhood. *Education Sciences* 3(2), 121–135.

Kolb, D. A. (1984) *Experiential Learning: Experience as the Source of Learning and Development*. Englewood Cliffs, NJ: Prentice Hall.

Kolb, D. A. and Kolb. A. (2018). Eight Important Things to Know About the Experiential Learning Cycle. *Australian Educational Leader*, 40(3), 8–14. Available at: https://learningfromexperience.com/research-library/eight-important-things-to-know-about-the-experiential-learning-cycle.

Lansing, A. (2014 [1959]). *Endurance: Shackleton's Incredible Voyage*. New York: Basic Books.

Lave, J. and Wenger, E. (1991). *Situated Learning: Legitimate Peripheral Participation*. Cambridge: Cambridge University Press.

Learning and Teaching Scotland (2010). *Curriculum for Excellence Through Outdoor Learning*. Glasgow: Learning and Teaching Scotland.

Leelawong, K., Wang, Y., Biswas, G., Vye, N., Bransford, J., and Schwartz, D. (2001). Qualitative Reasoning Techniques to Support Learning by Teaching: The Teachable Agents Project. In G. Biswas (ed.), *AAAI Qualitative Reasoning Workshop*. San Antonio, TX, pp. 73–81.

Lucas, B. and Claxton, G. (2010). *New Kinds of Smart: How the Science of Learnable Intelligence Is Changing Education*. Maidenhead: Open University Press.

Lucas, B., Claxton, G. and Spencer, E. (2013). *Expansive Education: Teaching Learners for the Real World*. Maidenhead: Open University Press.

Lucas, B. and Greany, T. (eds) (2000). *Schools in the Learning Age*. Sandford: Southgate Publishers.

Lucas, B. and Spencer, E. (2016). Written Evidence Submitted by the Centre for Real-World Learning at the University of Winchester and Others. Available at: http://data.parliament.uk/writtenevidence/committeeevidence.svc/evidencedocument/education-committee/purpose-and-qualityof-education-in-england/written/27451.html.

Lucas, B. and Spencer, E. (2017). *Teaching Creative Thinking: Developing Learners Who Generate Ideas and Can Think Critically* (Pedagogy for a Changing World). Carmarthen: Crown House Publishing.

Lucas, B. and Spencer, E. (2018). *Developing Tenacity: Teaching Learners How to Persevere in the Face of Difficulty* (Pedagogy for a Changing World). Carmarthen: Crown House Publishing.

Lucas, B., Spencer, E. and Claxton, G. (2012). *How to Teach Vocational Education: A Theory of Vocational Pedagogy.* London: City & Guilds Centre for Skills Development.

Lukianoff, G. and Haidt, J. (2018). *The Coddling of the American Mind: How Good Intentions and Bad Ideas Are Setting Up a Generation for Failure.* London: Penguin.

Marsh, H. and Kleitman, S. (2002). Extracurricular School Activities: The Good, the Bad, and the Nonlinear. *Harvard Educational Review*, 72(4), 464–514.

Maslow, A. (1943). A Theory of Human Motivation. *Psychological Review*, 50(4), 370–396.

Maslow, A. (1970). *Motivation and Personality.* New York: Harper & Row.

Miettinen, R. (2000). The Concept of Experiential Learning and John Dewey's Theory of Reflective Thought and Action. *International Journal of Lifelong Education*, 19(1), 54–72.

Minero, E. (2016) Talking in Class: Strategies for Developing Confident Speakers Who Can Share Their Thoughts and Learning. *Edutopia* (15 September). Available at: https://www.edutopia.org/practice/oracy-classroom-strategies-effective-talk.

Mitchell, T. (1982). Motivation: New Directions for Theory, Research, and Practice. *Academy of Management Review*, 7(1), 80–88.

Muñoz, S. (2009). *Children in the Outdoors: A Literature Review.* Forres: Sustainable Development Research Centre.

Newport, C. (2011). Flow is the Opiate of the Mediocre: Advice on Getting Better from an Accomplished Piano Player [blog] (23 December). Available at: http://calnewport.com/blog/2011/12/23/flow-is-the-opiate-of-the-medicore-advice-on-getting-better-from-an-accomplished-piano-player.

Newport, C. (2012). The Father of Deliberate Practice Disowns Flow [blog] (9 April). Available at: http://www.calnewport.com/blog/2012/04/09/the-father-of-deliberate-practice-disowns-flow.

O'Brien, L. and Murray, R. (2006). *A Marvellous Opportunity for Children to Learn: Participatory Evaluation of Forest School in England and Wales.* Farnham: Forest Research.

O'Neil, A., Quirk, S. E., Housden, S., Brennan, S. L., Williams, L. J., Pasco, J. A. et al. (2014). Relationship Between Diet and Mental Health in Children and Adolescents: A Systematic Review. *American Journal of Public Health*, 104(10), e31–e42.

Ofsted (2014). *Key Stage 3: The Wasted Years?* London: Ofsted.

Ofsted (2019). *The Education Inspection Framework*. London: Ofsted.

Olsen, S. (2009). Helping Children Find What They Need on the Internet. *New York Times* (25 December).

Oppezzo, M. and Schwartz, D. (2014). Give Your Ideas Some Legs: The Positive Effect of Walking on Creative Thinking. *Journal of Experimental Psychology: Learning, Memory, and Cognition*, 40(4), 1142–1152.

Park, N., Peterson, G. and Seligman, M. E. P. (2004). Strengths of Character and Well-Being. *Journal of Social and Clinical Psychology*, 23, 603–619.

Patel, P., Lamar, M. and Bhatt, T. (2014). Effect of Type of Cognitive Task and Walking Speed on Cognitive-Motor Interference During Dual-Task Walking. *Neuroscience*, 28(260), 140–148.

Pearcey, N. R. (2018). *Love Thy Body: Answering Hard Questions about Life and Sexuality*. Grand Rapids, MI: Baker Books.

Perkins, D. (2009). *Making Learning Whole: How Seven Principles of Teaching Can Transform Education*. San Francisco, CA: Jossey-Bass.

Peterson, C. and Park, N. (2010). What Happened to Self-Actualization? Commentary on Kenrick et al. (2010). *Perspectives on Psychological Science*, 5(3), 320–322.

Peterson, C., Park, N., Hall, N. and Seligman, M. E. P. (2009). Zest and Work. *Journal of Organizational Behavior*, 30, 161–172.

Peterson, C., Ruch, W., Beermann, U., Park, N. and Seligman, M. E. P. (2007). Strengths of Character, Orientations to Happiness, and Life Satisfaction. *Journal of Positive Psychology*, 2(3), 149–156.

Peterson, C. and Seligman, M. E. P. (2004). *Character Strengths and Virtues: A Handbook and Classification*. Oxford: Oxford University Press.

Peterson, J. B. (2018). *12 Rules for Life: An Antidote to Chaos*. London: Penguin.

Peterson, K. and Kolb, D. A. (2018). Expanding Awareness and Contact Through Experiential Learning. *Gestalt Review*, 22(2), 226–248.

Phelps, D. (2018). *Xientifica SOS*. Winchester: Planet Poetry.

Pink, D. (2009). *Drive: The Surprising Truth About What Motivates Us*. New York: Riverhead Books.

Plowden, B. (1967). *Children and Their Primary Schools: A Report of the Central Advisory Council for Education (England)* [Plowden Report]. London: HMSO.

Prior, K. S. (2018). *On Reading Well: Finding the Good Life Through Great Books*. Grand Rapids, MI: Brazos Press.

Provenzo, Jr., E. (2009). Friedrich Froebel's Gifts: Connecting the Spiritual and Aesthetic to the Real World of Play and Learning. *American Journal of Play*, 2(1), 85–99.

Quigley, A., Muijs, D. and Stringer, E. (2018). *Metacognition and Self-Regulated Learning: Guidance Report*. London: Education Endowment Foundation.

Rees, D. and Sabia, J. (2010). Sports Participation and Academic Performance: Evidence from the National Longitudinal Study of Adolescent Health. *Economics of Education Review*, 29(5), 751–759.

Reynolds, G. (2013). Easing Brain Fatigue with a Walk in the Park. *New York Times* (27 March).

Robinson, K. (2009). *The Element: How Finding Your Passion Changes Everything*. London: Penguin.

Robinson, K. and Aronica, L. (2013). *Finding Your Element*. London: Penguin.

Robinson, M. (2018a). Theology for This Moment. Honorary lecture delivered at the University of Lund, Sweden, 26 May 2016. In *What Are We Doing Here? Essays* [Kindle edn]. London: Virago, loc. 554–766.

Robinson, M. (2018b). The American Scholar Now. Presidential Lecture delivered at Stanford University, 29 October 2015. In *What Are We Doing Here? Essays* [Kindle edn]. London: Virago, loc. 1182–1448.

Robinson, M. (2018c). Our Public Conversation: How America Talks About Itself. The Page-Barbour Lectures delivered at the University of Virginia, 22–26 February 2016. In *What Are We Doing Here? Essays* [Kindle edn]. London: Virago, loc. 1889–2560

Robinson, M. (2018d). Mind, Conscience, Soul. Plenary address at the Religious Affections in Colonial North America Conference delivered at Huntingdon Library, San Marino, California, 27 January 2017. In *What Are We Doing Here? Essays* [Kindle edn]. London: Virago, loc. 2579–2879.

Robinson, M. (2018e). Old Souls, New World. The Ingersoll Lecture on Human Immortality delivered at Harvard Divinity School, 27 April 2017. In *What Are We Doing Here? Essays* [Kindle edn]. London: Virago, loc. 3847–4184.

Robotham, D., Chakkalackal, L. and Cyhlarova, E. (2011). *Sleep Matters: The Impact of Sleep on Mental Health and Wellbeing*. London: Mental Health Foundation.

Rottensteiner, C., Tolvanen, A., Laakso, L. and Konttinen, N. (2015). Young Athletes' Motivation, Perceived Competence, and Persistence in Organized Team Sports. *Journal of Sports Behavior*, 38(4), 1–18.

Sanderson, D. (2019). Google Maps and Sat-Navs Are Damaging Our Brains, Says Author David Barrie, *The Times* (27 May).

Sârbescu, P. and Boncu, A. (2018). The Resilient, the Restraint and the Restless: Personality Types Based on the Alternative Five-Factor Model. *Personality and Individual Differences*, 134, 81–87.

Sawyer, R. (2006). *The Cambridge Handbook of the Learning Sciences*. Cambridge: Cambridge University Press.

Schleicher, A. and Tang, Q. (2015). Education Post-2015: Knowledge and Skills Transform Lives and Societies. In E. Hanushek and L. Woessmann (eds), *Universal Basic Skills: What Countries Stand to Gain*. Paris: OECD Publishing, pp. 9–14.

Schnorr, C. (2000). Habits of Mind as Character Education. In A. L. Costa and B. Kallick (eds), *Activating and Engaging Habits of Mind*. Alexandria, VA: Association for Supervision and Curriculum Development, pp. 76–81.

Schuller, T. and Watson, D. (2009). *Learning Through Life: Inquiry into the Future for Lifelong Learning*. London: NIACE. Available at: https://www.learningandwork. org.uk/wp-content/uploads/2017/01/ Learning-Through-Life-Summary.pdf.

Scott, R., Reynolds, L. and Cadywould, C. (2016). *Character by Doing: Evaluation*. London: Demos. Available at: https:// www.demos.co.uk/wp-content/ uploads/2016/07/Character-By-Doing.pdf.

Scottish Government (2008). *Curriculum for Excellence. Building the Curriculum 3: A Framework for Learning and Teaching*. Edinburgh: Scottish Government.

Seligman, M. (2006). *Learned Optimism: How to Change Your Mind and Your Life*. New York: Vintage.

Seligman, M. and Csikszentmihalyi, M. (2000). Positive Psychology: An Introduction. *American Psychologist*, 55(1), 5–14.

Seligman, M., Reivich, K., Jaycox, L. and Gillham, J. (1995). *The Optimistic Child: A Proven Program to Safeguard Children Against Depression and Build Lifelong Resilience*. New York: Houghton Mifflin.

Semper, R. (1990). Science Museums as Environments for Learning. *Physics Today*, 43(11), 50–56.

Sennett, R. (1998). *The Corrosion of Character: The Personal Consequences of Work in the New Capitalism*. New York: Norton.

Sennett, R. (2009). *The Craftsman*. London: Penguin.

Sherrington, T. (2013). Great Lessons 10: Joy [blog]. *Teacherhead* (3 March). Available at: https://teacherhead.com/2013/03/03/ great-lessons-10-joy.

Shulman, L. (2005). Signature Pedagogies in the Professions. *Daedelus*, 134, 52–59.

Slade, P. (1954). *Child Drama*. London: University of London Press.

Smith, J. (2011). *The Good and Beautiful Life: Putting on the Character of Christ*. London: Hodder & Stoughton.

Solano, A. C. and Cosentino, A. C. (2016). The Relationships Between Character Strengths and Life Fulfillment in the View of Lay-People in Argentina. *Interdisciplinaria Revista de Psicología y Ciencias Afines*, 33(1), 65–80.

Spencer, E., Lucas, B. and Claxton, G. (2012). *Progression in Creativity: Developing New Forms of Assessment.* Newcastle: CCE. Available at: https://www.creativitycultureeducation.org//wp-content/uploads/2018/10/CCE-Progression-in-Creativity-Literature-Review-2012.pdf.

Squire, K. D. (2005). Changing the Game: What Happens When Video Games Enter the Classroom. *Innovate: Journal of Online Education*, 1(6). Available at: https://nsuworks.nova.edu/cgi/viewcontent.cgi?article=1168&context=innovate.

Stoet, G., Bailey, D., Moore, A. and Geary, D. (2016). Countries with Higher Levels of Gender Equality Show Larger National Sex Differences in Mathematics Anxiety and Relatively Lower Parental Mathematics Valuation for Girls. *PLoS ONE*, 11(4), e0153857.

Stone, M. and Petrick, J. (2013). The Educational Benefits of Travel Experiences: A Literature Review. *Journal of Travel Research*, 52(6), 731–744.

Swann, M., Peacock, A., Hart, S. and Drummond, M. J. (2012). *Creating Learning without Limits.* Maidenhead: Open University Press.

Swansbury, R. (2018). *A Fresh Approach to Collective Worship: Support and Guidance for Planning and Leading Collective Worship in Canterbury and Rochester Diocesan Schools.* Canterbury: Diocese of Canterbury. Available at: https://www.canterburydiocese.org/media/childrenandschools/collectiveworship/freshapproach/freshapproach.pdf.

Syed, M. (2011). *Bounce: The Myth of Talent and the Power of Practice.* New York: HarperCollins.

Syed, M. (2019). Andy Murray One of Britain's Greatest Sportsmen. *The Times* (11 January).

Taylor, M. (2019). 089: Planet Poetry & Xientifica SOS with Daniel Phelps. *Education on Fire* (31 March) [audio]. Available: https://www.educationonfire.com/education-on-fire/089-planet-poetry-xientifica-sos-with-daniel-phelps.

Telef, B. B. and Furlong, M. J. (2017). Social and Emotional Psychological Factors Associated with Subjective Well-Being: A Comparison of Turkish and California Adolescents. *Cross-Cultural Research*, 51(2), 491–520.

Telegraph, The (2012). 'Cotton Wool Culture' Stops Children Playing (4 September).

Tishman, S. (2005). Learning in Museums. *Harvard Graduate School of Education* (4 September). Available at: https://www.gse.harvard.edu/news/uk/05/09/learning-museums-0.

Ulicsak, M. and Wright, M. (2010). *Games in Education: Serious Games.* Bristol: FutureLab.

UNESCO (2005). *Educating for Creativity: Bringing the Arts and Culture into Asian Education.* Bangkok: UNESCO.

Walker, R. (2004). 25 Entrepreneurs We Love: Jeff Bezos, Amazon.com. *Inc.com* (April).

Wallop, H. (2016). Meet the Hunky Headmaster Who Teaches Kids to Use a Shotgun. *The Telegraph* (7 February).

Washor, E. and Mojkowski, C. (2013). *Leaving to Learn: How Out-of-School Learning Increases Student Engagement and Reduces Dropout Rates*. Portsmouth, NH: Heinemann.

Welsh Government (2019). *A Guide to Curriculum for Wales 2022. Draft Statutory Guidance*. Cardiff: Welsh Government.

Wenger-Trayner, E. and Wenger-Trayner. B. (2015). Introduction to Communities of Practice: A Brief Overview of the Concept and Its Uses. Available at: https://wenger-trayner.com/introduction-to-communities-of-practice.

Westling, S., Pyhältö, K., Pietarinen, J. and Soini, T. (2017). Intensive Studying or Restlessness in the Classroom: Does the Quality of Control Matter? *Teaching and Teacher Education*, 67, 361–369.

Wilkinson, I. and Anderson, R. (2007). Teaching for Learning: A Summary. In G. Nuthall, *The Hidden Lives of Learners*. Wellington: NZCER Press, pp. 153–163.

Wirtz, D., Stalls, J., Scollon, C. and Wuensch, K. (2016). Is the Good Life Characterized By Self-Control? Perceived Regulatory Success and Judgments of Life Quality. *Journal of Positive Psychology*, 11(6), 572–583.

WJEC CBAC (2015). *WJEC Level 3 Extended Project: Guidance for Teaching. Teaching from 2015 for Award from 2016*. Available at: https://www.wjec.co.uk/qualifications/extended-project/WJEC-Level-3-Award-in-Extended-Project-Qualification-Guidance-for-Teaching.pdf?language_id=1.

World Health Organization (2016). *Growing Up Unequal: Gender and Socioeconomic Differences in Young People's Health and Well-Being. Health Behaviour in School-Aged Children Study: International Report from the 2013/2014 Survey*. Copenhagen: WHO.

Yuen, W., Sidhu, S., Vassilev, G., Mubarak, S., Martin, T. and Wignall, J. (2018). *Trends in Self-Employment in the UK: Analysing the Characteristics, Income and Wealth of the Self-Employed*. London: Office for National Statistics.

Zosh, J. M., Hopkins, E. J., Jensen, H., Liu, C., Neale, D., Hirsh-Pasek, K., Solis, S. L. and Whitebread, D. (2017). *Learning Through Play: A Review of the Evidence*. Billund: LEGO Foundation.

Zuckerman, M. (1979). *Sensation Seeking: Beyond the Optimal Level of Arousal*. Hillsdale, NJ: Lawrence Erlbaum.